# *Development Design*

***Pitt Latin American Series***
Catherine M. Conaghan, *Editor*

# Development Design

HOTELS AND POLITICS IN
THE HISPANIC CARIBBEAN

**Erica Morawski**

University of Pittsburgh Press

This publication was made possible, in part, by a Design History Society Research Publication Grant

Published by the University of Pittsburgh Press, Pittsburgh, Pa., 15260
Copyright © 2025, University of Pittsburgh Press
All rights reserved
Manufactured in the United States of America
Printed on acid-free paper
10 9 8 7 6 5 4 3 2 1

Cataloging-in-Publication data is available from the Library of Congress

Hardcover ISBN: 978-0-8229-4860-5
Paperback ISBN: 978-0-8229-6797-2

Cover art: Postcard of the Hotel Jaragua's swimming pool. Author's collection.

Cover design: Alex Wolfe

Publisher: University of Pittsburgh Press, 7500 Thomas Blvd., 4th floor, Pittsburgh, PA 15260, United States, www.upittpress.org

EU Authorized Representative: Easy Access System Europe, Mustamäe tee 50, 10621 Tallinn, Estonia, gpsr.requests@easproject.com

*To my mother, who should still be here but is always with me.*

*To José, mi media naranja.*

# Contents

*Acknowledgments*

ix

*A Note on Terminology*

xiii

## Introduction
Development Begun

3

## 1. The Grand Condado Vanderbilt
Creating the "Switzerland of the Tropics"

23

## 2. The Hotel Nacional de Cuba
Symbol of Authoritarianism, Site of Revolution

57

*A color gallery follows page 92*

## 3. The Hotel Jaragua
Race and Nation Building in the Dominican Republic

103

## 4. The Caribe Hilton
Redefining Puerto Rico through Operation Bootstrap

133

## 5. The Havana Riviera
Cultural Capital and *Cubanidad* in 1950s Havana

167

*A color gallery follows page 198*

## Conclusion
Development Persistent

211

*Notes*

223

*Bibliography*

247

*Index*

261

# Acknowledgments

In some ways, a book is like one of the hotels discussed in this study—a representative tangible object of a much larger project. Although written in my voice, it comes about thanks to the immeasurable support and assistance of innumerable individuals, organizations, and institutions. Like many big projects, this book happened over a long period, starting as an abbreviated project for a course on the history of urban design at the University of Illinois at Chicago (UIC). Since then, the study has grown and changed. I will be forever grateful to those who helped me realize this task; their insight and assistance has made this a much more compelling project, though it would be remiss of me if I did not note I am solely responsible for all remaining shortcomings.

Robert Bruegmann first saw the potential of this project and encouraged and supported me every step of the way. He always had useful and often unexpected questions ready for me that deepened my thinking. He never let me lose sight of the forest for the trees. Everyone involved helped me hone in on the larger arc of the project, each in a unique way. Thanks to Robin Schuldenfrei for helping me think as a design historian; to Esra Akcan for pushing me to always think theoretically; to Bebe Baird for sharing her Puerto Rico with me and for being one of the first to get me to think of the personal within the scholarly; to the late Peter Hales, who helped me see how this project was connected to my childhood love for EPCOT Center; and to John D'Emilio, who opened worlds of history writing to me. A special thanks to Kathryn O'Rourke, who brought her expertise in modern Latin American architectural history and her compassion for a young scholar entering the world of academia. Also, the camaraderie and friendship of Monica Obniski and Katja Rivera injected so much joy into those years in Chicago during my time at UIC.

Work on this project was supported by the Department of Art History at UIC and by the Dean's Office. I have been fortunate to have subsequent scholarly homes that have provided me with space and time to think—namely, Kendall College of Art and Design at Ferris State University, Grand Rapids, Michigan; Smith College,

Northampton, Massachusetts; and Pratt Institute, Brooklyn, New York. My postdoctoral fellowship at Smith College was enhanced by the attention Laura Kalba, Barbara Kellum, Dana Leibsohn, and Frazer Ward gave to my growth as a scholar and a teacher. At Pratt Institute, my thanks go to the History of Art and Design Department—especially the two chairs John Decker and Sarah Lichtman who have always supported my work. I am thankful to Dylan Hill, who served as an able graduate assistant, and whose work on Hawai'i enriched my thinking on the Caribbean and US imperialism. Dylan was also part of a seminar in fall 2022 on Caribbean design. I am grateful to those students for thinking through so much Caribbean theory, design, and space with me. I am indebted to Maia Hirschler, whose exceptional attention to detail made all the difference in the last review of thsi book; I delight in all opportunities to work with her. Peter De Staebler has proved to be an incomparable office mate who is always willing to dive into debates about the discipline. At the school and institute level, Dean Helio Takai, Assistant Dean Karyn Zieve, and Provost Donna Heiland have supported this project in significant ways. I am grateful for funding from Pratt Institute's Faculty Development Fund and a publication grant from the Design History Society. Along the way, funding from the Graham Foundation for Advanced Studies in the Visual Arts, the Center for Advanced Study in the Visual Arts–National Gallery of Art, and the Society of Architectural Historians have made research and writing possible.

    The meat of this book would not exist if not for the archivists, librarians, and staff who welcomed me to their collections and helped me locate sources. In San Juan, these include people at the Archivo General de Puerto Rico (General Archive of Puerto Rico), Oficina Estatal de Conservación Histórica (State Historic Preservation Office), and the Archivo de Arquitectura y Construcción de la Universidad de Puerto Rico (Archive of Architecture and Construction at the University of Puerto Rico); my special gratitude goes to Elena for her help in the latter collection. In Santo Domingo, my thanks go to the staff at the Archivo de la Nación (National Archive). In Havana, my gratitude to the staff at the Biblioteca Nacional José Martí (José Marti National Library), La Oficina del Historiador de la Ciudad de La Habana (Office of the City Historian, OHCH), the Escuela de Altos Estudios de Hotelería y Turismo de la República de Cuba (School of Advanced Studies in Hospitality and Tourism of the Republic of Cuba, EAEHT), and the Unión Nacional de Arquitectos y Ingenieros de la Construcción de Cuba (National Union of Architects and Construction Engineers of Cuba, UNAICC). Of the latter, Clarita was of special help. Likewise, Maite of Plan Maestro (Master Plan) of the

## ACKNOWLEDGMENTS

OHCH and Pablo of the OHCH were always ready to lend a hand in any way they could. Research in Cuba, in particular, was possible because of the generosity of scholars, architects, and designers there. My deep gratitude to Daniel Bejerano, the late Mario Coyula, the late Juan de las Cuevas, Humberto Ramírez, and Eduardo Luis Rodriguez for graciously sharing their time and expertise. In the United States, the staff at the Wolfsonian-Florida International University, Miami Beach; the Cuban Heritage Collection at the University of Miami, and HistoryMiami Museum, Miami; the New-York Historical Society and Avery Architectural and Fine Arts Library at Columbia University, New York; and the Hilton Hospitality Industry Archives at the Massad Family Library Research Center, University of Houston, Texas, all received me warmly and shared enthusiasm for the project.

I am appreciative to those, whether known or anonymous, who have given feedback on my work along the way. I am indebted to the three reviewers of the manuscript who were so generous with their time and feedback. Their comments brought me to see this project anew in meaningful ways. My appreciation to panel chairs and audience members who heard versions of these ideas at conferences hosted by the Society of Architectural Historians, the College Art Association, the Vernacular Architecture Forum, Florida Atlantic University, and the Society of Historians of American Foreign Relations. A version of chapter 2 and some key themes of the book have been published in various venues and forms, and I thank Keith Eggener, Fredie Floré, and Cammie McAttee for their keen editorial eyes. Finally, the editorial team at the University of Pittsburgh Press—including but not limited to Joshua Shanholtzer, Kelly Lynn Thomas, and other support staff—have brought this into existence as a published book with a high level of care and attention for which I am grateful.

I have been part of two groups that somewhat bookend this publication and have provided the community needed to carry me through the book-writing process. In 2015, I participated in a seminar funded by the National Endowment for the Humanities and organized by the late David Raizman and Carma Gorman on design history beyond the canon. I am grateful for the lasting friendships that began during those two weeks in Philadelphia. Also, thanks to the determination of Bryan Norwood and John Davis, the Architectural History of the Greater Caribbean symposium took place in June 2022 at the University of Texas after years of delay. Those few days in Austin were an invitation (and indulgence) for us participants to linger in the Caribbean world, and as a result I developed the conviction that we are building a nurturing and inclusive space for architectural and design historians of the Caribbean and that the future holds much exciting collaborative work.

Besides those already mentioned, there are many individuals who have aided me along the way in small and big ways, whether by reading drafts, listening to me work out new ideas, answering emails for information, offering friendship, sharing a chat over coffee, or getting my mind off the project when most needed. These include Irene Brisson, Belmont Freeman, Joe Hartman, Timothy Hyde, Tara Kohn, Vladimir Kulić, Fernando Luiz Lara, Ana María León, Abigail McEwen, Dennis Merrill, Louis Nelson, Paul Niell, Patricio del Real, Fredo Rivera, Jonah Rowen, Alexis Salas, Nico Vicario, Carla Yanni, and Kimberly Zarecor.

Family is the counterpoint that makes projects like these possible. Mine is small but mighty, though across this project my family has grown in beautiful ways. My brothers, Jonathan and James; my sisters-in-law, Katie and Melissa; and my nieces, Alex, Zoey, and Ava bring levity and laughs, and I love them for that and so much more. Mi familia cubana in Havana, Miami, and Spain welcomed me without question. This is thanks to José who has lived this project with me and become my partner in so much more. He pushed me professionally in ways I know he will probably never understand, but he also taught me how to take the weekend off. He is the best travel companion (often for my research) one could ask for, and I always look forward to the next adventure. The unwavering support he offers and the sacrifices he has made are love in action. During this project, José and I welcomed Xavier and Xoan. They bring more joy than I could ever have imagined and put it all in perspective. In an inexplicable way, and despite the chaos of the day to day, they have brought clarity and purpose.

Finally, I owe the deepest gratitude to my mother, Cindy Morawski. This book is because of her in so many ways. She supported me throughout the years, encouraging me to follow my professional goals and passions. Early on, she let me come back home to write. She traveled with me, and we explored the world. She listened, even if she did not always understand. Her librarian side delighted in my research triumphs. She showed me what matters in life through the way she lived it. She has done more for me than I could ever possibly capture in words. More than anything I wanted her to see this finished. She is in every word written on these following pages.

# A Note on Terminology

**Within words and language we can find articulations and assertions of power**—dominance, violence, negotiation, resistance. Relevant to this book is the way coloniality and modernity are embedded in how we refer to people, places, and things. Throughout this book, I have opted to use the terms "US citizens" or "US travelers" rather than simply referring to people from the United States of America as "Americans," as this reinforces a violence against all the other people in the hemisphere who are also of the Americas. In the chapters that cover Puerto Rico, my language is a bit clunkier as I try to acknowledge that Puerto Ricans are US citizens by referring to those from outside Puerto Rico as being from the contiguous United States. I avoid the terms "US mainland" or "mainlanders" as they suggest that what is not "main" is "minor" or lesser.

The fact that this is a book written in English about predominantly Spanish-speaking societies means that I have had to make some choices concerning translation. Wherever possible, I refer to proper names in Spanish to maintain a sense of identity, whether of person or of place. Likewise, there are a number of terms that are important to present in their original Spanish as translations fail to capture the spirit of the thing or the concept represented by the word. Finally, unless otherwise noted, all translations from Spanish to English are my own.

# Development Design

# Introduction

# Development Begun

### From Colonialism and Modernity to Tourism and Hotels

**A series of tropical print shirts are suspended on hangers over backgrounds of** similar tropical prints; in some cases, it is almost impossible to distinguish between background and fabric patterns. Artist Joiri Minaya's *I can wear tropical print now series* (2018) asks viewers to pause and consider the politics of what many consider innocuous activities—wearing tropical print fabrics and partaking in tropical vacations (see plate 1). Using new and old fabrics, the artist brings into focus the persistence of a romanticization of tropical space—which she characterizes as a non-space constructed into a fantasy of "watered-down, decontextualized capitalist production" that "commits violence."[1] Having grown up in the Dominican Republic, Minaya astutely understands contemporary tourist geopolitics and the negative effects this has on the local population. For example, most significant infrastructure such as hotels and restaurants are owned by foreigners or Dominicans of colonist ancestry, locals are not adequately compensated for work, and many spaces (often through government corruption) are designated for tourists and made inaccessible to locals. The trends Minaya points out have persisted for well over a century and define late modern tourism systems throughout the Caribbean.

The connection between contemporary tourism and Minaya's contemporary artwork offers an entry point into tourism's past and its ties to colonialism and the project of modernity more broadly. As Minaya herself points out, the botanical illustrations produced by European colonists and "explorers" as a means to assert control over the Caribbean through knowledge and systems of production are directly linked to the tropical print of the textiles she uses. The vestiges of colonialism are not just European but are also of US imperialism, its global reach and exertion of power and control present in the history of tropical shirts. Those associated with the Caribbean were born out of the US occupation of Hawai'i and the ensuing interest in the aloha shirt on the part of those from the contiguous United States. This is another reminder that tropical paradise is a non-place as configured by US imperial agendas and US practices that exert power and violence over other societies through a manipulation and a disrespect for their culture and sovereignty.

The construction of the tropical paradise non-place enacts a violence against very real places. In this book I explore the history of how projects built in pursuit of tropical paradises were part and parcel of fraught geopolitics and complicated projects of development. A vacation in the Hispanic Caribbean conjures notions of quaint colonial architecture, fruity cocktails, and picturesque views of coconut palms and turquoise surf from a hotel window. Although easily dismissed, these vacation dreams reveal the interwoven histories of politics, design, and development in Puerto Rico, the Dominican Republic, and Cuba. Newly constructed hotels were a driving force in both the expansion of and the shifts in these insular economies and urban landscapes. The hotels functioned as sites and symbols of development, tied to notions of advancement, progress, and modernization as defined by European and US systems and values. Through attention to the intertwined politics and practices of twentieth-century design and development, I illustrate how tourism was seen as a means to arrive at economic prosperity and to accomplish social reform in Hispanic Caribbean countries, and I reveal how hotel design came to represent ideas about development that both coalesced and clashed with issues of sovereignty and autonomy, national identity, and international relations.

The modern hotel was positioned—discursively and physically—as one of the best public exemplars of modernization and progress in the Hispanic Caribbean. In contrast to other types of buildings associated with development projects and infrastructure, which were often viewed as utilitarian or mundane, representations of hotels were proudly and widely distributed; these representations, along with their material forms, allow us to parse out the ways in which the modern hotel projected idealistic, compromised, and negotiated visions of development. All aspects of hotel design, including industrially produced goods and furniture, vegetation and landscape, art, architecture, interior schemes, and urban planning, as well as graphic advertising material, contributed to positioning hotels as important sites for negotiating national identity vis-à-vis development and in turn shaping international relationships.

But who was positioning these hotels and to whom? Which people and groups saw tourism as a positive instance of development? In this study I dive into the muddy waters of the various agents who instigated and responded to the development of hotels and the tourism industry on these islands. In considering the varied relationships diverse people had with these hotels and what they represented, my aim is to give structure and detailed definitions by framing the study through different conceptual frameworks. These frameworks are interrelated on many layers and presenting them in a hierarchy is no easy task, but I attempt the best I can to bring clarity to the conceptual orientation of the book.

The book can be seen as engaging with two broad historiographic trajectories in architectural history. The first, the more established trajectory, is the history of modernization, with roots in the consideration of European and US architecture, which has since been used to view architecture and urbanism of the global South. The second trajectory, emerging more recently, is the historiographic account of colonization as a means to understand architectural and urban histories. This offers a different lens through which to view built environments such as those in the Caribbean. When I began this research, I initially conceptualized the project under the former trajectory. However, across the fourteen years I have been working on this topic, I have deliberately shifted more attention to the latter trajectory. Despite their differences, they are not mutually exclusive, and their connection gets to the heart of this book and its examination of tourism not in a broad ethnographic sense but as the concrete manifestation of a form of economic colonialism. Viewing tourism as economic colonialism—in particular, within the Hispanic Caribbean's twentieth-century colonial/postcolonial/imperial setting—offers a new lens through which to write architectural histories.

## *From Plantation to Hotel*

Modern hotels—their designs, the spaces they constitute, and the practices they support—reflect the persistence of an older colonial system. Changes to the system are made for the purposes of maintaining control over the colonized land and its people, with the main goal being to wield power for financial gain. As configured in the Caribbean, colonizers sought profit through the exploitation of labor for extraction of goods and resources that were then consumed primarily elsewhere in the world. This initially took the form of the plantation system, but over time it shifted to the tourist system, as Jamaica Kincaid so eloquently captures in her book *A Small Place*. Kincaid vividly describes how, after emancipation and independence, Antigua (though she could be referring to almost any postcolonial Caribbean island) was operated by locals in a manner similar to the previous colonizers, continuing a cycle of violence, corruption, and (for most locals) poverty. Visitors, like colonizers, have the ability to come and go as they please, take what they want, and may choose to shield themselves from the realities of local Antiguan life. Kincaid notes how Antiguans go to the Hotel Training School to learn how to work in the tourism industry and be good servants. She observes that, "in Antigua, people cannot see a relationship between their obsession with slavery and emancipation and their celebration of the Hotel Training School."[2]

The tourist system and the hotels of the twentieth century and today were built off earlier tourism practices born out of the modernity/coloniality project that has persisted for more than five centuries.[3] In analyzing Puerto Rico, Paul Niell captures Aníbal Quijano's configuration of modernity/coloniality when he states that it "identifies the darker and transnational side of Western modernity, that of the racism, genderism, and imperialism instrumental to capitalism's expansion worldwide," one that continues well beyond the seeming end of colonialism.[4] Indeed, the end of the Spanish-American War in 1898 can be seen most productively as the transfer of Puerto Rico and other Spanish colonies to the control of the United States (as well as its acquisition of other newly claimed places), rather than liberation.[5]

The possibility of travel by those in the contiguous United States to Caribbean islands was first facilitated by the fast fruit trade steamships that early travelers took in the nineteenth century.[6] This type of mobility was one of privilege, enacted by those who had the money and time to engage in leisure travel, and, as tourism became formalized, transportation dedicated to tourists became the norm. The New York & Porto Rico Steamship Company was marketed in Grand Condado Vanderbilt promotional materials and served as a transition zone from the everyday to the holiday as guests enjoyed deck games, dancing, and the "thoroughly modern and complete appointments" of the guest cabins.[7] Travel and its cost became easier, faster, and cheaper after this, as more tourism infrastructure and promotion created both the need for and the competition in this sector.

The failed agricultural reforms of the early 1940s that prefigured Puerto Rico's industrialization project Operación Manos a la Obra (Operation Bootstrap) were meant to move power from the few wealthy landowners to the masses of agricultural laborers who worked the land, but these land reforms were not adequately conceptualized to support an alternative system that empowered agricultural laborers. This is but one example of the failure to reconfigure the spatial arrangement of the plantation system, which invites questions about the hotel as plantation. Ian Strachan explores this question and unequivocally positions tourism as "an indispensable part of the plantation economy," a conclusion he supports through the invocation of Antonio Benítez Rojo's configuration of the plantation as a repeating machine, a "proliferating regularity in the Caribbean sphere." Concurrently, Strachan also reminds us of Edward Kamau Brathwaite's observation that plantation discourse may be as much a trap as a tool.[8] Thinking about plantation discourse and hotels in terms of consumables, profit, and labor is a way to leverage it as a tool.

Undergirding the spatial shift from plantation to touristic landscapes was the change in focus concentrated less on extractive practices of raw and agricultural goods and more on the consumption associated with tourism. However, the two are not so far apart; tourism participates in cycles of extractive practices. Some of the materials and products cultivated in Puerto Rico—coffee, pineapple, or sugar, for example—and their literal ingestion invite connection to tourist consumption, which can happen on visual and cerebral levels. The product of consumption for these tourists is a highly constructed one and often the result of a careful negotiation between foreign fantasies and local agendas.

As Kincaid, Strachan, and others have articulated, one parallel between the plantation system and the tourist system is the extraction of profits. Just as plantation owners often lived outside the islands and funneled profits to their homes elsewhere, so too hotel owners were often foreign corporations. Profits leaving the islands impoverish these places, a process compounded by the attendant colonial practice of importation, which promotes further impoverishment and dependency. As Strachan points out, costly imported foods have seeped into local culinary traditions, making locals dependent on these imports, which often comprise the familiar dishes that visitors wish to consume on vacation. Tourism monopolizes not only food resources, both imported and the prime locally produced foods, but other resources such as electricity, clean water, and labor (often inadequately compensated or exploited). Even when hotel owners are not slave owners, the state, as Kincaid compellingly captures in her work, repeats the same corrupt and violent practices of the previous colonial government, perpetuating societies of extreme disparity between the "haves" and "have-nots." A similar way to think of this is through Silvia Rivera Cusicanqui's discussion of the internal colonialism that persists in many postcolonial states.⁹ A section of elite—often white—society continues to implement the same practices of colonialism that existed before state sovereignty.

Consideration of resource extraction in cultural terms reveals significant implications for the built environment.¹⁰ Examination of the impulse to visit historic sites provides some insight. Tourism boosters and guidebooks from the nineteenth century to the present encourage visitors to experience what are deemed to be significant Spanish colonial monuments, in effect privileging a white European heritage over the history of Indigenous, Black, and Asian communities.¹¹ As a result, resources were allocated to facilitate the visitor's movement to and consumption of these sites. To be sure, locals did find ways to profit from this, whether by driving a taxi or selling souvenirs outside a sixteenth-century cathedral, but the emphasis on Spanish heritage also wrought negative economic consequences and shaped urban and rural landscapes and their circuits and routes—in terms of people, goods, and money—in forms that were often contrary to the needs and concerns of locals.

## *Tourism (As) Development*

Underscoring the complex and varied approaches to state involvement in and use of design as integral to tourism development, I utilize an interpretative framework that foregrounds insular agency in these hotel projects. Looking across three islands during periods of colonial governments, democratically elected governments, and dictatorships, in this study I underscore governments' use of hotel design to promote a development agenda as well as local engagement with hotels to enact resistance and to project desires. Eschewing a colonialist viewpoint, I focus less on the tourist experience in order to contemplate what the representations and spaces of the hotel were meant to convey in terms of local concerns. However, I am not interested in an uncritical celebration of local agency. Rather, I explain insular perspectives through the framework of the legacy of colonialism-imperialism, which allows for a contextualization of insular projects as bound to the legacy of modernity/coloniality.

In this study I attend to all that is associated with development—progress, modernity, and the idea that with development comes higher living standards, a better national economy, and more international prestige, though development was not without critics. I illustrate how this history is represented through hotel design and, more broadly speaking, how design was seen as a mode of visualizing and materializing development. However, the focus remains on how development projects and programs meant to elevate and liberate places deemed under- or undeveloped in reality often deepened dependence and inequality, both on a national level to developed countries and on individual levels to the state. In the case of the Hispanic Caribbean, development was heavily colored by US imperial impulses, most formally structured in its maintenance of Puerto Rico as a de facto colony, on the one hand, and more ambiguously charted in back-channel financial and political dealings in the Dominican Republic (as well as multiple occupations by the US Marines), on the other, with Cuba positioned as a quasi-vassal state until the abrogation of the Platt Amendment in 1934.

In this book I renounce partiality toward US imperial perspectives, but US foreign relations and imperial politics—and the fact that tourism to the Hispanic Caribbean was comprised predominantly by visitors from the contiguous United States—played a notable role in how development played out on these islands. Tourism in the Hispanic Caribbean was bound to the history of Spanish colonialism and the past and persistent legacy of US imperialism. Despite the realities of unequal power relations and the fact that the adopted forms of development ultimately deepened imbalances, both insular governments and other individuals embraced development in a genuine and optimistic manner.

The general characteristics of this development were a move toward industrialized production, whether in manufacturing, agriculture, or resource extraction; the attention to and enrichment of urban centers; and enhanced modern infrastructure, generally in the form of large urban works programs, electrification, water and sewage systems, and transportation systems. Development was not just a process, I argue, but came to be embraced as a notable facet of insular identity. Hotels came to symbolize these larger projects, which I demonstrate as I connect, for example, modernist lobbies to factory construction and wicker furnishings to paved road programs. I make a pointed argument about the specific ways in which hotel design worked as part of a larger network of systems and structures of development. Through hotel design, I sketch out the larger picture of development by offering a visual and material critique.

The modern hotel is employed here as a means to expand outward to capture a larger system or infrastructure of development in the Caribbean, a system in which it is but one instance of the built form of development and but one instance of the way in which development was a negotiated arena. Therefore, the focus here is on tourism as a development program and practice. Tourism is certainly not the only approach to understanding development in the Caribbean, but the heavy investment in tourism on the part of many Caribbean nations and the large part of the GDP that it comprises for many Caribbean states set it apart. Moreover, tourism policies and practices do much to create powerful representations of the Caribbean that reverberate throughout the world.

The development programs and tourism practices that define the decades under study here (from roughly the 1910s to the 1960s) were established through an embrace of the modernity/coloniality project across more than five centuries. Quijano defines coloniality as "the most general form of domination in the world today" after the world order of colonialism was destroyed.[12] This system of domination relies upon the construction of race and gender as determining factors in questions of labor and the world capitalist system. As products of coloniality, I situate these hotels as a continuation of—rather than a rupture from—the colonial project. By doing so, I show that a more comprehensive picture emerges of how, why, and when development was valued and implemented by powerful local and US businessmen, and how hotels were instrumental in the lasting effect this has had on the islands.

## *The Modern Hotel*

Although the modern hotel—in the nineteenth and twentieth centuries referred to the world over as the "American hotel"—was understood to be a unique product of the United States, its implementation in the Hispanic Caribbean complicated simplistic understandings of geopolitics and agency.[13] Constructing "American" hotels in the Hispanic Caribbean thus proffers a paradox—at once, trying to raise the level of the island through modern buildings and social practices while relying on models of imperial and economic dominance inherited from historic colonial relationships. The capital cities of the Hispanic Caribbean offered temporary accommodation before modern hotels were built, usually in the form of lodging and guesthouses. Employing the most modern technologies in order to ensure the satisfaction of large numbers of guests, the modern hotel was known as a machine of efficiency, which differentiated it from its predecessors. The specific technologies incorporated in these hotels changed over the long arc of the modern hotel's evolution from the nineteenth into the twentieth century, but hotels were consistently some of the first spaces where new technologies were integrated and employed, technologies such as running water, indoor bathrooms, machines to aid in laundering, equipment for cooking and cleaning on a large scale, gas and then electric lighting systems. Also integral to the definition of the modern hotel was a specific attention to cleanliness, privacy, and social propriety. Modern hotels were understood to be good business, especially in places that were otherwise not considered to be beacons of modernity.

Modern hotels first took hold in cities, because they relied upon water and sewage infrastructure, gas and later electricity, and other utilities, services, and systems initially developed in urban areas. Marked by the comings and goings of large numbers of people who needed temporary lodging, cities provided modern hotels with the steady flow of guests upon which they relied; they were considered public spaces for locals of a certain social standing to utilize as much as foreigners. In the Hispanic Caribbean, this hotel typology quickly moved outside urban areas as destination tourism to more remote locations became increasingly accessible and popular in the nineteenth century, largely thanks to improved technologies of transportation such as the railroad and steamships. Coincident with this spatial move was the shift in the hotel's public areas, which increasingly became reserved for hotel guests, who were predominantly from the contiguous United States.

In the context of Hispanic Caribbean development and its politics, this urban form was tied to Spanish colonialism, US imperialism, and insular movements for self-determination. The most influential modern hotels, I argue, were those that were constructed at the peripheries of cities, what can be called suburban resort hotels, and which urged urban growth while still reinforcing the centrality of the historic core. I trace this type of hotel from its first instance in the 1910s to its decline in the 1960s, when secluded and more removed resort hotels became the dominant form. I do this through a sustained examination of a number of hotels that were instrumental in advancing development agendas and that were significant in shaping local politics and foreign relations at critical moments in history. In each chapter I analyze history beyond the design and construction of these sites as a strategic move to capture some of the voices, viewpoints, and controversies that otherwise are not represented in traditional archival narratives.

## *Modern-Tropical-Historic*

I engage throughout with three motifs or categories that were central to tourism development in these three nations and to more broader development programs— the modern, the tropical, and the historic. All three themes have shifted and changed depending on time, place, and other contexts. The variety of forms and configurations taken by these themes, especially as regards their relationship to one another, does matter on a detailed level but is additionally revealing in terms of why and how these themes are leveraged for larger political aims, whether at a state or an individual level.

Across all the objects presented in this study, the notion of the modern was tied to modernity. Modernity was, more or less, understood according to European and US definitions and standards. Insular governments, both foreign and local, sought to develop an environment of modernity, one in which the built environment and material culture supported and impelled social and cultural practices that aligned with definitions of modernity. However, alignment did vary—from desires of exact replication to more differentiated manifestations, which sought to realize modernity in a manner that was unique to the Puerto Rican, Cuban, or Dominican context.

Design was harnessed as a means to represent the modern. It addressed modernity through style but also through its capacity to create spaces or situations to promote specific behavior considered representative of modernity. Therefore, although it was important for something to look modern (whatever that might mean at any particular moment), it was also paramount that it supported modern comportment and values. Tourism itself was seen as a practice born of modernity and leisure time—supported through the design of beaches, swimming pools, golf courses, and other amenities that surrounded the hotel—that allowed visitors to realize their modern selves. (How this played out for locals was a bit different, depending upon one's opinion of tourism and of the government.) Government officials who were driving tourism saw these hotels as first steps in creating and publicizing modernity in these insular places. While projects of the modern were certainly seen as necessary for a number of reasons, Hispanic Caribbean tourism developers needed to call out something unique about the locale—something visitors would not find at home.

Circling back, it is useful to question tropical space as a non-space in order to understand the constructed nature of the tropical. Geographer David Arnold is specific in proposing the term "tropicality" as a means to indicate the constructed or discursive representation of the tropics. Arnold considers this notion of tropicality to be parallel to Edward Said's notion of Orientalism as a cultural and political construction of Europe and the United States. However, this does not preclude Caribbean folks from then participating in practices of resistance, redefinition, and negotiation of tropicality in order to stake their own claim to the concept.[14]

For visitors, tropicality was—and is—largely associated with the exotic and with escape from the quotidian, and although it is desirable on the part of the tourist, it comes with attendant dangers or a dark side. The concept of the tropical bound elements such as climate, geography, time, and people together in unique ways that usually served to reinforce ideas of the superiority of modernity, European and US culture and society, and whiteness. For visitors, tropical climate and vegetation were unfamiliar and exotic. Coconut palms and flamboyant trees were enticing and guests swooned for the warm ocean breezes, but other visions of the tropical environment invoked fear of invasive and uncontrollable vegetation, stifling heat, and oppressive humidity.

Indeed, there has been a changing European and US discourse on health and the tropical environment. This fear of and danger associated with the tropics were based on more than just a fear of illness. Historian Nancy Leys Stepan uses visual culture to explore how the tropical region of the world—at one point or another all colonized by Europe and/or the United States—elicited fears in colonists and colonizing nations because of the appearance and the unfamiliar practices of Indigenous groups that foreigners found unusual and uncivilized.[15]

Often fashioned as a tropical paradise, the Caribbean landscape in discourse was often connected to the biblical Garden of Eden. Art historian Katherine Manthorne traces how these connections between tropical space and the Garden of Eden are based on associations between the tropical environment and notions of the primordial, primitive, and uncivilized.[16] To many foreigners, Europe and the United States were marching forward with progress, modernity, and development as their guides, while these tropical places were changed either very little or not at all over time. Outsiders viewed this in more than one way, both as a pretext for colonizing and interfering with the sovereignty of these places and as a desirable antidote to the stresses and enervation of modern life.

Art historian Krista Thompson defines tropicality, as it relates to tourism, as "the complex visual systems through which the islands were imagined for tourist consumption and the social and political implications of these representations of actual physical space on the islands and their inhabitants."[17] She traces the construction and negotiation of notions of tropicality for nonlocals, in particular through the "exoticism and overabundance of nature."[18] Tropicality was visually captured through the picturesque, which allowed for the manipulation and containment of tropical nature in a way that allayed nonlocals' fears that this foreign vocabulary was dangerous. This ability to control was important for visitors from the North, who associated these locales with tropical disease and a lack of sanitation. Historian Catherine Cocks charts how, over time, US visitors came to consider Latin America, often conceived as tropical, as safe enough for travel as ideas shifted about health and disease, race, climate, and the relative modernity of places in Latin America.[19]

Thompson illustrates how discourse around tropical travel was about much more than vegetation—discursive representations worked to conflate local people and their culture with the landscape, allowing visitors to see exoticness and a lack of development (for this was seen in contrast to civilization and progress) in the landscapes and people around them. This conflation of people and landscape meant that locals were also ascribed both positive and negative traits in a fashion similar to tropical nature. For example, many guidebooks would describe locals in appealing terms such as humble, warm, and connected to nature, only in the next sentence to warn travelers that they were lazy, licentious, and deceitful. Moreover, these differences were cemented through the racialization of local bodies. Not all local bodies were racialized equally; as Thompson shows, many local elites took pains to align themselves with white visitors.[20] Connecting locals to tropical nature and racializing them mutually reinforced their being understood as others by the visitors. The practice of seeing them as others, especially in its racial aspects, was used as justification for European and US colonialism and imperialism in the Caribbean.

Locals were not without agency in engaging with outside conceptions of tropical space and "tropical people," and they responded in a variety of ways. Some, as we see in the case of Puerto Rico under the governorship of Luis Muñoz Marín, sought to proudly claim tropicality as a positive feature of national identity. Many other individuals reacted in ways that have not been recorded, and unfortunately, their voices are not as present here as they should be. On the other hand, on a state level, government officials perpetuated these tropes in promotional material and the type of tourism development they undertook. We will perhaps never know what those decision makers thought—did they figure it as a compromise for more revenue, did they exclude themselves from the others, or something else?

Despite the discursive practice of ascribing these places and people a timeless or unchanging quality, officials were interested in fashioning a conception of the historic that belied the false narrative that these cultures and places were unvarying and constant. Establishing narratives of the historic played a key role in modernity projects as it helped to delineate differences between past and present. The historic was a malleable arena in which history could be shaped to suit present values and prerogatives. In other words, the national identity campaigns I discuss in most of these chapters relied heavily on careful construction of a colonial past.

Tourism and the built environment played a significant role in this. Modern hotels built in newly developing areas were in direct contrast to new or renewed interest in restoring and conserving a colonial core in each city. State promotion of colonial monuments and areas as essential to any visit to these cities cemented these historical narratives as both important and legitimate. During the period under study here, the historic entailed a celebratory engagement with the Spanish colonial past, with value placed on European roots and Spanish colonial "accomplishments" and little attention or value placed on Indigenous or African roots or the violences suffered by these groups. The celebration of the colonial past helped justify the imperialistic tourism taking place in the present.

## *Crucible of Modernity*

The hotel designs under study are manifestations of the complexities, nuances, and contradictions inherent in framing a national identity in each of the three Caribbean islands. These hotels also played a role in the unique urban histories of San Juan, Santo Domingo, and Havana. Both national identities and built environments are themselves born out of the longer history of these islands, in particular the spatial practices and history writing that happened after Europeans started colonizing the Caribbean at the end of the fifteenth century. While governments positioned the historic or old nature of the colonial period or the colonial urban core as a foil to the modernity of these new hotels, the Caribbean has in fact been quite modern for more than five hundred years. However, the persistence of the modernity/coloniality project continues to obscure recognition of the Caribbean as a leading site of modernity.

Sidney Mintz dedicated his professional career as an anthropologist to insisting that we see the Caribbean as a crucible of modernity. As he points out, it is the original European colonial site for expansion. Not only is the Caribbean a product of that encounter, but the production of the Caribbean has created the world we know today. It is worth quoting him at length, because his words capture the perspective from which my study is positioned:

> In the view espoused here, Caribbean peoples are the first *modernized* peoples in world history. They were modernized by enslavement and forced transportation; by "seasoning" and coercion on time-conscious export-oriented enterprises; by the reshuffling, redefinition and reduction of gender-based roles; by racial and status-based oppression; and by the need to reconstitute and maintain cultural forms of their own under implacable pressure. These were people wrenched from societies of a different sort, then thrust into remarkable *industrial* settings for their time and for their appearance, and kept under circumstances of extreme repression. Caribbean *cultures* had to develop under

these unusual and, indeed, terrible conditions. The argument here is that they have, as a result, a remarkably modern cast for their time.[21]

Mintz's presentation of the Caribbean is one that foregrounds the history of enslaved people, most of whom were brought to the Caribbean from Africa. However, these are not the people who have usually had much say in how twentieth-century histories were written at the time these hotels were built. Nor have we yet rectified that problem, as the Caribbean is still often left out of histories of modernity; for example, while there has been increasing recognition of the role of slavery in creating the conditions that made the Industrial Revolution possible, the standard narrative is still that the Industrial Revolution came out of Europe. There is little recognition of the Caribbean systems and processes of labor, technology, and capital that influenced—and financed—the Industrial Revolution on the other side of the Atlantic. Therefore, although this study is grounded in certain decades of the twentieth century, it is informed by a much larger temporal lens, both past and present/future. I follow in the footsteps of scholars such as Mintz who consider the Caribbean to be critical to the project and path of modernity by telescoping out to the twentieth century as Hispanic Caribbean nations were still struggling for sovereignty and grappling with how to construct twentieth-century identities.

The attention to three Hispanic Caribbean nations is not meant to suggest that tourism development was taking place only at these sites in the Caribbean. Hispanic Caribbean governments often looked to other countries—such as Jamaica, Mexico, the Bahamas, and more—for inspiration and as competition. Limiting the study to these three Hispanic nations is a means to hone in on the relationship between development and economic colonialism, through their shared, though certainly not identical, histories of Spanish colonialism followed by US imperialism. I do not intend this study to be strictly comparative in nature, nor do I suggest these islands are equivalent or congruent. All three places are quite distinct in their history, urban development, culture, and the way they utilized tourism as a form of development. Rather, my focus on these three places is based on research that has led me to the conclusion that the modern hotel as an international phenomenon had important roots in the Hispanic Caribbean.

## *People-Agency-Voices*

Wherever possible, my aim in this book is to move beyond the voices of those who held power in these island nations, though this a challenge because of the silencing in the archives of the voices of the oppressed and disempowered. Very real politics and power at work in how the archive is made render certain histories either invisible or incredibly challenging to bring to light. The many layers of production involved in the history of these hotels and in what they represent more broadly in terms of development and tourism are often hard to address evenly, but occasionally there are openings through which to focus on different voices. Government officials and the designers often shine through, though other agents are difficult to trace; it is hard to capture all of the texture of these histories because of the problematic ways in which we preserve materials and the consequences of what gets lost in the process. Although this makes writing a truly equitable history impossible, my aim is to question these conditions.

Other studies have thoroughly covered tourist perspectives from the search for authenticity to the escape from modernity and beyond. The focus here is more on what the host countries were trying to create, not on how those countries were interpreted by visitors from the contiguous United States. It is worth bearing in mind that the host countries working on tourism and development were complicit in perpetuating coloniality. Leading insular governments usually subscribed to values and ideologies similar to those of Europe or the United States, especially when it came to development and modernity. However, they often aimed to fashion these values in their own terms; to say it another way, values are not always aligned across countries but are not always contrary to colonial/imperial precedents and values. Thus, what was created by host countries was in certain ways itself detrimental to local communities. For example, indigeneity, for the most part, was simplified and tokenized when incorporated into tourism. As has been argued in tourism theory, this outcome can be expected from a system that revolves around consumption.

Looking to different local voices is not to suggest that the different groups always held opposing views but, rather, to recognize that there are so many different voices other than the few that have been recorded and preserved. What constitutes "locals" is not a homogenous body of citizens but, rather, a diversity of people who engaged with one another within systems of power negotiation based on factors such as race, class, and gender. Although the hotel projects studied here were often projects of the state, I employ other frameworks that open up these histories to consider other local groups, even if in an incomplete manner.

One means of acknowledging representation of different groups and individuals is to consider the urban and the rural in relation to one another. All of these hotel projects are in capital cities, but it is helpful to look outward toward rural contexts and toward larger insular programs and phenomena that affected both rural and urban areas. In chapter 3, I consider border and agrarian politics and the 1937 Haitian Massacre in order to bring into relief the work the Hotel Jaragua was intended to do in terms of racial politics and national identity. In the case of Cuba, favoring Havana at the expense of the rest of the island was a factor in the revolutions of both 1933 and 1959, which involved the targeting of hotels as contentious sites. To look across both the urban and the rural is to consider labor. Laborers are usually not represented or well accounted for in the archives, but it is through local labor that these hotels were built and that visitors negotiate their expectations and imaginaries with the experiences they have with real people, whether through the service industry, the entertainment sector, or something else.

Another approach that has been helpful in opening up this history is considering not just the mobility of tourists but also the mobility of locals. Looking at the movement of locals within the island (between capital city and rural areas) or abroad (either for short-term visits or more permanently to live in diaspora communities) reveals the consequences, both positive and negative, of development practices and programs. For example, when the Grand Condado Vanderbilt was being built, Puerto Ricans were newly minted US citizens, and this had a direct result in how many went to fight in World War I and World War II. From a different angle, Trujillo enacted agrarian policies that limited peasants' mobility, which allowed him to shore up the borders and monitor his state more thoroughly, all of which fed into his larger national identity project. Although rural areas often provided the material resources that brought money to the islands, they were often viewed by governments as spaces that needed to be firmly controlled, whereas the city was more readily viewed as representing the state's values.

## *Objects/Spaces of Study*

I take on one hotel as a main focus in each of the chapters that follow. In each case, I cover the history of the hotel—its conception, design, construction, funding, and operation—in detail, but larger contexts or adjacent histories are also critical to the narrative. This approach allows for the interrogation of each hotel's inextricable connection to the urban environments within which it is located, to the rural environments that engage in a mutually constitutive relationship with it, and even to built environments abroad. My aim is to capture how the hotel participates in a variety of flows—capital, labor, people, goods, imaginaries—and to suggest some of the effects that come out of these circulations.

In chapter 1, I focus on the Gran Condado Vanderbilt (1919) in San Juan, which serves as the most imperial example, because this is the only hotel under study that was built in a context where there was no local representation in government. I trace the imperial history of Frederick Vanderbilt's patronage of the architectural firm Warren & Wetmore to design a hotel as part of the effort to develop Puerto Rico as the "Switzerland of the Tropics" during a period of insular administration by contiguous US politicians and bureaucrats. The hotel's design promoted the tropical climate as being safe and pleasant for US visitors. As a case in point, an analysis of promotional brochures illustrates how the design's attention to sanitation and hygiene was understood to mediate the tropical climate—in its use of wicker furniture and technologically advanced refrigeration systems, for example. The hotel was a powerful tool for development extending beyond the hotel grounds; it facilitated a type of imperialistic tourism. Guests were encouraged to consider the hotel a home base from which to explore the natural splendor of the island through automobile touring—a new, modern leisure pastime that celebrated other infrastructure development such as paved roads and bridge building. Brochures also illustrate how the consumption of leisure was parallel to contemporaneous extractive economies that were often for the financial benefit and enjoyment of US citizens from the contiguous states. Extending beyond the completion of the hotel, I conclude the chapter by analyzing the Puerto Rican government's subsequent interest, in the 1930s, in acquiring the hotel as a potential revenue source that could aid in achieving financial independence for the island, a stance that sets the stage for the involvement of insular governments in the rest of the hotels under study.

In chapter 2, I consider President Gerardo Machado's Hotel Nacional de Cuba (1930) project in Havana within the context of the corruption and totalitarian policies that ultimately led to the Revolution of 1933. The hotel displayed its stature as the number one national hotel through design details that referenced the Cuban flag and Spanish colonial tradition and through the incorporation of vast quantities of fine Cuban wicker and mahogany furniture, a point of Cuban pride. I pay particular attention to the contractual and construction requirements faced by McKim, Mead & White in overseeing the project, which reveal complex Cuban-US business and political relations. I utilize publicity ephemera to trace how the hotel was marketed as one of the monuments of the city, a destination unto itself, a position reinforced by the way the hotel was incorporated in a contemporaneous master plan for Havana. This attention to the urban planning of the time underscores the considerable significance of tourism in tying together different parts of the city. I follow the history of the hotel through 1933 in order to investigate the passionate local response. The Hotel Nacional served as one of the major sites of the

Revolution of 1933 because, for many, it symbolized a corrupt and authoritarian government at odds with the needs and desires of the majority of Cuban people.

In chapter 3, I continue to examine government patronage of hotels in my study of the Hotel Jaragua (1942), President Trujillo's commission for Ciudad Trujillo (his renaming of Santo Domingo). I position the Hotel Jaragua as a space intended to legitimize the dictatorship and to promote a homogenous Dominican identity by paying attention to the hotel's plan, which allocated a disproportional amount of space to social areas rather than to guest rooms. Architect Guillermo González Sánchez's bold use of a modernist idiom in the design—groundbreaking in the Caribbean and beyond—not only differentiated the *trujillato* from previous governments but also was a global message of the progress and modernity of Trujillo's Dominican Republic. I explore the role of the hotel in Trujillo's program by setting it in the context of Trujillo's urban plans for designing Ciudad Trujillo as a modern first world city in the wake of the 1930 Ciclón de San Zenón. González's design and the confidence the hotel inspired within the government led the Trujillo regime to commission fourteen more hotels across the country. This is a shorter chapter because of the impact of COVID-19 on travel and research practices, though this very fact raises salient points about the precarious nature of development when travel and tourism play a dominant role.

The Caribe Hilton (1949) was also meant to legitimize the insular government—in this case the first popularly elected government of Puerto Rico. In chapter 4, I illustrate how the Puerto Rican government envisioned the Caribe Hilton as the symbol of Operación Manos a la Obra (Operation Bootstrap), a development program meant to bring progress and modernity to the island through manufacturing. Through an analysis of the hotel's design, I reveal the politics attached to the tropical modernism employed by local architectural firm Toro, Ferrer y Torregrosa and the importance of the hotel in legitimizing architectural modernism on the island. This was done, in part, through a careful construction of notions of a historic Puerto Rico, which were set in relief against the innovative new hotel. In particular, I argue that tropical modernism was a tool used in promoting a cultural nationalism in order to avoid a political nationalism that would only underscore the contentious issues of Puerto Rico's status vis-à-vis the United States. This form of tropical modernism suggested that modernity and exoticism, usually understood in oppositional terms, coexisted harmoniously in Puerto Rico. Internationally recognized as a success, the hotel was claimed simultaneously by Puerto Rico as a symbol of the national agenda and by the United States as evidence of both US benevolence and the virtues of adopting capitalist modernization practices.

In chapter 5, I focus on the Havana Riviera (1957), a privately owned hotel characterized by significant influence from government policy. My aim is to recuperate a history of the hotel that has been drowned in revolutionary rhetoric that dismisses its design as tourist kitsch; in this chapter I present a more complex picture. For example, I juxtapose the rampant land development and influence of US culture in Havana—spurred by President Fulgencio Batista's policies that favored foreign investment in the island—with a reading of the interior spaces as a proclamation of a cosmopolitan *cubanidad*. Filled with Cuban-made furniture, materials, and artworks displaying Cuban avant-garde engagement with themes of heritage, modernity, and identity, I argue that the Havana Riviera presented a mixture of the expected stereotypes and experiences with design elements that suggested a commitment to expressing a more authentic Cuban identity. It is this conflict between developing the island for foreigners or for Cubans that made hotels significant sites of resistance in the Cuban Revolution in 1959. The Revolution—a discussion of which brings to light many of the inherent conflicts in the type of hotel under study—marked the end of large-scale international tourism to Cuba for some time. The Cuban Revolution also coincides with a shift in hotel design practice in Puerto Rico and the Dominican Republic to more remote, secluded resort hotel models, which, through spatial design, minimized the type of local and visitor interaction previously provided in suburban resort hotels. I conclude the study by directly connecting certain trends and histories from across the chapters, linking to subsequent hotel and tourism trends, addressing continuities and ruptures in local concerns past and present, and drawing contemporary connections.

This study is part of a growing body of scholarship that connects modern architecture and design across many styles and across the world wars by focusing on prevalent overarching discourses such as hygiene, technology, and climate. The modern hotel in the Hispanic Caribbean was not a simple instance of imperial imposition, despite its "birth" in the United States. In fact, Caribbean hotels were driving innovation in the field of modern hotel design and tourism infrastructure. These hotels played a fundamental role in shaping notions of a tropical aesthetic, in establishing modern notions of the touristic zone, and in reinforcing the importance of a contained historic center. All of this was influential in other locations in the Caribbean, in parts of the United States, in other areas of Latin America, and in other places around the globe, in the tropical zone and elsewhere. Through exploration of the centrality of hotels and tourism in development projects, in this study I shed light on the profound impact of these designs both locally and internationally.

Figure 1.1. Postcard of the south façade of the Grand Condado Vanderbilt showing the Condado Lagoon. Author's collection.

# The Grand Condado Vanderbilt

### Creating the "Switzerland of the Tropics"

**An image of San Juan Viejo (Old San Juan) and its harbor opens the section on** Puerto Rico in the 1899 *Picturesque Cuba, Porto Rico, Hawaii, and the Philippines*.[1] The caption from the image locates the photograph (and, by extension, the position from which the viewers imagine themselves) as taken from the Hotel Inglaterra, underscoring the fact that the hotel is the base point, both physically and metaphorically, from which the visitor looks out into San Juan. This book captured the normal lodging and visiting experiences at the turn of the century—an urban hotel catering to guests who were in the city for business with perhaps some time for leisure activities. Advertised amenities included features that would appeal to business visitors, such as reading and writing rooms, and services such as translators; business took place in the lobbies and other spaces that were accessible to guests and nonguests of an acceptable social standing.[2] The hotel was an important meeting space used as a location for conferences to discuss the evacuation of Spanish military presence after the conclusion of the 1898 Spanish-American War, for example.[3]

The type of visiting promoted to contiguous-US visitors in *Picturesque Cuba, Porto Rico, Hawaii, and the Philippines* and supported by hotels such as the Inglaterra Hotel was the norm until the Grand Condado Vanderbilt opened in 1919 (figure 1.1).[4] The Grand Condado Vanderbilt not only marked a shift in hotel design in Puerto Rico, but its resort format also promoted a particular mode of leisure vacationing, which included activities such as golf and tennis. Despite some notable shifts in vacationing practices and different ways of understanding the insular possession between 1898 and 1919, the Grand Condado Vanderbilt underscored long-standing imperial rhetoric and promoted a vision of Puerto Rico and tourist experience of the island that was informed by and designed to reinforce imperial attitudes. Although in 1919 the island lacked sufficient progress in the contiguous-US popular imagination, the ability to experience it in a safe and refined manner was facilitated through the thoroughly modern and luxurious Grand Condado Vanderbilt—at least this is what was promised in the promotional materials. Thanks to the Grand Condado Vanderbilt, contiguous-US travelers could now experience Puerto Rico in an acceptable manner, according to the promotional materials published by the hotel. The idea of vacationing in Puerto Rico, especially according to the Grand Condado Vanderbilt publications, was grounded in the notion of a juxtaposition of the modern and the exotic or primitive.

The Grand Condado Vanderbilt story brings up a broader argument about imperialistic tourism—that is, a tourism based on imperial desires that functions to strengthen imperial agendas and dovetails with pro-development mentalities.[5] The hotel serves as an example to illustrate the spatial shift from plantation to touristic landscapes. The rather restrained Mediterranean Revival style of the hotel at once announced the luxury possible through US development and also suggested that Puerto Rico was still an outpost of empire (figure 1.2). Along with the structure, the representation of the hotel, both visual and textual, performed significant work in defining the hotel and in promoting imperialistic tourism. The Grand Condado Vanderbilt booklets were a new kind of propaganda literature that, in the quest to drum up more business, shaped a new way of understanding Puerto Rico as a vacation destination. They evidence the connection between the extractive practices of raw goods and agriculture and the consumption practices of tourism. Analysis of the hotel design and promotional materials points to the ways in which we can consider tourism development as much more related to other imperial business ventures than has been previously acknowledged.[6]

Perhaps overlooked because it does not involve the consumption of a tangible commodity, tourism, especially in the colonial/imperial context, was directly related to the historic flow of goods and money and also the power relations by which that flow was negotiated. Because imperial imperatives had to be justified through a paternalistic, professed commitment to helping local populations,

Figure 1.2. Photograph of the north façade of the Grand Condado Vanderbilt just before it opened in 1919. Folder 10, box 19, Warren & Wetmore Architectural Drawings and Photographs, 1889–1938, Avery Architectural & Fine Arts Library, Columbia University, New York City.

business ventures and tourism were bound to projects of development that were explained in terms of beneficial progress for the oppressed society. As it related to notions of progress, development extended to such diverse fields as urban development and resource extraction. When considered more holistically (with tourism as one of many types of businesses), a more comprehensive picture emerges of how, why, and when development was valued and implemented by powerful Puerto Ricans and US businessmen and the lasting effect this development had on the island in the decades that followed.

Two characteristic promotional brochures explore how the Grand Condado Vanderbilt was tied to conversations of imperialism and development. Meant to be understood as a transplant of US design, modes, and meaning, the hotel was set up as one end of a continuum of US style lodging in the booklet "Porto Rico: The Island of Enchantment." Travelers traded their everyday accommodation for those of the "modern luxurious steamers" of the New York & Porto Rico Steamship Company. The vacation started on the boat, as travelers enjoyed warmer climes and the entertainment provided during four days at sea. The brochure depicts deck games, dancing, and the "thoroughly modern and complete appointments" of the guest cabins. These accommodations were meant to be an extension of the United States and to provide all the comforts of domestic life associated with the contiguous United States. Images of the Grand Condado Vanderbilt that follow are comparable in level of comfort and luxury. This notion of the Grand Condado Vanderbilt as something not insular but of the contiguous United States is reinforced through the graphic commingling of images of interiors of the steamer and the hotel.[7]

The booklet "Porto Rico: 'The Switzerland of the Tropics'" also connects the Grand Condado Vanderbilt to US traditions through its ads for other Vanderbilt hotels in the contiguous United States, reminding the reader that the Grand Condado Vanderbilt was to be understood unequivocally as being of the United States. These connections to the modernity of the steamship or the Vanderbilt hotels in the contiguous states reasserted the Grand Condado Hotel's connection to the United States and reinforced broader touristic and imperialist discourses. Despite the fact that publications often reasserted Puerto Rico's status as part of the United States, there was no mistaking the island for one of the contiguous forty-eight. At this moment in time, Puerto Rico was a territory of the US empire that was understood to be inferior to the United States. The printed publications for the Grand Condado Vanderbilt reinforced these beliefs through its association with the United States and through its work in promoting a tourism based on imperialist prerogatives. The hotel was a product of and an instrument for reinforcing imperial imperatives and, importantly, shaping an imperial imaginary for contiguous-US citizens. The brochures—and the real experience they promoted—constructed and defined a vision of Puerto Rico that underscored the island's availability for US consumption and possession through the seemingly innocent action of leisure travel.

### *The Switzerland of the Tropics*

Shortly after its opening in 1919, the Grand Condado Vanderbilt hotel published a promotional brochure for Puerto Rico, proudly declaring Puerto Rico, "The Switzerland of the Tropics" (plate 2). The brochure explained that it was Theodore Roosevelt who first applied this sobriquet to the island in a letter home to his children. Roosevelt, one of the most ardent of US imperialists, returned to this idea more than once, including in a speech he gave to Congress on December 11, 1906, when he noted "the mountains of the interior, which constitute a veritable tropic Switzerland."[8]

Although recounted as an offhand comment made by Roosevelt, this moniker conjured a certain image of Puerto Rico that served the purposes of Roosevelt's imperial politics. The low-stakes context invoked in the brochure—an inconsequential letter from a father to his children—seemingly strips the phrase of political implications. However, his repetition of this expression in Congress suggests otherwise, and there was much at stake in employing this phrase. Images and ideas related to Switzerland—Old World, cultured, civilized, beautiful landscapes, no unbearably hot or humid climate—were thus transposed onto Puerto Rico, even if Roosevelt claimed he was only talking about the mountains. Roosevelt, who had already traveled multiple times to the US West, was no stranger to lofty ranges, many of which loomed over the likes of those in Puerto Rico, suggesting ulterior motives to this tagline rather than an innocent comparison based on geographic characteristics.

At the time Roosevelt first uttered this sobriquet, Puerto Rico had been under the control of the United States for less than ten years after the Spanish-American War. The "splendid little war," as John Hay famously called it, left the United States with new territorial possessions, including Puerto Rico.[9] The United States was mostly interested in Puerto Rico as a coaling station and as a means to establish a stronger presence in the Caribbean.[10] However, other imperial concerns soon came to the fore, including an attention to "civilizing" Puerto Rico so it could be used as an exemplar of the positive effects of US empire and also attention to how the island could be exploited for agricultural purposes.

After two years of military administration, the Foraker Act instituted a civil government in May 1900, giving the United States controlling power over the island—to the disdain of many Puerto Ricans. As a result, the act was amended to give Puerto Ricans more of a role in the government, but by the time of the 1909 Olmsted Act, Washington still wielded extensive and ultimate control over the insular government. Colonial relations and the lived experiences of Puerto Ricans were further complicated by the Jones Act of 1917, which granted US citizenship to Puerto Ricans and expanded Puerto Rican participation in the US government while at the same time affirming Puerto Rico's status as a permanent territory of the United States.[11]

When "The Switzerland of the Tropics" was splashed across the front of the Grand Condado Vanderbilt brochure, published after the hotel's 1919 opening, the island's status was essentially the same as it had been twenty years earlier—the

US government was still exerting significant imperial control in Puerto Rico, specifically in limiting Puerto Rican self-governance. The Jones Act conferred US citizenship upon Puerto Ricans but did not grant much in the way of self-determination. This act and earlier twentieth-century maneuverings reinforced a concept of Puerto Rico that was concretized in the 1901 US court case *Downes v. Bidwell*, which was concerned with whether oranges coming into New York from Puerto Rico would be subject to import duties. Since the Constitution provided that all import duties shall be uniform throughout all of the United States and since there were no duties on oranges from other parts of the United States, the contention was that there should be no duty on oranges from Puerto Rico. However, the court's holding was that the Constitution does not necessarily apply to territories and that Congress had the jurisdiction to create laws within territories in certain circumstances. In explaining Puerto Rico's role as an unincorporated territory in this series of cases known as the Insular Cases (1901–1905), the Supreme Court declared Puerto Rico's relationship to the United States as "not part of it and not *not* part of it." Oranges, Puerto Ricans, and the island itself were treated interchangeably after the Insular Cases and were positioned as open to an interpretation of being both within and without the United States in ways that economically and politically privileged the contiguous United States.[12]

This classification contributed to the ways in which development on the island could either be attributed to the United States or be claimed as a Puerto Rican accomplishment. This dual status was exploited by tourism boosters as a way to promote a destination that simultaneously promised the safety and comfort of the United States and the excitement and exoticism of a foreign country. The variation of the phrase from "Switzerland of the Tropics" to "Switzerland of America," which appeared in some later promotional publications, further suggests the extent to which imperial politics were bound to the promotion of tourism to Puerto Rico. The shift in words demonstrates less concern with the tropical nature of the island and more attention given to locating Puerto Rico as part of the United States.

The Grand Condado Vanderbilt is but one example of how the interests of US captains of industry in overseas development aligned with US government and social reasons for justifying empire. As Greg Grandin summarizes, foreign policy officials applied soft power—that is, the assertion of US authority through nonmilitary means such as culture and commerce—throughout various places in Latin America. The Spanish-American War had opened the Hispanic Caribbean to US corporate interests, as banks and corporations looked to move into the region to take advantage of postwar opportunities. When the United States took control of Puerto Rico in 1898, the idea of US expansion was supported by US citizens of various stripes as economics, intellectual analysis, and emotional involvement converged to promote an imperial outlook.[13]

Within this broader context, Frederick Vanderbilt's interest in business abroad was quite typical, though the type of business venture he launched was not. Surely inspired by the resort hotels popular in the United States, Vanderbilt commissioned, under the auspices of the Vanderbilt Hotels Company, a luxury resort hotel that was located outside of the urban core of San Juan. Vanderbilt was breaking new ground—this was the first resort hotel on the island and his first hotel venture outside the continental United States. Vanderbilt probably understood the value of building a resort hotel for the upper class at this particular moment and in this specific place. With the temperance movement gaining ground in the United States and talk of a prohibition on alcohol, businessmen started to think of alternative ways to profit from alcohol consumption. Vanderbilt may have considered the potential profits of a resort in Puerto Rico if alcohol consumption were forbidden at resorts in the contiguous United States.[14] Moreover, with World War I raging in Europe, Puerto Rico was an alternative for the US elite who usually traveled to the French Riviera or other places in the temperate Mediterranean. The island offered the Old World charm and warmer climate associated with the Mediterranean while being well removed from the war zone.

Ensconced in the world of railroad transportation, Vanderbilt was well aware of the effects that increased transportation technologies and networks were having on tourism and may have felt that he wanted a piece of the pie. Perhaps inspired by the success of Henry Flagler and Henry Plant in moving into uncharted territory to develop Florida as a leisure destination, Vanderbilt looked to Puerto Rico, which had some hotels but was not developed for leisure tourism in the same way as Florida. John E. Berwind, whose family had owned the New York & Porto Rico Steamship Company for a short time, may have guided Vanderbilt's gaze toward Puerto Rico. Berwind sold the company in 1907, but he may have used his experience to talk up Puerto Rico as an untapped market. Indeed, Berwind was no minor character in the history of the Grand Condado Vanderbilt; he was a major partner with the Vanderbilt Hotels Company and fought to see the project constructed.[15]

The figure of John E. Berwind reminds us of how design and tourism were bound to larger imperial projects grounded in capitalist expansion and resource extraction. Like many other powerful white capitalists of the United States, Berwind sought to profit from a variety of ventures that were not necessarily seen as unrelated. In addition to his connection to the Grand Condado Vanderbilt and his role as director of the New York & Porto Rico Steamship Company, Berwind was a founder of the South Porto Rico Sugar Company, president of the Puerto Rico Coal Company, and vice-president of the Havana Coal Company.[16] The coal magnate's involvement in multiple coal companies suggests his perspective that numerous resource sites and companies ensured greater and more consistent profits. It also reminds us that in cases such as these, capital was almost always flowing outward from these imperial islands to the contiguous United States—and more specifically, into the pockets of white businessmen well connected with politicians and government. However, when we look to structures of leisure, in this case at the Grand Condado Vanderbilt, we do not see reference to extracted resources such as coal or sugar. The narrative has been wiped clean of the othered bodies whose sweat, blood, and (in many cases) ultimately lives provided Berwind with the capital to invest in the hotel project.

Moreover, Puerto Rico was a particularly attractive location for a hotel project for US businessmen because in several enticing economic and juridical ways it was still part of the United States. Setting up businesses in the territories of US empire was often read as a forward-looking, albeit risky, business move. Echoing the sentiments expressed in the ethos of Manifest Destiny, the acquisition of territories in 1898 was justified by, among other things, the science-inspired idea of political gravitation. According to this theory, it was only natural that the "weaker" societies (such as Puerto Rico) would be drawn to the "stronger" United States—scientific ideas rendered absorption into the United States as being both natural and inevitable.[17] Continuing along this line, it was believed to be natural that the United States would have its influence and that strong men, such as Frederick Vanderbilt, would reach out to mold these underdeveloped places.[18]

Those who developed Florida for tourists created transportation and lodging infrastructure together, but Vanderbilt did not create parallel transportation and lodging ventures that economically benefited and reinforced one another.[19] Instead, the hotel established a symbiotic relationship with the Porto Rico Steamship Company. Up to this point, travel to the Caribbean was reserved for the elite, who had the requisite time and money to travel. As mobilities scholar Mimi Sheller notes, the network of tourism in the Caribbean that developed in the late nineteenth century was based on the fast steamship routes that grew up with the fruit trade, which travelers used as a major means of transportation to get to and from the Caribbean islands.[20] Headquartered in New York, the Porto Rico Steamship Company was the major steamship line to Puerto Rico, conveying passengers in as few as four or five days in 1917. The steamship company invested between forty thousand and fifty thousand dollars in the construction of the hotel, and the Grand Condado Vanderbilt relied on the Porto Rico Steamship Company to deliver visitors to the hotel.[21]

At the time it opened, the Grand Condado Vanderbilt's primary competition was the hotel industry in Palm Beach and Miami. Although we will never know exactly why Vanderbilt decided to build a hotel in Puerto Rico, it was a logical choice given the mindset of the time.[22] Puerto Rico was positioned as part of the US empire, a natural extension further south from Florida, and was promoted as being ripe for development opportunities. The Grand Condado Vanderbilt offered its financial backers the opportunity to get in on the ground floor of the next big vacation destination for contiguous-US travelers.

## *Urban Development*

The Vanderbilt Hotels Company and John Berwind took advantage of the urban development project of Condado. The grandeur of the subsequently constructed hotel and the prestige of the urban development of Condado contributed to Condado's reputation as a modern, progressive, and desirable part of San Juan. Bordered by the Atlantic Ocean to the north and the Condado Lagoon to the south, the Condado area is a small peninsula that juts out west from the mainland and reaches toward, but does not touch, San Juan islet (containing Puerta de Tierra and San Juan Viejo), to the west. During the early twentieth century, two brothers—Sosthenes and Hernan Behn—invested significant time and money into making Condado an upper-class residential neighborhood of San Juan. The Grand Condado Vanderbilt was the first monumental, nonresidential structure to be built in Condado, and it was fundamental to the development of this area.

At the time the hotel was built, San Juan islet was connected to the mainland by four major roadways with bridges. Three of these roadways connected by bridge to the rest of the island south of the Condado Lagoon. The other major thoroughfare to the mainland was the Puente Dos Hermanos, known in English as the Behn Brothers Bridge. Built by the Behn brothers, the bridge fed into Avenida Ashford, Condado's main thoroughfare. The bridge and the direct connection it provided to San Juan islet contributed greatly to the area's development.

In 1908, while building the bridge, the Behn brothers were also involved in developing a residential park in Condado along the streetcar line.[23] Engineer Juan Bautista Rodríguez drew out the subdivision in Condado, dividing the area into sixteen hundred lots of varying sizes, which radiated out from a focal point.[24] The bridge allowed the Behn brothers to run telephone cables to Condado, which probably received telephone service earlier than other elite neighborhoods of San Juan such as Santurce and Miramar, located to the south of Condado.[25] In short, they were building a thoroughly modern neighborhood, and they enticed the social elite to purchase land in Condado by offering a level of amenities and infrastructure commensurate with a modern built environment, including rainwater drainage systems, a streetcar line, wetland infill, three acres of parks, an esplanade, a kiosk, and three new boulevards.[26]

The character of the development resembled contemporary suburban developments in the United States and other cities in Latin America such as Havana, Buenos Aires, São Paulo, and Mexico City, among others.[27] By the end of 1909, local publications advertised that the upper-class Condado residences of M. Rodríguez Serra, F. Ramírez de Arrellano, Ralph Swigget, and José Llompart had been completed and the value of the lots had more than doubled in the first year.[28] This year also marked the incorporation of the Borinquen Park Company, which operated Borinquen Park in Condado, responsible for providing amusements to Condado residents that echoed what was fashionable in large metropolises in the Americas and Europe. The park became a social venue for *sanjuaneros* to dress up and parade—to see and be seen.

The Behn brothers—foreigners who, through their business interests, positioned themselves as part of San Juan's elite society—laid the groundwork for urban development in Condado.[29] Even though a few residences were constructed as early as 1909, Condado remained largely unbuilt until ten years later when the Grand Condado Vanderbilt was constructed. The hotel established an approach to building that was copied throughout the area and that cemented the reputation of Condado as a place of sophistication and luxury. Its prominent position along Avenida Ashford made the hotel a visual focal point; it gave the hotel access to the infrastructure of the Condado Residential Park and provided guests access to attractive natural and man-made amenities. While the hotel was located on a plot of land on the north side of Avenida Ashford and its north façade butted up against a rocky outcropping touching the Atlantic Ocean, its property also extended south of Avenida Ashford to the more tranquil waters of Condado Lagoon. Designers converted this area into gardens and spaces for other activities such as tennis for the guests.

Besides access to two bodies of water, the Condado area provided more spacious grounds to build upon. San Juan Viejo was an area of interest to tourists who wanted to discover the old colonial city or go shopping and dining, but there was not much space within the walled city to build a grand hotel with resort amenities such as outdoor gardens and tennis courts. However, after the construction of the Puente Dos Hermanos, access was easy from Condado to San Juan Viejo. Condado offered hotel developers the opportunity to plan for more expansive grounds, while still being conveniently located near the city center. In fact, when the Grand Condado Vanderbilt was first built, areas to either side of the hotel were populated with only palms and conifers, offering the ambiance of nature and seclusion that one expected to find at a grand resort hotel.

## Warren & Wetmore and the Mediterranean Revival

Perhaps the most productive way of understanding the design of the Grand Condado Vanderbilt is as a representation of architectural firm Warren & Wetmore's understanding of what it meant to design for clientele expectations for a resort hotel in Puerto Rico.[30] The stripped-down Mediterranean Revival design of the exterior of the hotel indicates the firm's use of formalism to shape the guests' experience, and the more restrained design was probably the reflection of their understanding of Puerto Rican architecture. We can read this lack of ornamentation as a deliberate design choice meant to reinforce the location as an outpost of empire. Here, the design suggests the notion that the colonial outpost always strives to mimic the greatness of the metropole, but because of its nature as colony it never can reach the same magnificence, thus reinforcing the notion of US superiority. However, the goal was not to create an architecture that could be dismissed easily, and the monumentality of the building commands respect.

Known for their Beaux Arts approach, the firm had already designed a number of residences for the Vanderbilt family and had played a central role in the Vanderbilts' Grand Central Terminal project in New York, including the design of three of the four hotels in the terminal complex. However, a resort hotel in what was considered an outpost of empire was a project quite different from the urban hotels in Manhattan to which Warren & Wetmore were accustomed. Their 1917 design for the Grand Condado Vanderbilt unquestionably achieved the goal of creating a grand resort that reinforced the power and prominence of the Vanderbilt family. One of the firm's drawings of the projected hotel and grounds illustrates how Warren & Wetmore intended to create a sense of grandeur and monumentality through the restrained use of decoration and the creation of expansive, carefully designed gardens that would spread from the hotel's main façade south across Avenida Ashford to Condado Lagoon (see plate 3).[31] The landscape design connected across Avenida Ashford, insisting on a larger symmetrical and highly regulated design suggestive of French gardens. The similarity between the hotel's building and grounds and Mediterranean villas and landscape architecture evoked the grandeur and refinement of these luxurious properties of the European nobility.

The structure was completed in 1919, built of reinforced concrete with a hipped terracotta tile roof, a popular feature for Mediterranean Revival style buildings. The Mediterranean flavor was reinforced underneath the roof overhang, where wood support beams imitated those of Spanish architecture both in Spain and in its colonies. The smooth plaster cement finish of the exterior and interior walls, the decoration, and the fenestration and openings that reinforced openness to the temperate climate all referenced Mediterranean architectural traditions.

Whitney Warren and Charles D. Wetmore's Beaux Arts architectural education and the tendency of this school to favor eclecticism undoubtedly informed the Mediterranean Revival style of the hotel. Their Beaux Arts education predisposed them to a primary concern with program, symmetry, and grandeur achieved through the use of historical styles that architects freely borrowed, combined, and adapted. Architects, and society in general, considered Beaux Arts design a modern building approach during the earlier part of the firm's architectural practice.

Warren & Wetmore's reference files for the project in the Avery Architectural and Fine Arts Library contain a number of photos and reproductions of architecture in Puerto Rico, Cuba, and Spain. Much of the Spanish architecture in the files is highly ornamented Moorish architecture; there are numerous photos of the Alhambra Palace. However, images of Puerto Rican architecture in the files may have influenced the more restrained design of the Grand Condado Vanderbilt. These photographs depict architecture of basic design with simple lines and little to no decoration, including many images of simple wooden houses with tiled roofs and *bohíos*.[32] In addition, the colonial architecture in San Juan was, in general, rather plain and did not have as much ornament as that found in Spanish colonial architecture in other Latin American locations. Warren & Wetmore may have been thinking of their design in terms of the context of extant architecture in Puerto Rico, as the Grand Condado Vanderbilt was a relatively undecorated building, save for the neo-Plateresque windows and ornamental swags.[33] Whether or not this is how the designers really understood Puerto Rican architecture, this is the image of Puerto Rican architecture they chose to engage with in their design.

The few decorated windows project a recognizable Mediterranean Revival character. Perhaps the most striking of these are the two neo-Plateresque windows on the third floor whose decoration continues upward to the windows above, on the fourth floor. Elaborate detailing surrounds the simple rectangular window openings, and this cast concrete ornamentation is the most extravagant feature of the entire façade. Although rich with neoclassical elements such as Corinthian columns and cornices with decorative keys, this ornamentation also contains some maritime elements such as mermen and fish, reinforcing the hotel's oceanfront location.

Another focal point of the main façade is a large ornamental coat of arms located between the fourth and fifth floors. To either side of the large central coat of arms, crowned with a seashell, floral garland swags drape outward and connect to two smaller coats of arms.[34] These two coats of arms contain anchor designs in the center, adding another maritime reference to the hotel's decoration. The maritime details—anchors, fish, seashells, and mermen—have multiple interpretations. They could be a reference to the hotel's proximity to the ocean (a point on all visitors' minds as they would have come to Puerto Rico by ship) and could also be a reference to the Vanderbilt family, who amassed their first fortune in international maritime shipping.

After the Grand Condado Vanderbilt Hotel, Warren & Wetmore designed a number of more heavily ornamented hotels and monumental buildings for locations outside the United States, most of which were territories or under heavy US influence. Sometime around 1919, the firm designed a proposal for an extension for the Sevilla-Biltmore in Havana.[35] Decidedly Spanish Revival in style, the design has a strong Moorish flavor, which is completely absent from the Grand Condado Vanderbilt.[36] In the proposal for the Havana hotel, the uppermost part of the hotel is highly decorated with pinnacles, windows surrounded by elaborate ornamentation, and textured surfaces that recall elaborate brickwork in Moorish architecture. The lower portion of the hotel aims to garner attention through its balconied windows and arches, both punctuated by Spanish Revival decorative elements. And while the Condado Vanderbilt has a relatively unadorned central area, save for the coat of arms and neo-Plateresque windows, the Havana hotel's central portion is marked by heavy repetition of highly elaborated balconied windows interspersed with the application of decorative elements to the walls.

Warren & Wetmore also proposed a project for a new presidential palace in Havana. A sprawling three-story structure, the proposed palace had a strong neoclassical character, with Corinthian capitals, pedimented windows, floral swag ornamentation, and a balustrade topped with urns. A design such as this was quite fitting for Havana. Not only did the neoclassical style probably lend an air of sophistication and status to the palace, it was visually similar to other neoclassical designs in Havana. In particular, it shares a number of decorative elements with the iconic neoclassical Hotel Inglaterra, of which the firm had a photograph in their reference files.[37]

Warren & Wetmore also developed a design for a hotel in Mexico City that was never realized (figure 1.3). Probably dating to somewhere between 1917 and 1924, the proposed hotel is a massive rectangular structure that appears to take up at least one-quarter of the city block and dwarfs the buildings around it. The Spanish Revival style of the Mexico City hotel proposal was more subdued than that of the Sevilla-Biltmore design, but it was still more decadently ornamented than the Condado Vanderbilt. The design incorporated fewer Moorish details and focused more on the classical vocabulary used in Spanish Renaissance and baroque architecture. For example, lower and upper floors boasted pedimented windows articulated in a classical language and the four corners of the building thrust upward to create square areas pierced by archways and topped by open cupolas. Despite their differences, projects such as these show just how prominent urban hotels were in the city landscape as beacons of modernity and good living.

Based on the external appearance of the Mexico City and Havana projects, it appears the architects were following an established hotel design practice of locating public spaces on the first two floors, similar to the Grand Condado Vanderbilt design, and on top floors, which were usually dedicated to banquet halls and ballrooms. Despite their programmatic similarities, however, of the three hotels Warren & Wetmore designed for Latin American cities, the Grand Condado Vanderbilt stands out as the most visually subdued with clean lines and little ornamentation. Given the island's status as a territory of the United States and the fact that it was not yet established as a vacation destination for the elite, the more restrained use of architectural elements referencing far-flung exotic locations reinforced the idea that Puerto Rico was not too foreign—perhaps primitive, by continental US standards, but not too exotic.

Their experience with the Grand Condado Vanderbilt and other country clubs and hotels also helped Warren & Wetmore gain commissions for projects in other parts of the Caribbean. In 1922, the British steamship company Furness, Withy and Company hired Warren & Wetmore to design the Bermuda Golf Club in Tucker's Town, Bermuda. Warren & Wetmore complemented the club in 1925 with the Hotel Bermudiana, which was part of a later phase of the development plan of Bermuda's Trade Development Board.[38] Another well-known Mediterranean Revival style hotel by Warren & Wetmore—the Royal Hawaiian on Waikiki Beach in Honolulu, Hawai'i—was designed in 1925 and completed in 1927. The Royal Hawaiian was built to fashion Waikiki into an upper-class resort and residential community and to accommodate the hordes of US tourists arriving by steamship.[39] Historian Christine Skwiot analyzes the manner in which guests could understand

Figure 1.3. Proposal for a hotel in Mexico City by Warren & Wetmore. Folder 9, box 19, Warren & Wetmore Architectural Drawings and Photographs, 1889–1938, Avery Architectural & Fine Arts Library, Columbia University, New York City.

the Royal Hawaiian simultaneously as both luxuriously modern and associated with the perceived primitive simplicity of the residences of Hawai'i's native chiefs and chieftesses. The property grounds were supposedly royal grounds of the kings and queens of Hawai'i, and the pink stucco of the hotel made an allusion to the coral house of King Kamehameha and Queen Ka'ahumanu.[40]

In the hands of Warren & Wetmore, the Mediterranean Revival became a tool to promote imperialist visions that justified the US presence on these islands. The leisure activities of tourism promoted through these hotels masked the dark sides of these imperial relationships—such as the extraction of resources and labor that in many cases provided the initial capital for investment in the development of the tourism industry. Along with benefiting US capitalists, Warren & Wetmore also profited from their foray into imperial projects. Their work on the Grand Condado Vanderbilt begat invitations for more work in the US empire, as they developed a reputation for designing in imperial landscapes.

## *Planned for Luxury and Efficiency*

The vast amount of architectural and building publications that were printed in the United States in the first decades of the twentieth century served as a forum and material sourcebook for contemporary architects. Although published about ten years after Warren & Wetmore first conceived their design for the Grand Condado Vanderbilt, architectural historian Rexford Newcomb's explanation of the Mediterranean Revival would have held true in the 1910s: "Spanish, Italian, Moorish, Byzantine—all Mediterranean types generally—instead of being archeologically segregated, are under the orchestral process merged, as were those golden threads long ago, into a new, sun-loving style which, while eminently American in its plan and utilities, is never-the-less distinctly Mediterranean in its origins and spirit."[41] Newcomb clearly thinks this contemporary style combines the best of both worlds—the attention to functionality and efficiency associated with US practices and the architectural richness of blending historical styles. It was a style that could be considered quite alluring and desirable by potential tourists. The Grand Condado Vanderbilt complemented its outward appearance with interiors that referenced history but also spoke to the modern efficient nature of the hotel.

The restrained Mediterranean Revival hotel was composed of a major central hall with two flanking wings. The organization of the fenestration on the main façade reinforced the style of the hotel and referenced the rational organization of the interior space. The division between the two first floors (dedicated to public

Figure 1.4. Photograph of the colonnaded gallery on the ocean side of the Grand Condado Vanderbilt just before opening in 1919. Folder 10, box 19, Warren & Wetmore Architectural Drawings and Photographs, 1889–1938, Avery Architectural & Fine Arts Library, Columbia University, New York City.

spaces) and the three upper floors (the guest rooms) was clearly demarcated by a stringcourse integrated into a decorative balcony that ran along the central portion of the main hall.[42] Consistent with European villa and palace design, the grandest floor of the hotel, the *piano nobile*, was located on the second floor. This was echoed in the façade and in the nine double-height arched openings located above the rectangular openings of the first floor, which marked the importance of the second floor.

The oceanfront façade was designed to allow guests to enjoy the ocean views.

The arched openings on the second floor of the north façade provided expansive vistas of the Atlantic Ocean. In the main hall, these archways opened up to a patio with a central hexagonal garden surrounded by a colonnaded gallery, which culminated in a covered pavilion at the point closest to the sea (figure 1.4). Warren & Wetmore positioned views of nature within an architectural framework using this colonnaded gallery along with the arched openings on the second floor. The open colonnaded gallery allowed guests to feel connected to the ocean as waves crashed up to the rocky shore just below the building. An assortment of wicker furniture decorated the gallery, encouraging guests to relax while still maintaining an openness that facilitated easy movement throughout this area.

The interior spaces of the hotel were designed in a layout conducive to an efficient hotel that also projected Puerto Rico's Spanish heritage in a monumental fashion. Guests first entered through an unassuming entrance under the porte-cochère on the south façade where they encountered a grand staircase to take them up a floor to the main level of the hotel. The double-lyre-shaped flying staircase was dramatic, partly because the staircase widened moving upward. Created out of reinforced concrete, the staircase was surfaced with black terrazzo, which complemented the other terrazzo floor designs of the first and second stories and further underscored the elegance and grandeur of the Grand Condado Vanderbilt lobby.[43]

Grand moments in the hotel's public spaces were complemented by services and amenities to ensure that guests were comfortable. For example, the first floor included ladies' and men's rooms, a barbershop, a restaurant, a billiard room, and a bowling alley. There were services on the first floor that were hidden from the guests but that were vital to the operation of the hotel, such as trunk storage, kitchens, pantries, and a stewards' department. The second floor, which was dedicated primarily to social functions, also included utilitarian services including offices, telephones, and a ladies' parlor.

Beyond this front area, which revolved around the grand staircase, the second floor was divided into three other spaces: the dining room, the lounge, and the patio (figure 1.5). The open patio area was located in the center, with a dining room and a lounge room of the same size symmetrically flanking it. These indoor and outdoor spaces were all connected by a network of loggias that fostered a form of leisure entertainment where guests could stroll around to take in the fresh air and the views outside, socializing and watching what was happening in the rooms with opened doors. Arched openings in the loggia were topped by wooden transoms and glass transom windows; they had wooden louvered doors that could either fold open to allow a cross breeze to ventilate the area or be kept closed for privacy

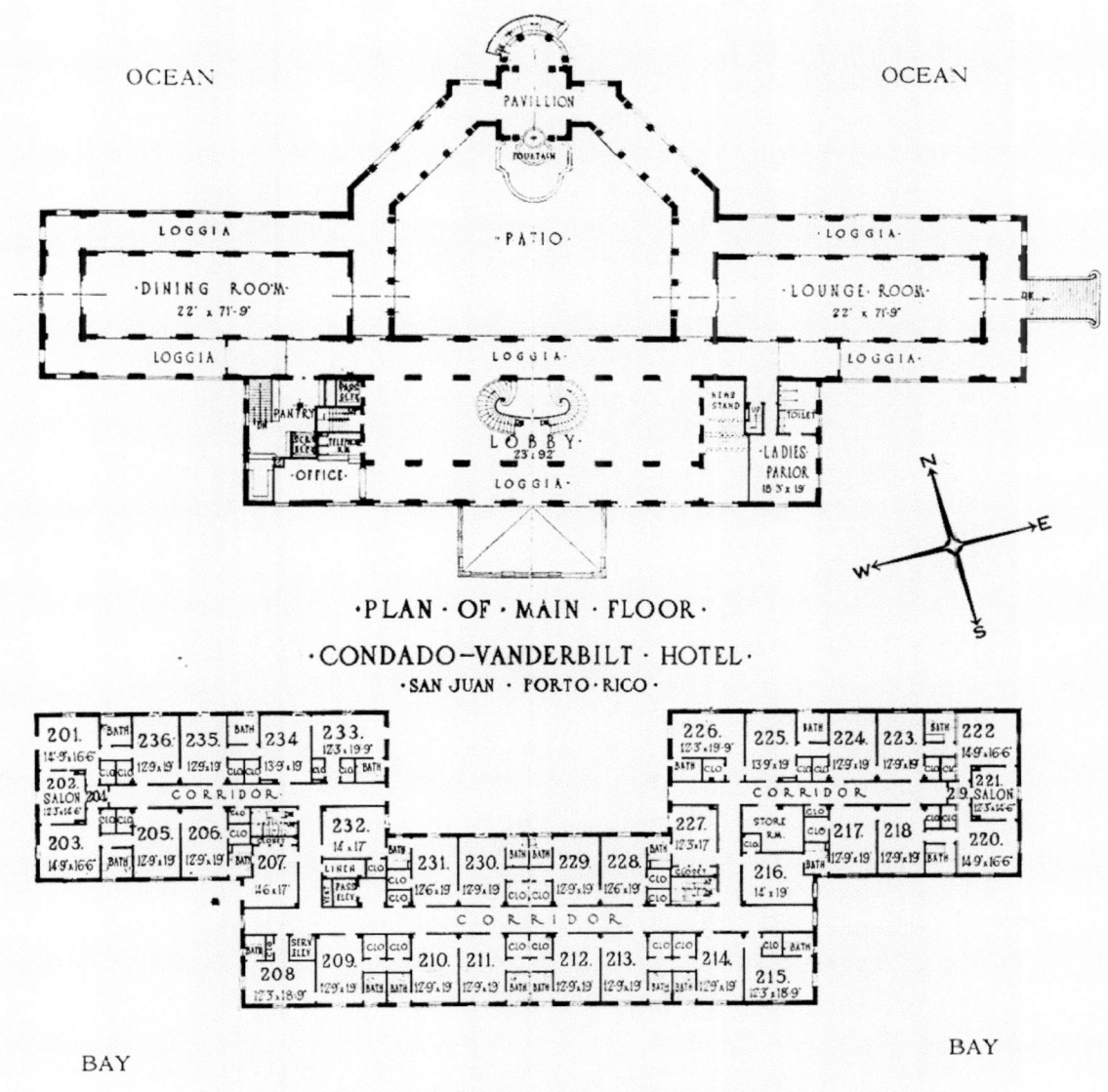

Figure 1.5. Plan of the main floor (second level) and typical guest-room floor from a brochure for the Grand Condado Vanderbilt. Archivo General de Puerto Rico.

or for protection from the elements. Some of the loggias and rooms on the second floor contained traditional Spanish style ceilings, with exposed wooden beams that were either plain or intricately carved with classical decoration and human figures. Other sections of the loggia and the rooms had pointed cross vaults with electric lamps that looked like candle lanterns hanging from the center.

A postcard of the public space near the grand staircase on the second floor illustrates how the interior design of the hotel conjured notions of the historic, tropical, and modern (plate 4). The space is equipped predominantly with wicker furniture, considered particularly appropriate for warm climates. Since the nineteenth century, in US and European thought, wicker was considered a more sanitary option to upholstered furniture. In the United States in the 1900s and 1910s especially, scores of popular magazines and domestic guides touted wicker as naturally hygienic because it was airy, vermin-free, and thoroughly sanitary.[44] Wicker was especially valuable in the hot humid climate of Puerto Rico as it did not absorb moisture, allowed air to circulate freely, and could be cleaned easily. The wicker furniture in the postcard, designed for comfort and lounging, references the tropical climate, and so do the potted tropical plants in the interior. Visually prominent furniture, such as centrally located tables surrounded by chairs, are wooden Mediterranean Revival style pieces that point to history. Recalling a European-rooted past, perhaps real or imagined, the table in the postcard conjures notions of a romantic Spanish colonial past, the type of furniture Spanish nobility used to furnish their residences in the New World. The heavy wooden legs and stretchers of the table recall fine handcrafted furniture in a baroque style, the curves and turns of which bring a visual liveliness to the space. The table stands on a rug with a simple checkerboard pattern, which appears light enough to be easily removed for cleaning. The interior is modern, creating a hygienic interior.

In contrast to grand hotels further north in the United States, the Grand Condado Vanderbilt was not filled with plush carpets, thick drapes, and stuffed furniture. The restrained decoration of the public spaces indicated not only notions of a simpler past but also an approach to interior design that considered ease of cleaning and issues of sanitation in a modern civilization. This was a necessary counterpoint to any references to the tropical or the historic, which, on their own, may have reminded guests too much of an underdeveloped or unsafe place.

The third, fourth, and fifth floors were dedicated to guest rooms, each of which had a window (plate 5).[45] Rooms boasted practical furniture that did not crowd the space, lending a sense of airiness to the room. The wicker chaise longue and armchairs promoted relaxed corporeal positions, and the limited color palette and patterns in the room reinforced the sense that the Condado Vanderbilt, even in the outposts of empire, offered comfortable accommodations. At the end of the wings on these floors, a salon between two rooms allowed for the possibility of a large suite of rooms. Many rooms had a private "American style" bathroom, which contained a toilet, a sink, and a shower with a tub, as was customary in the contiguous United States. The bathrooms were decorated with the white fixtures popular at the time, and wherever possible, bathrooms were located next to one another, an efficient design so as to cut back on the number of pipes running throughout the structure. Other bedrooms, most commonly those in the outer wings, had a shared bath. In almost all instances, rooms that shared a bath had connecting doors to the rooms to either side, allowing the management greater flexibility in locating guests based on what rooms were already occupied.

As the hotel was meant to entice elite society and to represent the Vanderbilt name, the focus of its design was on luxury and comfort. Modern bathroom and kitchen design assured guests of comfort through hygiene. Certain interior elements such as the double-lyre-shaped flying staircase imparted a sense of grandeur and status to the hotel. The design struck a necessary balance to convince guests that they were safe and comfortable in an exotic and primitive setting.

## *Printed Propaganda and Imperial Agendas*

The Grand Condado through its design represented US involvement in Puerto Rico and the possibilities of progress, and so did the promotional material published in the early years of the hotel. The promotional material was meant to circulate throughout the contiguous United States in order to entice travelers to stay at the hotel, and it influenced a greater number of people than just those who stayed at the hotel. Indeed, we are reminded that the tourist gaze is not confined to actual travelers alone but also includes those perusing promotional material in the comfort of their own home.[46]

The Grand Condado Vanderbilt promoted an imperialistic tourism through its printed publicity, which was didactic in prescribing specific tourist behaviors and experiences. This printed literature is notable because the intention is to promote Puerto Rico in general just as much as the focus is specifically on a stay at the Grand Condado Vanderbilt. This approach appears to be a conscious reiteration of a kind of promotional literature that had been published about Puerto Rico and other US territories since 1898. Promotional literature for the Grand Condado Vanderbilt echoed much of the established discourse of these other publications, but it was unique in the sections that positioned the hotel and the amenities and activities it offered as a key part of a contiguous-US visitor's experience of Puerto Rico—more broadly, as the true way of knowing the island. Reading one of these publications was not meant to be an end in itself, but a prescriptive preview of the experience that lay ahead. In this sense, the aim was to define the quintessential visit to Puerto Rico in terms of what travelers would do and see, and, more specifically, how that would be realized through their staying at the Grand Condado Vanderbilt.

In 1912, seven years before the opening of the Grand Condado Vanderbilt, the Insular Government Bureau of Information in San Juan published a book in English titled *Porto Rico: The Riviera of the West*.[47] Through its celebratory imperialist language, this book served as propaganda to entice US businessmen and average folks to invest in Puerto Rico and echoed much of the information and rhetoric that had been published about the island since 1898. With titles such as *Our Islands and Their People As Seen with Camera and Pencil*, *Everything about Our New Possessions*, *Our New Wonderlands*, and *Picturesque Cuba, Porto Rico, Hawaii and the Philippines: A Photographic Panorama of Our New Possessions*, other publications were likewise dedicated to justifying US imperialism and superiority as well as cataloging and displaying the assets and resources of these newly acquired territories, which served as a "bridge spanning a gap of unintelligibility."[48]

Faye C. Caronan explains: "The goal of these travel guides is seemingly benign. . . . [h]owever, these guides construct 'objective' information about places and people from particular privileged vantage points." Caronan uses this as a springboard for diving into an analysis of how similar the packaging of these islands for colonial purposes is to the packaging for tourism, and indeed they are interwoven, as both forms of packaging positioned the islands as something to be consumed. Often framed through the rhetoric of westward expansion, the islands were constructed as undeveloped and untouched, with quaint locals "more suited for tourist consumption than their own economic production."[49]

A comparison of the 1912 publication *Riviera of the West* and the two Grand Condado Vanderbilt booklets preserved in the Archivo General de Puerto Rico reveals the continuity of discourse as well as some significant divergences, especially in the promotion of tourism in the latter. Just like the 1912 book, they sport enticing titles—"Porto Rico: 'The Switzerland of the Tropics'" and "Porto Rico: The Island of Enchantment." Both are similar in the content they present, but their visuals, formatting, and arrangement of content are different.[50] The 1912 *Porto Rico* and the Grand Condado Vanderbilt brochures use specific content to promote investment in business and leisure, respectively, and in doing so, they define a particular vision of the island. Both book and brochures offer basic information that the visitor, whether entrepreneur or vacationer, would want to know pertaining to climate, conditions, and transportation. All touch on important cities and landmarks, in effect defining what spaces are important on the island.

The focus of the book is extensively on the economy, particularly on agricultural production and manufactures; trade and agriculture are also mentioned in the hotel booklets as a way to suggest both the development and the exoticness or picturesqueness of the island. The uniqueness of Puerto Rico and what it can offer the United States as its possession is underscored in the attention paid to crops such as coffee and pineapples, which are hard to grow in the contiguous United States. Puerto Rico is presented as a possession whose abundance is available for US consumption.

As the reader turns from general boosterist publications to the Grand Condado Vanderbilt materials, there is a shift in emphasis, and tourism supplants resource extraction as the focus. Here is international business, but with a twist. Rather than extract natural resources from the island, the product—vacation—is produced and consumed on the island. US vacationers travel to Puerto Rico to enjoy everything the island has to offer from the safety and luxury of the Grand Condado Vanderbilt. In a move that both reaffirms the status of the Grand Condado Vanderbilt and promotes Vanderbilt hotels in general, both hotel publications include images to promote other Vanderbilt hotels—in effect, reinforcing the prestige of the Grand Condado Vanderbilt and promoting the entire Vanderbilt hotel chain.

The book and the two brochures, following on from other post-1898 imperialist publications, include a romantic history of Puerto Rico that revolves around its "discovery" by Europeans and their enchantment with its natural beauty. This history reinforces the Spanish heritage of the island, which is portrayed as quaint and enchanting. Describing and defining the island's Spanish roots in these terms served a number of purposes. One was to lend an air of exoticism and history to the island. These characteristics were important for characterizing Puerto Rico in a manner that positioned it as a foil for the contiguous United States. The Old World charm and natural beauty of the tropical setting were meant to be read in contrast to the industrialization of modernity associated with the United States. Of course, the United States could not be accurately defined in such unequivocal terms any more than Puerto Rico could be, but the juxtaposition worked to create palatable and desirable visions of both places.

Both the 1912 book and the Grand Condado Vanderbilt publications take on the topic of tourism, and it seems the brochures took much inspiration from the book, though with a pointed emphasis on positioning the hotel itself as a key attraction in Puerto Rico. The book includes a section dedicated to appealing details for tourism in Puerto Rico, commenting on the island's history, its ideal climate, and the ease of traveling there. However, the authors admit that, when it came to accommodations, the options in Puerto Rico were "rough and not comparable to one of the gilded palaces found on Broadway."[51] This was exactly the condition that Vanderbilt sought to remedy with his hotel project in San Juan; it is quite understandable that the hotel's promotional booklets highlighted certain features that set it apart as exceptional.

In the brochures, the hotel itself was a key attraction in Puerto Rico. Its refined design and modern amenities offered reassurance that the hotel provided comfortable spaces; sections in the brochures describing grounds committed to golf and tennis and access to water sports let readers know there were countless ways for the well-heeled vacationer to while away the hours. These publications firmly circumscribed tourist activities to include leisure sports and entertainment taking place on the hotel's grounds, but they also worked in a broad sense to codify touristic experiences in a more specific way than in other publications. Through visual images of the hotel and textual descriptions in the promotional booklets, there emerged a clear vision of tourism in Puerto Rico. The connection of the hotel to other places in Puerto Rico through the promotion of certain leisure activities invited the tourist to consume the island both visually and spatially, in an imperial performance of possession through leisure activities.

## *Science and Control*

Just as the social Darwinism thought to justify US imperialism drew from the scientific theories of Charles Darwin's natural selection, so too did the emerging vision of the social practice of tourism presented in the Grand Condado Vanderbilt brochures rely on science in noteworthy ways. The invocation of various branches of science such as biology, chemistry, and geology in these promotional booklets was used to justify imperialism and acts of possession through systems of knowledge.[52] The way in which science is embedded in these booklets is nothing new, but the way in which tourism in Puerto Rico was mapped onto an older legacy of scientific exploration was. The fact that tourism was erroneously considered inconsequential or innocuous makes the connection to science all the more significant.

Certain aspects of Puerto Rico (such as pirates and colonial religious history) are rendered romantic and vague, but other aspects are available for US domination through analysis, measurement, and classification. In one of the booklets, "The Switzerland of the Tropics," a diagram of a motor boat is followed by a list of all the fish one could catch in the waters around the island. This list not only evokes the idea of natural bounty but, coming just short of providing Latin names, conjures up notions of classification and taxonomy. By understanding the boat and how it functions through this Diderot-esque diagram and learning the names of the fish one might catch, the tourist can master the experience of boating and fishing in Puerto Rico. This trend continues in the following section, which offers an analysis of the waters at Coamo Springs. Listing each chemical element in the water with the corresponding quantity per liter of water, the analysis concludes, and in capitals no less: "CLASSIFICATION: SULPHATED MIXTURE VARIETY SODA CHLORURATED WITH BROMO IRON AND LITINA."[53] The springs thus offered the romantic connotations of Ponce de León's fountain of youth and, at the same time, functioned as an entity that could be analyzed and thus made safe for consumption through scientific understanding.

The long legacy of cartography as a means of colonial conquest and domination left its imprint on the hotel booklets. Maps not only respond to the need for control and surveillance but, as Mark Monmonier elucidates, implement it by "legitimizing territorial conquest, economic exploitation and cultural imperialism." Far from being objective, cartographic representations reveal a specific point of view and set of values; even the blanks on a map are powerful in the way they indicate gaps in knowledge or, according to Chris Tiffin and Alan Lawson, the "erasure of existing social and geocultural formations in preparation for the projection and subsequent emplacement of a new order."[54]

We are reminded in the brochure that touristic desires are, in fact, imperialist desires with a map of the hotel golf course followed by a map of the Caribbean basin. Lines and numbers tracing the distance from tee to hole are not dissimilar to the lines and numbers charting the routes and distances of US steamships that ran from the United States to various locations throughout the Caribbean basin. These routes mark the business ventures and interests of US businessmen and politicians and the expansion of US markets and exploitation of raw materials. Marking the US desire to expand and control surrounding areas, these routes were the basis for the tourist trade, as the first tourists from the contiguous United States traveled to the Caribbean on steamers dealing in bananas, pineapples, coffee, and other "exotic" products. Just as the straight line from tee to hole suggests the way to master each hole of the course, so do the ship routes mark the US domination of the Caribbean. Placed next to each other, the cartography of imperial ambitions, vacation paths, and leisure activities become one and the same, defining the underlying nature of leisure travel to the Grand Condado Vanderbilt.

Messages of race and class, which at this time were believed to have scientific underpinnings, were inscribed through the hotel publications in other ways. In one brochure, the header graphics depicted a woman playing golf with the hotel in the background (plate 6).[55] In the foreground, a man, presumably the woman's caddy, is depicted in the labor of extracting or inserting a club in the golf bag. What is striking is the caddy's depiction, which is evocative of blackface or a caricature of a person of African descent. Clearly not meant to be a humorous image, this depiction of race, then, suggests certain attitudes of the time. Presumably, this is a local person working as a caddy, which implies that Puerto Rico is an island composed, at least in part, of Black labor. Even though many potential contiguous-US travelers would know from literature that Puerto Rico was not defined as a "Black" island compared to other Caribbean islands, it was still regarded as a racial other, and the marking of the caddy as Black (or at the least, not white) reinforces US popular belief at the time that Puerto Ricans were less racially (and thus less socially) evolved than Teutonic or Anglo-Americans.[56] Visualizing US imperial attitudes, the booklets construct Puerto Rico as a place to be consumed and possessed by the United States, facilitated by local labor that was naturalized by casting Puerto Ricans as a racial other.

The discourse of science was part of the scaffolding that held up the juxtaposition of modern and tropical in these booklets and in popular discourse. The modern is that which has harnessed science and technology for the sake of progress, and it is marked in contrast to the tropical. However, there is the romance of the other—the exotic, tropical, historic, quaint—and this is constantly evoked in juxtaposition. These qualities are enticing precisely because of their contrast to modernity and all that it entails; they offer both an antidote to modernity and reinforcement of the superiority of these vacationers.

## *From Car Trips to Water Cures*

The Grand Condado Vanderbilt was presented as a landmark destination for the traveler, but one whose identity emerged fully only through its broader geographical environment and a more expansive conceptual terrain of tourism. Although the island's modernization projects were conceived as a way of domesticating the landscape, the touristic experience relied on the consumption of untamed or only-somewhat-tamed wilderness and natural beauty, facilitated through modern conveniences such as automobiles and modern hotels. While automobile touring in Puerto Rico was endorsed in other publications such as the *Riviera of the West*, the Grand Condado Vanderbilt brochures promoted automobile touring as an activity that was bound specifically to a stay at the hotel and a visit to the island.

The act of touring in automobile aligned with imperatives of scientific control in many ways. Here advancements in technology—specifically automotive technology—were harnessed and employed to realize imperialistic tourist acts of dominating the island through experientially based knowledge. As Cotten Seiler argues, "automobility was an apparatus that coincided with, facilitated, and illustrated the United States' spread across its continental borders and its imperial rise." According to Seiler, driving expresses a dominant subjectivity, and mobility is a form of capital, so moving feely is an index of power.[57] Contiguous-US visitors thus performed their dominance of Puerto Rico and its people through their automobile touring of the island.

Hotel publications advertised that cars were available for rent, or one could bring one's own car to the island with relative ease. "Porto Rico: 'The Switzerland of the Tropics'" offered a road map of the island with a number of suggested automobile trips (plate 7).[58] Like the lists of fish or the chemical makeup of the sulfur springs, this vehicular cartography allowed the visitor to possess the island through knowledge, in this case through the clear delineation of the road network crisscrossing the island accompanied by exact mileage counts of distances between different locales. Short descriptions accompanying each numbered motor trip not only help the vacationer choose what is most appealing but educate the traveler as to what is significant on each trip, whether it is a certain geographic feature, a notable restaurant, or a landmark site linked to a Spanish conquistador. Road maps were widely reprinted in promotional material for Puerto Rico, and through their lines and distances they function similarly to the previously discussed golf course and steamer maps.

Automobile trips were a form of celebrating the modernization of the island. In the minds of many visitors and locals, the roads were part of a larger move toward modernization that, although it began under Spanish rule, intensified under US authority after 1898. The term "Americanization" was often employed in the nineteenth and twentieth centuries as a synonym for modernization, showing the tendency to consider the United States as at the forefront of technological, organizational, and economic innovation. "Americanization" also refers specifically to the adoption of US systems, technologies, values, and attitudes, and this was very much the case in Puerto Rico and other US territories. The changes taking place in Puerto Rico were, at the core, directed at furthering US interests through a rhetoric of paternalism. While it was a colony of Spain, Puerto Rico had undergone programs to improve sanitation, health, transportation, and other infrastructure, but US publications about Puerto Rico made little mention of these types of initiatives. In the 1899 *Picturesque Cuba, Porto Rico, Hawaii and the Philippines*, careful note is made that the "incompetence of Spanish officials prevented anything like adequate service being given." As Niell notes, these publications cast Spain as a "backward imperial power" and configured Puerto Ricans as needing redirection into the world of US capitalism.[59]

The slew of publications that came out in the wake of 1898 often paid much attention to the potential for the island through a departure from the old Spanish ways and the adoption of Americanization. William Dinwiddie's survey of the island, *Puerto Rico: Its Conditions and Possibilities*, was geared toward a US audience and was meant to provide "a comprehensive grasp of the administrative problems which confront us, and the possibilities for the embarking of American business enterprises." In a discussion of the water works of San Juan, Dinwiddie eloquently summarized the general US conception of modernity in Puerto Rico: "The awakening to the needs of modern life and the possibilities in the direction of mechanical comforts has come only in the last few years, and then principally through the instrumentality of progressive Americans."[60] The Grand Condado Vanderbilt and its promotion of leisure activities such as automobile touring were a celebration of the island's awakening to modern life. These leisure activities reified the foreign guest as a modern subject, the hotel as a modern space, and the roadways as modern, precisely through the comparison with what was promoted on these automobile tours as wild or undeveloped.

The promotion of automobile touring in the Grand Condado Vanderbilt further tied the hotel and tourism to other connotations and motivations for improved transportation infrastructure. Better roads suggested insular progress overall, which was largely driven by US business interests, especially those in the sugar, tobacco, and coffee markets who desired the framework necessary for profit. Many projects wrought significant changes in the Puerto Rican landscape. At the end of Spanish rule there were only 254 kilometers of road, and after six years of US occupation in 1904, 1,179 kilometers of macadam roads had been laid down. Establishing a network of roads was not just beneficial for businesses to transport goods but also for promoters of tourism to sell Puerto Rico as a modern, navigable island, especially at a moment in which automobile touring had become an accepted and established practice in the continental United States.[61]

Images related to automobile touring can be found throughout the Grand Condado Vanderbilt promotional booklets and play a particularly significant role in the "Switzerland of the Tropics" booklet. Besides the image of golf, another header graphic is a depiction of the hotel with four cars traveling along the roads in front of the building. A car in the left foreground draws the viewer into the image and suggests the experience of moving to and from the hotel by automobile. Other photos in the booklet depict automobiles, and yet others suggest the views of the island one would enjoy from a car, including thatched houses on the side of the road and a view of mountains and valley with a road winding away, which the viewer has presumably used to arrive at this outlook. These photographs reinforce an idea of experiencing the island by car and link this experience specifically to the hotel—the hotel provides the car and the safe comfortable quarters from which one can venture out during the day to discover the natural beauty of the island.

The booklets promote movement in automobile as the easiest way to travel from the Grand Condado Vanderbilt to Coamo Springs, a site highlighted in all publications about Puerto Rico. A visit here was marketed as a complementary counterpoint to the Grand Condado Vanderbilt. The positioning of the springs as a foil furthered the tactic of contrasts or juxtapositions, which effectively positioned the Grand Condado Vanderbilt as a modern luxurious hotel and a valuable touristic experience. Promotional material marketed Coamo Springs as a quaint place where one could step back in time and connect with nature through the enjoyment of the mineral springs (plate 8). Should a traveler be anxious that provinciality meant backwardness or lack of sanitation, the promotional materials commented on the "modern-trained" chef, highlighted the recently remodeled rooms, and reminded potential visitors that the Coamo Springs hotel was operated by the same company as the Grand Condado Vanderbilt.

The Grand Condado Vanderbilt had a financial stake in encouraging travel to Coamo Springs, but the regularity with which other publications discuss the springs suggests that all sorts of parties considered them a point of interest serving as an asset in tourism development. Coamo Springs did much to help promote the Grand Condado Vanderbilt through this relationship of contrast and connection. The springs was one of the main ways tourists could consume nature, and not just any nature, but this very rare mineral springs that had been around for ages. The history of the springs told in publications was anecdotally similar to other desirable water features in the contiguous United States, and thus the use of Coamo Springs by contiguous-US visitors was consistent with the formula employed in the North, wherein colonists appropriated the appreciable behaviors of Indigenous groups, who had discovered and enjoyed these mineral springs before European presence.

Contiguous-US visitors in Puerto Rico echoed the behaviors of their colonial ancestors up north, who in turn had been mimicking the fashion for water cures and treatments popular among the European society they had left behind. Initially, water cures in Europe were reserved for the aristocracy. Likewise, although the various publications from 1898 through the first quarter of the twentieth century insisted that one could travel to Puerto Rico quite affordably, real leisure vacationing in Puerto Rico at the time of the opening of the Grand Condado Vanderbilt was reserved primarily to those with financial means. Although the monied contiguous-US vacationers in Puerto Rico had, by and large, gained their wealth through modern capitalism and had not inherited their wealth through noble bloodlines like their earlier European counterparts, they used vacationing as a tool of social distinction. By the early twentieth century, Coamo Springs did not just represent the traditional water cure but was grounded in the idea of temporarily escaping the enervating effects of modernity, which was also a way to reinforce US superiority over its territories vis-à-vis modernity and progress.

## *Tourism Development Becomes an Insular Government Concern*

In a letter to Governor Blanton Winship, Henry L. Hartzell, a lawyer practicing in Puerto Rico, recounted the history of the Grand Condado Vanderbilt as a precursor to his earnest call for the local government to spearhead the development of tourism on the island and purchase the hotel.[62] This letter lends insight into the way the hotel was viewed as a means to control a narrative of insular identity as well as to shape a future economy for the island. When Hartzell penned the letter in 1934, Puerto Rico was reeling from the impact of the Great Depression, and Governor Winship was looking for ways to rehabilitate the island's economy. The insular government focused on the recovery of established industries and markets, but Winship was also open to new revenue options, and he saw the value of developing contiguous-US tourism to Puerto Rico. The 1930s was also a time of great unrest in Puerto Rico, as the independence movement was gaining popularity and was agitating for change.[63] Hartzell saw government control of the hotel as being key in ensuring a continued focus on the US imperial project in Puerto Rico.

The economic prosperity of the years between World War I and the Great Depression was certainly partially responsible for what Hartzell recounts as the golden age of the hotel. After the stock market crash of 1929, the economic situation of the hotel changed. By 1930, the contiguous-US-based San Juan Hotels Corporation was operating the hotel as the Condado Hotel. In 1931, Manuel González Martínez acquired the hotel for three hundred thousand dollars, the golf course was sold off separately, and the lease of the Coamo Springs Hotel was cancelled. In his letter, Hartzell noted that the decline of the Grand Condado Vanderbilt was largely a result of the onset of the Great Depression. Because of the decrease in visitors, the result of economic hard times, the hotel could not afford the normal upkeep and maintenance, which forced "economies of management." This in turn decreased patronage, and according to Hartzell the two factors continued to negatively impact one another from that point on.[64]

All of Hartzell's history is a prologue to the ultimate goal of his letter: to convince Governor Winship that the Puerto Rico government should become involved in the fate of the hotel. Hartzell was concerned with developing the Grand Condado Vanderbilt as a symbol of Puerto Rico—a Puerto Rico that was part of the US empire—rather than using the hotel as a representation of insular identity.[65] He also underscored his opinion that the elite tourism associated with the Grand Condado Vanderbilt could be maintained only if the hotel was under US management or ownership.[66] Ultimately, Hartzell felt the best course of action was for the Puerto Rican government to acquire the hotel with federal aid. Governor Winship agreed with Hartzell that this option promised the insular government the maximum amount of control over the fate of the hotel.

In 1934, Governor Winship retained an option for the purchase of the hotel at the price of three hundred thousand dollars and was very interested in obtaining the hotel but was still searching for funding.[67] In a telegram to the Bureau of Insular Affairs in Washington, DC, from July 1934, Winship expressed his hope that the proposition be put to the Emergency Relief Administration with the idea of funds coming from the Civil Works Administration. He concluded by expressing his belief that the development of the tourism industry in Puerto Rico was dependent upon the government purchase of the hotel.[68]

Despite Winship's devotion to the cause, the US government did not offer financial support and the insular government never purchased the Grand Condado Vanderbilt. The hotel continued under the ownership of González and experienced a rather unremarkable history until the post–World War II tourism boom. A ballroom was added to the first floor, as well as an addition known as the East Wing, which provided more guest rooms in the 1940s. In 1962, a new West Wing created even more rooms. In 1976, the Condado Convention Center was built, and this

Toro y Ferrer design connected to the Grand Condado Vanderbilt where the now demolished East Wing once stood. Later, in the 1990s and 2000s, the Condado Convention Center and West Wing were demolished, practically returning the hotel to its original form.

Although the Grand Condado Vanderbilt never quite found a way to compete with the new modern hotels popping up in Condado in the 1950s, it was fundamental in laying the foundation for the tourist landscape that would develop in San Juan throughout the twentieth century. The appeal of the Grand Condado Vanderbilt to the US elite defined the trajectory of postwar tourism. Even before the end of World War II, other new hotel projects in San Juan were designed to attract a wealthy clientele.

The Hotel Normandie, inaugurated in 1942 and located just across the Puente Dos Hermanos in Puerta de Tierra, was the next modern luxury hotel to be built in San Juan. Conceived and financed by Félix Benítez Rexach, a wealthy Puerto Rican engineer, the Hotel Normandie was an homage to the luxury ocean liner, and the hotel carried all the connotations of the modernity and opulence of this magnificent vessel. The building's rounded front and balconies running along the side referenced the form of an ocean liner, conjuring notions of transnational travel, cosmopolitan society, and a world made smaller and more accessible through technological advancements in design. Like the interior decoration of the SS *Normandie*, which featured works by famed Art Deco designers such as René Lalique, Jean Dupas, and Jean Dunand, Benítez spared no expense in furnishing the Hotel Normandie's interiors, commissioning artists and craftsmen from as far away as France and Spain to create the sumptuous interiors.[69]

The Hotel Normandie functioned as a bridge between the historicist Beaux Arts Grand Condado Vanderbilt and the International Style inspired hotels that would be built in San Juan after World War II. The hotel displayed Art Deco interest in the historic, and the sleek lines of the hotel were a preliminary gesture of the way modernity could be displayed in the style of the hotel. Though stylistically more contemporary, the Hotel Normandie followed in the footsteps of the Grand Condado Vanderbilt in significant ways. The Hotel Normandie's design and location reinforced the emphasis on upper-class tourism, further anchored a tourist home base outside of San Juan Viejo, and engaged with tropical nature through style.

The proposal that the Grand Condado Vanderbilt become a property of the state and a symbol of the US empire was innovative in Puerto Rico at the time. While it was not unheard of for hotels to be owned or operated by the government, this happened almost entirely on the municipal level. For example, in 1905, the city of Tampa acquired the 1891 Tampa Bay Hotel for $125,000.[70] Similar to the situation of Grand Condado Vanderbilt in the 1930s, the Tampa Bay Hotel was struggling as a business, and the municipal government was interested in preserving it as an economic asset of the city. A notable difference here is the interest in local boosterism in the case of the Tampa Bay Hotel versus the imperial overtones of the acquisition of the Grand Condado Vanderbilt.

The Puerto Rican government's interest in owning a hotel that represented the government resonates with contemporaneous hotel projects in other parts of the Caribbean. For example, the Machado government's hotel project in Havana resulted in the opening of the Hotel Nacional de Cuba in 1930. Although the economic prosperity of the times encouraged the conception of the Hotel Nacional project in 1928, the depression that plagued Puerto Rico in the 1930s was the primary impetus to get the insular government to seriously consider an investment in tourism as a means to end immediate fiscal problems and create a path for a prosperous financial future for the island. The Hotel Nacional de Cuba may have served as an inspirational model of the possibilities of a state-owned hotel for the Puerto Rican government.

The Grand Condado Vanderbilt firmly established Condado as a place of tourism, evidenced by the numerous hotels, motels, and tourist apartments built in Condado in better economic times in the 1950s and 1960s. The residential neighborhood the Behn brothers had designed gave way to a strip of land crowded with hotels and motels. The Grand Condado Vanderbilt persisted as the anchor of this expansion in temporary lodging. Its Beaux Arts design is a reminder of the hope and vision many had in the early part of the twentieth century of fashioning Puerto Rico into a modern island.

Figure 2.1. Page from *Album fotográfico de los actos celebrados con motivo de la toma de posesión de la Presidencia de la República por el General Gerardo Machado y Morales*. Mitchell Wolfson Jr. Collection, Wolfsonian-Florida International University, Miami Beach, Florida.

# The Hotel Nacional de Cuba

Symbol of Authoritarianism, Site of Revolution

**El Capitolio (Capital Building), the Hotel Nacional de Cuba, El Morro, the** Monument to the USS *Maine*, a pair of rumba dancers, and a ship in a distant horizon—these are the places, objects, and people that decorate a ceramic souvenir ashtray that was available for purchase after World War II (plate 9). This souvenir proposes a shorthand identity of Cuba. The geographic limits of the island are described in the outline of the object; highlighted with gold trim, the island is a blank white ceramic punctuated with discrete images. Beaches, mountains, plantations, and small towns are erased, and instead the island nation is represented by a set of icons removed from context. The island is not reduced to images of palm trees or tropical cocktails but, rather, presented as a site of architectural monuments above all else. Notably, the ashtray defines Havana with structures, but Guantanamo Bay is referenced with a dancing couple—positing the capital as a space of modernity and the country's built accomplishments and other parts of the island as sites of traditional culture.

Although President Gerardo Machado y Morales and his administration—invested in the design and construction of a number of the monuments on this ashtray—would have taken issue with the decontextualization of these buildings, based on their commitment to promoting their achievements in urban infrastructure, this souvenir squares quite nicely with their imagining of Cuba as a first-class nation, articulated specifically and somewhat narrowly through the city of Havana. The success of these efforts on an international scale is evidenced in the ashtray, an object from the post–World War II period that equates a number of Havana's built projects of the *machadato* (Gerardo Machado's presidency from 1925 to 1933) with the identity of the country.[1]

President Machado's attention to urban works as a means to define the nation and his legacy was communicated on a more local scale as well. In a commemorative book meant to legitimize his second term in office (starting in 1928, and a result of highly contested manipulations of the Cuban Constitution), images of uniformed military marching in celebratory parades and crowds who are meant to be read as supporters worked in part to figure Machado as powerful and beloved (figure 2.1).[2] Half of the album is focused on the achievements of the machadato as evidenced in the urban works of Havana. Here, power and popularity (the latter more imagined than actual) are expressed through Machado's ability to manipulate and shape Havana into a city of cutting-edge modernity. However, this was a modern city imagined to serve the few rather than the many. Machado's urban works were ultimately about supporting and elevating a white elite and, as Joseph Hartman illustrates, were characterized by designs that "reiterated a socioracial hierarchy based on collective and traumatic memories of Cuba's recent colonial past," as well as laying clear touchpoints with ongoing colonial projects around the world.[3]

The effort Machado put into tying his power and legacy to the built environment means it comes as no surprise that architectural spaces were the object of attacks by groups revolting against the machadato in 1933. The Revolution of 1933 was multilayered; the US-backed military officers who ousted Machado soon found themselves overthrown by a number of activist groups who represented middle-class and working-class interests. Unrest had been fomenting throughout the island for some time—strikes and protests and other forms of revolt were often quite violent, as were reprisals by the machadato.

One main site of confrontation in the Revolution of 1933 was the Hotel Nacional de Cuba. It was meant to be the preeminent hotel of Cuba, expressing the island's national identity and sovereignty as envisioned during the machadato. The hotel reflects the machadato's commitment to and reliance on architecture and urban development as a main venue for expressing a successful sovereign state, but for many Cubans the building represented an authoritarian government that pandered to US interests. Indeed, the original popularity that Machado enjoyed in the first years of his presidency was based on an improved economy, which was made possible through loans he secured from J. P. Morgan and Chase National banks.[4]

The story of the Hotel Nacional de Cuba is not a traditional tale of patronage. Rather, it is the story of the government of an essentially neocolonial nation trying, not surprisingly, to gain legitimacy through the consolidation of a national consensus on state identity, enrich itself through economic profit, and maintain its political power. In 1929 the Machado government contracted the US-based National Cuba Hotel Corporation to finance and realize the hotel project. This conglomerate was composed of entities such as the architectural firm McKim, Mead & White, the Plaza Operating Company of New York of hotel management fame, and the National City Company of New York, a financial powerhouse at the time. Known for its nationalist agenda, the government's choice of a US corporation seems particularly odd, though the realities of Machado's deep ties to the corporate United States provide clarity; the conglomerate, formed expressly for the purpose of pursuing this project, was attractive because it included the famed US architectural firm of McKim, Mead & White, though at this point that architectural firm was no longer as innovative as it once had been.[5] This project was perhaps beside the point for this well-established firm, but it was exactly the point for the Cuban government that commissioned it. In the end, the story of the Hotel Nacional de Cuba reveals complicated imperial power relations by highlighting how the machadato defined the project's terms and outcomes, leaving the architectural firm without the last word. The resulting architecture carried such significance, even if not exactly the symbolism the Machado government hoped it would convey, that only three years after its opening the Hotel Nacional de Cuba was the site of one of the bloodiest confrontations defining the Revolution of 1933.[6]

By giving due consideration to the hotel project within this political context, especially through the application of an international framework to a project conceived within an overtly nationalist discourse, we can begin to understand the hotel's significance in this period.[7] Rather than tell the story solely through the lens of the state's interests, a more inclusive approach acknowledges heterogeneity and dives into not just the messy entanglements between the newer nation and the imperial presence but also the contradictions within the nation itself—the plurality of voices that variously supported or opposed the project or proposed alternative visions. The 1933 attack on the Hotel Nacional de Cuba by insurgent groups allows us an entry point into considering the multiple meanings of the hotel and also shows us how the site could be mobilized as an active space for resistance and conflict. Not only did the hotel exist as an image (as in the souvenir ashtray), for example, but also as a dynamic space of contestation.

## Picturing Luxury Tourism

Tall, graceful palms foreground an image of the 1930 Hotel Nacional de Cuba on the front of a promotional brochure, the composition echoing the experience of arriving at the hotel via the striking palm-flanked drive that culminates at the hotel's main entrance (figure 2.2). Designed for potential US visitors, the brochure promotes the hotel through a description of the hotel and its relation to the larger world of tourism in Havana. Beyond the front page awaits an image of the lobby, with the Spanish-inspired tiles and wood beam ceilings, native mahogany furniture representative of the respected tradition of Cuban furniture craftsmanship, and arches running down the sides of the room all working together to convey colonial charm (figure 2.3). The accompanying text underscores the features of the hotel most likely to appeal to US tourists, positioning the architecture as providing an experience of comfort and luxury. The interior of the trifold brochure offers an appealing collage of photographs taken from a variety of viewpoints (figure 2.4). Images capture the hotel's majestic position on Taganana Hill, the

Figure 2.2. Front of brochure for the Hotel Nacional de Cuba. McKim, Mead & White Architectural Records Collection, Department of Prints, Photographs and Architectural Collections, New-York Historical Society Museum & Library, New York City.

Spanish-inspired towers reinforcing its commanding presence over the surrounding Vedado neighborhood, and the expansive palm-dotted lawn asserting its dominance in the urban landscape. The luxury of the hotel is rendered visible in the images of its monumental front drive, the modern swimming pool, and the chandeliers and fine furniture that define its interiors. Situating the hotel in relationship to other noteworthy landmarks, including El Morro and the casino, the text explicitly locates the Hotel Nacional de Cuba as "the very heart" of urban life.

Although many hotels in Cuba catered to the needs of both locals and tourists in this period, various visual and textual references underscore the hotel's function as temporary lodging for primarily foreign visitors. The sheer size of the H-shaped building, coupled with the repetition of a multitude of windows punctuating the surfaces, indicate the interior layout of the hotel: double-loaded hallways with guest rooms on all sides offering vistas of the hotel grounds and surrounding city and ocean. The commingling of traditional Cuban design elements with modern amenities was most likely interpreted by

Luxuriously equipped to meet your every need and whim, the National Hotel affords many a delightful retreat when you leave your comfortable rooms to mingle with fellow guests . . . Outdoor dancing and dining terraces . . . the magnificent Café . . . the monumental Bar . . . the Grand Ballroom . . . Gala nights and fiestas . . . loggias looking out to sea . . . broker's office and smart shops . . . Life here moves at any pace you choose, but always surrounded by deft service and the bewitching charm of Havana.

Figure 2.3. Inside of brochure for the Hotel Nacional de Cuba. McKim, Mead & White Architectural Records Collection, Department of Prints, Photographs and Architectural Collections, New-York Historical Society Museum & Library, New York City.

Figure 2.4. Inside spread of brochure for the Hotel Nacional de Cuba. McKim, Mead & White Architectural Records Collection, Department of Prints, Photographs and Architectural Collections, New-York Historical Society Museum & Library, New York City.

guests as an experience of the foreign, while still providing the comforts of home. The text reinforces the idea that tropical attractions were not limited to the hotel but were part of the larger experience of other landmarks and destinations in the city, underscoring the attraction of Havana as a place of history, culture, fun, and entertainment.

The back of the brochure sports an image of the Monument to the Victims of the USS *Maine* with the Hotel Nacional de Cuba clearly visible in the background (figure 2.5).[8] Besides indicating their geographic proximity, the juxtaposition of these two architectural works reveals the political context of Cuba in that period. The Maine Monument was designed in 1925 to commemorate those who died in the sinking of the USS *Maine*, the event that marked the entry of the United States into Cuba's fight for independence, which ultimately resulted in extensive US involvement in Cuba that frustrated true national sovereignty. For many Cubans, the entry of the United States into the Cuban Guerra Necessaria (Necessary War) and the subsequent monument that was erected represented US intervention and imperialism.[9] These monument and the hotel, built within a few years of each other, represent the conflict inherent in a country of citizens trying to build and express a free state while also being severely limited in their sovereignty by foreign imposition.

The Hotel Nacional de Cuba was one of the principle architectural projects of the machadato. It is representative of an important facet of Cuban architectural history that has only just recently begun to be accounted for—the manifestation of US-Cuban entanglements in the built environment of Cuba during a period of national turmoil (figure 2.6).

Figure 2.5. Back of brochure for the Hotel Nacional de Cuba. McKim, Mead & White Architectural Records Collection, Department of Prints, Photographs and Architectural Collections, New-York Historical Society Museum & Library, New York City.

Romantic Havana, where the climate is perfect . . . "Paris of the Americas" . . . blending mellow Old-world charm and New-world luxury! What is your pleasure? Name it, and Havana will produce it. Every outdoor sport . . . racing at Oriental Park, yachting, bathing at La Playa or the hotel's salt-water swimming pool. Tennis courts at the hotel and golf courses nearby. A city teeming with fascinations, day and night, lies temptingly at hand. Theatres, music, open-air cafés, parks and plazas, quaint churches and palaces of olden times. A gloriously "different" city in a land where it is Springtime all the year. To this playland, the golden key is the National Hotel . . . For reservations and further particulars, apply to your own travel agent, to the hotel direct, or the New York office—The Plaza Hotel, Fifth Avenue at 59th St. Representatives meet you at the pier, take charge of luggage, and facilitate your transportation to the hotel.

*The*
**NATIONAL HOTEL**
*of Cuba*
**HAVANA**

Henry A. Rost, President
Will P. Taylor, Manager

Figure 2.6. McKim, Mead & White, Hotel Nacional de Cuba, 1930. Photograph taken at time of completion. McKim, Mead & White Architectural Records Collection, Department of Prints, Photographs and Architectural Collections, New-York Historical Society Museum & Library, New York City.

Architectural studies that consider this period often focus on stylistic groupings: the more avant-garde, such as the exuberant Art Deco tradition in Cuba, exemplified by the Edificio Bacardí; the proto-rationalism developing among a select group of innovative Cuban architects; or the historicist architecture of the Cuban elite, defined by the revivalist mansions of Vedado.[10] These types of studies invariably overlook or give only a brief mention of the Hotel Nacional de Cuba, whose eclectic design refuses stylistic categorization. Certain features look directly to Spain, such as the two bell towers that top the structure, which recall Spanish Renaissance and baroque architecture. However, the sheer size of the hotel clearly indicates a connection to US Beaux Arts grand hotels, such as the Biltmore hotels and other resorts being built across the United States. On this level, the hotel suggested certain notions of US elitism and excess associated with the affluent clients who would stay at this caliber of hotel.

Yet, the hotel is not a mere copy of US prototypes. Uniquely Cuban features—often referred to as creole—are expressed in the interior attention to iconography and materials associated with Cuba, which effectively highlight vibrant local design traditions.[11] For example, the patio area that defines the back of the hotel, which underscores the traditional attention to climate in Cuban design, is defined by a classically styled loggia punctuated with Art Deco stylized marine motifs. This type of architecture was meant to speak to various groups of people, including locals and visitors, but in escaping any clear stylistic classification it has been relegated to the margins of architectural history. A narrow stylistic analysis can at best celebrate the hotel as an example of creolization but at worst can lead to its prompt dismissal as a less than thoughtful pastiche lacking a unified vision. In either case, a study that emphasizes form from the point of view of taste or dichotomies of avant-garde and traditional architecture fails to account for a more compelling history of the structure. If we enter into the analysis of the Hotel Nacional de Cuba's design as a story of patronage, shaped by the context of foreign relations and domestic inequality and unrest, a far more interesting and complex history is revealed, allowing us to begin to understand the politics of the hotel and its potent symbolic function.

## *Building a Modern State, Defining National Identity*

When President Gerardo Machado released Presidential Decree No. 1867 on October 30, 1928, announcing an open competition for designs for a new national hotel, it was apparently a foregone conclusion that the commission would be awarded to the National Cuba Hotel Corporation. Drawings for the Hotel Nacional de Cuba in the McKim, Mead & White archives date back to 1925, which indicates that the machadato and the architectural firm had been in communication about a hotel project since Machado took office that same year.[12] The charade of an open competition served as a public relations opportunity for government leaders to widely publicize their patronage of this grand project. Even after the competition was over, the project was consistently presented as a government project, and the architects and financiers were rarely mentioned. The machadato took full credit for the project, using large billboards as propaganda of its beneficence in building for

Figure 2.7. Billboard for the inauguration of the Hotel Nacional de Cuba, photograph taken at the time of construction. McKim, Mead & White Architectural Records Collection, Department of Prints, Photographs and Architectural Collections, New-York Historical Society Museum & Library, New York City.

the country, conveniently failing to note that the government was not responsible for the design, the financing, or the construction of the hotel. One such billboard invokes the US-based management company in order to suggest the level of hotel, while Machado and Dr. Carlos Miguel de Céspedes, secretary of public works, are named in such a way as to suggest that the project only exists because of them (figure 2.7). The creation of complete state control over nation building was, in fact, very much dependent on international collaboration and the politics of foreign relations.

Indeed, the Hotel Nacional de Cuba was conceived as a celebration of Cuban progress and modernity under President Machado; it also served to reinforce Machado-defined nationalism. The machadato deployed a paradigm of nationalism that they called *cooperativismo*, which was grounded in a conviction that a healthy body politic was organized from the top down.[13] This authoritarian approach ensured that a sanctioned definition of national identity was transmitted from the elite government to the populace. The Hotel Nacional de Cuba exemplifies the production of architecture under cooperativismo, which provided the framework for Machado to consolidate his power and increase government profits. Under the aegis of building national identity and civic pride through architectural projects, government leaders were also controlling urban development, which allowed them to shape the appearance and dynamics of Havana and to profit financially from this lucrative sector of the Cuban economy.[14]

Government corruption and social inequality largely define the legacy of the machadato, despite the regime's campaign slogan of "¡Agua, caminos, escuelas!" (Water, roads, schools) and the initial 1925 Ley de Obras Públicas (Law of Public Works). Hartman chronicles the machadato's engagement with public works from those first years, including the response to the Ciclón de '26 (Hurricane of 1926), into Machado's second term as president, revealing how even projects seemingly conceived for the populace were merely a "simulacrum of republicanism," calculated vehicles meant to reinforce histories of socioracial hierarchy through the amplification of Spanish colonial identity and the erasure or diminishment of Indigenous, Black, and Asian identities and histories. Like Hartman, Carlos Venegas Fornias analyzes the machadato's program of urban development in Havana in light of the urban transformations under colonial governor Miguel Tacón in the 1830s, ultimately concluding that the two regimes were counterpoints in the history of urban design in Havana.[15] Not until almost one hundred years later, with the arrival of President Machado, was another colonial or republican government to embark upon an urban development plan as grand as Tacón's. Urban development promised to provide clear visual evidence of the reform serving as the basis of Machado's platform that won him his first term as president, and he harnessed architecture and urban planning as means of national development.[16]

The machadato relied heavily on the representation and discourse of urban development as evidence of successful government in order to justify President Machado's second term in office, which was not gained through democratic means.[17] The commemorative photo album of President Machado's second-term inauguration serves as material evidence of how the machadato attempted to demonstrate his popularity and legitimize his legal right to power through architectural and infrastructural means.[18] Not only does the album contain countless images of ceremonies and parades, with plenty of pomp, circumstance, and numerous uniformed Cubans, but it also contains an extensive selection of images of architecture and public works, the majority of which were completed during Machado's first term in office. Images of highways, bridges, and train lines as well as privately funded works serve as testament to the flourishing of public works

Figure 2.8. Page from *Album fotográfico . . . por el General Gerardo Machado y Morales*. Mitchell Wolfson Jr. Collection, Wolfsonian-Florida International University, Miami Beach, Florida.

and private endeavors under Machado's rule. By curating all this in the album and through other forms of state propaganda, Machado took credit for these public and private accomplishments as well as for a number of works in progress, including plans for a Ciudad Universitaria (University City) and the Hotel Nacional de Cuba (figure 2.8).[19] Cubans would certainly benefit from improved transportation infrastructure, but spaces they might never experience such as the university or a hotel meant for foreigners were presented as important works that every Cuban should be proud of, because these works symbolized the country's status as a modern nation. The rhetoric of the machadato's urban improvement program was about more than just improving the lives of everyday Cubans, it was part of a larger effort to position Havana internationally as a cosmopolitan city and Cuba as a country that rivaled other great nations of the globe. Development, particularly through the urban design of Havana, was championed by the machadato as the key marker of modernity—though, as bound to coloniality, this meant Western attitudes and prerogatives were valued above all else.

The detailed requirements outlined in Presidential Decree 1867, a call for bids for a national hotel, and the subsequent lease contract for the Hotel Nacional de Cuba echoes a nationalist top-down approach grounded in the conviction that government leaders were best equipped to define the major monuments of the country. Bidders were required to "submit the plans of their projects in the most detailed manner, especially the plans of the facades and gardens," as it was "the intention of the Government that the building which is to be constructed and also the gardens, are to be of the greatest beauty, in this way becoming a public ornament to this city."[20] As this passage suggests, the terms provided means for the machadato to manage the design, ensuring that the resulting hotel would adhere to the grand national monument envisioned by the government. The terms of the project determined, for example, the location of the hotel and called for the hotel and grounds to exist "in perfect harmony" with the Plaza del Maine, a major monumental area that was part of the 1920s urban plan for Havana and that included the Monument to the Victims of the USS *Maine*.[21]

Additionally, to ensure the creation of a hotel of such grandeur that it rivaled hotels around the globe, the contract required a minimum investment of three hundred million dollars for construction and at least four hundred guest rooms.[22] Revealing the machadato's desire to exploit the propagandistic potential of the hotel as a national symbol, the contract also specified that the hotel must include a deluxe apartment of no less than six rooms for government guests of honor to be used free of charge whenever desired. Adherence to the contract requirements was ensured by the decree's charge of responsibility to the Secretaría de Obras Públicas (Office of Public Works). A final attempt to control the pace of the project is evident in the terms requiring that the hotel open within two years. The importance attached to this hotel and the governmental insistence on maintaining control over the project were clearly expressed in the presidential decree, which required the submission of plans, especially of gardens and exteriors, so that leaders could be sure the project was of "greatest beauty, in this way becoming a public ornament to this city."[23]

Representation of machadato nationalism found expression in the Hotel Nacional de Cuba's design through its overall monumentality and luxuriousness and through specific design details that referenced the Republic of Cuba. In an effort to establish the Hotel Nacional as defining the Republic of Cuba, the contract for the hotel stipulated the inclusion of a suite of the most opulent rooms, which was called the Suite of the Republic. This had its own separate budget earmarked for its interior design to ensure that these were the most sumptuous rooms in the hotel. Located on the ground floor in one of the wings that jutted out alongside the main entry, the Suite of the Republic was composed of six rooms that were built and outfitted with the finest of materials and furnishings. Archival documents show that furniture for the Suite of the Republic was commissioned from Meras y Rico, and the mahogany furniture for this suite was much more elegant than the furniture that was provided for the regular guest rooms.[24] Fittingly, the theme of Cuba was strongly suggested in the suite's decoration. An ornamental cartouche over the entrance included a shield emblazoned with the Cuban flag, flanked by two cornucopias. On one hand, the suite was a financial concession for the National Cuba Hotel Corporation, which had agreed to let the Cuban government use these rooms for free whenever desired. However, the inclusion of such a luxurious suite helped raise the overall status of the hotel in public opinion, something the US company directors might have considered a fair exchange for the monetary expense of decorating the rooms.

The Suite of the Republic provided another means for the Cuban government to project the Hotel Nacional as a symbol of the Republic of Cuba. Such sumptuous apartments at the disposal of the government basically guaranteed that all visiting important heads of state would be staying at the Hotel Nacional, positioning the hotel as a key space in diplomatic exchange. The Cuban government could also offer the Suite of the Republic to important foreign businessmen, creating a way for the government to publicly endorse certain business interests. And of course, the Hotel Nacional played a vital role in conveying to those visiting businessmen and dignitaries the fact that Cuba was a country of the highest stature.

More broadly, the interiors of the Hotel Nacional were designed to convey a sense of comfort and luxury through modern amenities and design, above all concerned with expressing a Cuban identity and place specificity. Although the architecture incorporated modern design elements such as details revealing an Art Deco influence, the public interior spaces were decorated in a decidedly more Spanish colonial theme, injected with references to the Cuban republic. For example, the small decorative cement tiles designed to create a type of basket pattern were Spanish colonial in overall aesthetic appearance, but the specific images contained in these tiles referenced Cuba in particular. One tile had a five-pointed star in the center, iconography often used in depictions related to the Republic of Cuba, as the star held a prominent position in the Cuban flag. Another image was a small fortress or castle, similar to the three castles depicted on the coat of arms of Havana, which referenced colonial fortresses that were considered iconic of the island.

In total, $500,000 was budgeted for the hotel furnishings, and final costs were reported at just over $406,000.[25] According to correspondence, the "greater part" of the hotel furniture was contracted for in Cuba.[26] The interiors reflected general Cuban furnishing tendencies, which were still strongly reminiscent of colonial decorating approaches. These tendencies favored furniture of caned wood and wicker, because of their ventilation characteristics; mahogany furniture; and potted plants, especially in the patios and the spaces open to the outdoors. Furniture in public areas included fern stands, palms, and stick willow furniture. In general, wicker was widely incorporated throughout the hotel, and the majority was provided by the Cuban company Casa Mimbre.

Cuba had a long tradition of fine mahogany furniture and quality furniture craftsmanship. Two Cuban companies—Meras y Rico and Theodore Bailey & Company—provided the majority of the mahogany furniture for the hotel and showed attention to expressing local identity in the interiors. In contracts for the furniture, McKim, Mead & White made it clear they expected nothing less than the finest materials and the best craftsmanship. Although the lobby lounge had a Spanish colonial theme, the furniture was rather plain, with only a few focal pieces of more complex design, such as a mahogany table with spiral double legs made by Theodore Bailey & Company.[27]

Guest rooms were decorated in a similar manner that negotiated modern amenities and traditional Cuban wicker and mahogany furniture. Invoices indicate that all of the beds, tables, and mirrors were mahogany.[28] A typical guest room included an armchair, a dressing table, a chiffonier, a chair, a night table, and a valise stand. Although rooms contained the same furniture pieces, the pieces were often arranged differently in each room, especially when the room layout diverged from the standard. Adherence to US expectations of a modern bathroom positioned these as modern guest rooms. Tubs, toilets, sinks, and fixtures were supplied by Crane Company of Cuba (a local iteration of a US business) and Kohler, a company based in Wisconsin that was considered a leader in modern bathroom furnishings. The private baths in each room had hot and cold running water; in general, this type of bathroom design functioned to underscore that Cuba was a place of hygiene and sanitation.

A sense of national spirit or place distinctiveness was also conveyed in the exterior decoration. Most visually apparent was the inclusion of escutcheons and flags of Havana and Cuba in the design. Ornamental details in the stone tympanum depict the Cuban flag on a shield form, flanked by cornucopias and topped with a folded banner form that bears the word "CUBA." In fact, the contract stipulated that the hotel convey a national spirit—Machado did not want to leave any doubt that this was *the* national hotel of Cuba—and the details that include national symbolism were meant to legitimize the machadato as the rightful arbiter of national identity. Although financed and constructed with private funds, the overall effect was not unlike that of a national monument or a civic building.

## Machado's City, the Tourist City

In keeping with the basic tenets of cooperativismo, the hotel project allowed high-level functionaries to present themselves publicly as benevolent guardians of the nation and its people.[29] A case in point is Carlos Miguel de Céspedes, who served as secretary of public works under President Machado. A businessman turned public servant, Céspedes had skillfully transferred his entrepreneurial skills to his government position and achieved financial gain through political corruption.[30] Céspedes understood the importance of public image (especially given public knowledge of the government's rampant corruption), and he did not waste opportunities to position himself as a dedicated patriot. During the public signing of the contract for the Hotel Nacional de Cuba, Céspedes dramatically refused to stamp the contract, because, due to a typographical error, it was missing a clause that stated only the Cuban flag could fly over the hotel.[31] Positioning himself as a passionate national patriot who did not bow to the United States, Céspedes improved his public image when the press took up the story as an admirable act of patriotism.

During his tenure as secretary of public works, Céspedes supervised other urban planning projects, which included the machadato's most comprehensive urban planning project, "El Plan de Embellecimiento y Ampliación de la Habana" (Havana City Project), in which the Hotel Nacional de Cuba was to play a major role both symbolic and practical.[32] This grand master plan highlighted Vedado as a new center of the city, with a web of clearly defined major arteries connecting parts of this area to other parts of the city east and west. In 1925, Céspedes invited French architect Jean-Claude Nicolas Forestier to come to Havana to collaborate with a Cuban team to "embellish and plan the expansion of the city of Havana."[33] Although Forestier was formally invited to run the project (his presence was meant as much to impart a cosmopolitan air to Cuban urban planning as it was to actually design the plan), he and his team worked closely with a group of Cuban architects, engineers, and urban planners who had a firm grasp of local conditions and international trends in urban reform and civic art.

The resulting master plan was a comprehensive scheme that linked the dispersed areas of metropolitan Havana. The plan was designed in 1925–1926 and revised in 1928, and it drew heavily upon work and studies done by other Cubans, especially Pedro Martínez Inclán, whose publication *La Habana actual* (*Havana Today*, 1922) outlined grand avenues connected by a system of axes and monuments, with an emphasis on large amounts of public art and gardens.[34] Through the development process, the team determined the existing principal nodes in the urban fabric, proposed new points of confluence, and connected all of them through a system of roads designed to facilitate the functional needs of the city and to highlight prominent landmarks. The plan identified some of the key sites in the city—the shipping terminal in Habana Vieja (Old Havana), Estación Central de Ferrocariles (Central Train Station), Plaza Cívica (Civic Square), and the Hotel Nacional de Cuba—and situated them as convergence points connected by a system of dominant boulevards.[35]

Although large portions of the plan were never realized, the plan usefully reveals how politicians and urban planners envisioned a modern, well-functioning city; the shipping terminal and train station demonstrate the desire for transportation efficiency by connecting major streets to other sources of transportation, and the Hotel Nacional made a neat connection to these points of arrival/departure to meet the need for temporary lodging.[36] Moreover, as Hartman notes, Forestier's plan "appeared to extoll the virtues of Havana's Spanish colonial legacy, a heritage dependent on the domination of Indigenous populations and, later, African slaves."[37] The nodes not only serve as a gesture to a colonial past but also represent the realities of the Cuban present in the 1920s, in which the sugar economy was still booming, relying upon the underpaid labor of Cubans (often, in this era, working for US-owned sugar mills).

However, the incorporation of the Hotel Nacional as a convergence point in this network could not have been a decision based solely on practical concerns for functional efficiency. The network was also meant to highlight national landmarks, and it positioned the Hotel Nacional as just as much of a national symbol as the Plaza Cívica. The construction of the Hotel Nacional de Cuba, and more generally the development of Vedado, strengthened and connected the urban network of tourism in Havana. Tourism in Havana was already robust, and the machadato took additional pains to amplify the tourist industry starting in 1925.[38]

Although a number of US citizens traveled to Cuba in the nineteenth and early twentieth centuries, the 1920s marked the first period of full-fledged mass tourism, thanks to an investment in tourist infrastructure, improved transportation, and increased spending power on the part of US citizens. Also playing a decisive role in the establishment of Cuba as a vacation destination in the 1920s was the implementation of the Volstead Act in the United States in 1919. Prohibiting the production, sale, and transportation of alcohol, the Volstead Act was expected to put a damper on drinking in the United States. Just as Frederick Vanderbilt had hopes of people flocking to Puerto Rico to escape a dry United States, so did many from the United States and Cuba envision Havana as the future bar for US citizens. Cuba was only ninety miles from the United States; it already had a nascent tourism history and was heavily Americanized by the time the new amendment went into effect in October 1919. Prohibition in the United States had a profound effect on tourism in Cuba—not only in terms of the number of tourists but also on the type of tourism. The Munson Steamship Company had announced in 1903 that Cuba would be the next tourist mecca and tourism had continued to grow, but it was Prohibition that sealed Havana's fate as a destination for pleasure seekers and partiers.

Before Prohibition, the type of tourist who went to Cuba was fairly similar to that in Puerto Rico. The wealthy elite had the time and the money to make the time-consuming and expensive journey to the Caribbean. However, because of Prohibition in the United States, US citizens of all classes wanted to travel to Cuba. The travel industry met their demands by offering different levels of transportation and lodging that were accessible to the working and middle classes. This diversification in the tourism industry resulted in huge increases in the number of tourists throughout the 1920s. Fifty thousand US travelers went to Cuba in 1920, for example, and by 1928 the number of US tourists topped ninety thousand.[39]

Tourists arrived primarily by steamship and had different choices in the level of transportation and the route of travel.[40] Numerous ports in the United States, including New York, Baltimore, Charleston, Philadelphia, and New Orleans, offered steamship service to Havana. In 1928, for example, the Ward Line offered round-trip service from Manhattan to Havana for $160.[41] If this sixty-hour boat ride from the northeast to the Caribbean cost too much, one could also take a train to Key West, where the P&O Steamship Company's SS *Florida* crossed to Havana in six hours for a round-trip ticket price of $30. Or, for tourists interested in bringing their automobile with them, the Florida East Coast Ferry also offered service to Havana.

Throughout the first decades of the twentieth century, advertisements and magazine articles linked travel to Cuba with notions of adventure, entertainment, romance, and indulgence. In 1919, the *New York Times* featured a major article focusing on the future of Havana in the face of US Prohibition. Favorable conditions on the island—such as the weather, cheap drinks, and proposals to distribute more gambling licenses—had spurred many travelers to flock to Havana. The article proclaimed that "the Pearl of the Antilles deems the present an auspicious occasion to establish herself as the Monaco of America—a playground at the doorstep of a puritanical nation."[42] The early 1920s saw the establishment of a number of Cuban institutions such as the Dos Hermanos Bar, Ballyhoo, and Sloppy Joe's, which all became requisite stops for US tourists visiting the city. Sloppy Joe's, located only one block from the Hotel Sevilla-Biltmore, was the most famous of these bars at the time. The slogan of the bar, "First port of call, out where the wet begins," captured the popular image of the drinking frenzy that ensued as soon as US tourists stepped foot on Cuban soil. This reputation was reinforced in visual culture that circulated through the United States, such as promotional postcards depicting fashionably dressed tourists crowding the establishment, sipping drinks, chatting, dancing, and enjoying the festive atmosphere of Sloppy Joe's Bar.

The wild and romantic image of a Cuban vacation helped solidify the island nation as the most popular destination in the Caribbean for US travelers. In 1920, 50,000 of the roughly 73,400 US citizens who traveled to the Caribbean chose Cuba over all other Caribbean islands. This trend continued throughout the decade, and in 1928 Cuba captured approximately 90,000 of the 116,500 US travelers in the Caribbean. Cuba was by far the most popular destination for US tourists in the 1920s, and it continued to capture the majority of the Caribbean-going US tourist market well into the post–World War II period.[43] Cuba seemed wide open for tourism and for business development. Averse to missing out on potential profits, Cuban leaders looked for ways to benefit, both collectively as a nation and as individuals working within the political system.

Up through the late 1920s, the majority of hotels were located in or immediately surrounding the historic center of Havana. The three hotels built in Vedado in the 1920s—Hotel Presidente (1927), Palace Hotel (1928), and Hotel Nacional de Cuba (1930)—are evidence that focus was shifting to Vedado as a new area to support the tourist industry and more generally to reinforce urban growth and cohesive ties between municipalities.[44] These hotels justified the previous attention to making better transportation networks in the form of roads, bridges, and trams, and they incited further development of transportation infrastructure, with the effect of encouraging tourists to stay further out from the historic center.[45] Between the urban core and the edges of the city, between the historic center and the tourist attractions in Marianao, the Hotel Nacional de Cuba's location positioned it in the best of both worlds; it was at once a resort oasis and yet closely connected to the city.

Although these three hotels were located in the same neighborhood, the Hotel Nacional's design provided a markedly different experience from that of the Hotel Presidente or the Palace Hotel. This was in part because of the quality of

Figure 2.9. Aerial view of the Hotel Nacional de Cuba taken around completion. McKim, Mead & White Architectural Records Collection, Department of Prints, Photographs and Architectural Collections, New-York Historical Society Museum & Library, New York City.

furnishings and the level of detail in the architecture, but it was largely because the government appropriated the lands necessary for an expansive resort in an area of the city that was already carved up into smaller plots (figure 2.9). The government allocated thirteen acres of land for the Hotel Nacional de Cuba while the urban zoning regulations of Vedado (which private developers had to adhere to) limited both the Hotel Presidente and the Palace Hotel. With their smaller plot sizes, these two hotels have a vertical emphasis; they have no landscaping or grounds and their entrances are quite close to the street. This type of design is similar to many of the urban hotels in Centro Habana and Habana Vieja, where space is at a premium. Hotels are limited to only one city block, and therefore the buildings usually have little or no transitional space between the sidewalk and the entrance as a means to most efficiently profit from the space.

Aside from these hotels in more densely developed urban areas, other lodging options included a couple of sprawling resorts located further afield. The Hotel

Almendares (1921), an elegant resort built to address the need for hotels in Marianao, was located close to the casino, yacht, and country clubs and offered a golf course. In effect, it promoted a vacation experience that was focused on remaining in Marianao.[46] Other similarly positioned resorts likewise focused on elite leisure activities such as golf, yachting, and country club culture. Both the Hotel Almendares and the Hotel Nacional de Cuba were located in largely non-Cuban enclaves that targeted US tourists, but the Hotel Nacional de Cuba was unique in that it played an important symbolic role as national hotel, and Cuban politicians and elite, as well as visiting dignitaries, commonly used its public spaces.

A comparison of these urban and suburban examples underscores how astute the machadato officials were in selecting Taganana Hill in Vedado as the site of the Hotel Nacional de Cuba. Although it was not the first modern resort hotel in Havana, the Hotel Nacional de Cuba was the first to be integrated into a zone that was close to the historic center and that still could offer the escapism of a secluded resort. It was the best of both worlds. Moving down the grand driveway, the flanking palms rhythmically flashing past, guests left the city and everything else behind, yet the alluring diversions of the city could be found just beyond the hotel gates.

## *Negotiating the Contract*

President Machado awarded the commission to a conglomerate powerhouse of a corporation—a veritable Who's Who in the world of US finance, architecture, construction, and hotel operations, the majority of whom already had interests in Cuba. The organization was composed of the National City Company of New York, Purdy & Henderson, the United States Realty Company, the George A. Fuller Company, the Plaza Operating Company of New York, and McKim, Mead & White.[47] Many of these organizations already had significant experience of working in Cuba or extensive investment in urban development.

The creation of the National Cuba Hotel Corporation in 1929 was consistent with general US attitudes toward Cuba at this moment. That the commission for the Hotel Nacional de Cuba went to a US conglomerate spoke to the general desires of US businesses to dominate the Cuban economy, an imperialist attitude encouraged by the US government.[48] US leaders' long-standing concern with maintaining Cuba as a friendly neighbor went beyond goodwill to include an interest in molding the island into a source of wealth for the United States through both official policy and unofficial plans and practices. To justify this stance, the involvement of the

United States in Cuba had been promoted as natural since the early nineteenth century when, as historian Louis A. Pérez illustrates, an understanding of Cuba as a natural extension of the United States was widely assumed in public opinion.[49] This attitude magnified when the United States declared war on Spain in 1898 and mounted an armed intervention in the Cuban war for independence, which scholars have argued was motivated, ironically, by a deep aversion to the idea of Cuban independence.[50] In the first decades of the twentieth century, the autonomy and agency of the nation and its citizens was severely restricted by multiple US military interventions, constant monitoring and strong-arming of the Cuban government by the United States, and pervasive and substantial positioning of US businesses across the island.[51] US government officials subsequently charged themselves with supervising the establishment of Cuban sovereignty, which existed in little more than word in the period following Cuba's release from Spanish colonial rule.[52]

In some respects, the Hotel Nacional de Cuba project seemed quite in keeping with general design and building trends in Cuban public, commercial, and elite residential sectors. McKim, Mead & White was just one of a number of US architectural firms and construction companies working in Cuba.[53] Purdy & Henderson, the construction company for the hotel project, was based out of New York and quickly established an office in Havana in 1901 at a moment when many US firms were eager to enter the Cuban market.[54] Their projects in Havana included a mix of public and private projects for Cubans and foreign entities, including the expansion and renovation of the Hotel Plaza and the Hotel Inglaterra; completion of the Lonja de Comercio, the Capitolio, and the railroad station; and construction of the Centro Asturiano, the Centro Gallego, the Havana Yacht Club, the Royal Bank of Canada, and the Banco Nacional de Cuba. They were also responsible for building some of the grandest residences in Vedado in the 1910s. Purdy & Henderson's quality construction, use of the latest building technologies, and relationships with US material suppliers most likely explain why they were the favored construction company in Cuba, especially with high-level government officials.[55] Moreover, many may have considered them a local firm, as the president of the company, Leonard E. Brownson, announced in 1925 that Purdy & Henderson had a 90 percent Cuban ownership.[56]

Although some architectural firms and construction companies had long been working in Cuba, the Hotel Nacional de Cuba was McKim, Mead & White's first project in the island nation. One of the most famed architectural firms of the Gilded Age, McKim, Mead & White had built extensively throughout the United States since 1879, adhering to Beaux Arts principles and often preferring neoclassical styles.[57] By the mid-1920s, the firm's influence and accomplishments were widely acknowledged, including in the form of a published monograph, all of which was surely attractive to the machadato leaders.[58] The Cuban government was acquiring celebrity with this well-established competent firm, even if it was no longer considered either progressive or innovative. Even if a US firm may have posed something of a mixed message for the design of a national hotel, the association of US architects with modern hotel design would have been a major factor in the machadato's selection of McKim, Mead & White.

Along with the architectural firm and construction company, the other entities involved in the National Cuba Hotel Corporation illustrate how building projects of the period were woven into the fabric of Cuban culture, politics, and economics. For example, the National City Company, part of the National City Bank of New York (now Citibank), was the chief financier of the project. It was the first US bank to establish a foreign department in 1897, and its history of business in Cuba was already established by the time the Hotel Nacional project began. National City Bank opened an office in Havana in 1915 and had already hired Walker & Gillette to design their impressive neoclassical headquarters in Habana Vieja in 1925.[59] Likewise, Machado had close ties to National City Bank; in fact, when he visited New York in 1925 he met with bank officers in order to entice future capital investment and to nurture a healthy relationship with the bank that owned huge amounts of Cuban debt.[60]

The inclusion of the Plaza Operating Company of New York in the corporation, for the purposes of operating the hotel upon its opening, was fitting for a first-rate hotel. As the operators of New York's Plaza and Savoy Hotels, the prestigious company had a reputation for excellence in hospitality.[61] The implementation of US management and operating companies in Havana was common practice by the late 1920s and was probably expected for this project.[62] The National Cuba Hotel Corporation, composed of various types of businesses and corporations, provided the machadato with an attractive bid that covered every aspect of the designing, siting, building, financing, and operating of a modern luxury hotel.

North of the Straits of Florida, the hotel project was presented as a US venture in order to help finance the project. After signing the hotel contract, the National City Company announced the public sale of 62,500 shares of common stock in the hotel at one hundred dollars a share.[63] In its advertisements, the National City Company played up the project as a US enterprise, and the Cuban government was portrayed as being involved only insofar as providing "favorable terms" for the project. The advertisements stressed the National Cuba Hotel Corporation's incorporation in the state of Delaware, highlighted that the architects were a US firm, and underscored the fact that the US company that ran New York's Hotel Plaza and Plaza Savoy would operate the new hotel in Cuba, all of which emphasized the stability, seriousness, and Americanness of this venture. That this project was grounded in public investment illustrates the pervasive nature of US investment in Cuba. Investment was not limited to a faceless company but, rather, was enacted by individuals who, in this case, could pull together one hundred dollars or more to become stockholders in a business venture in Cuba. These systems of financial investment reinforced a general conception of Cuba as being up for sale for all those interested in purchasing it.

The US perspective was in stark contrast to the way the Cuban government designed and advertised the project as a decidedly Cuban one, and discrepancies such as these underscore the fraught relationship between the machadato and the National Cuba Hotel Corporation. Despite an environment that furthered Cuba's subordination and supported the imperialist desires of the National Cuba Hotel Corporation, the Hotel Nacional de Cuba project proved not only that US-Cuban entanglements ran deep but that the power structures of these relations were not unilateral. Indeed, a reading of the McKim, Mead & White papers at the New-York Historical Society reveals that the National Cuba Hotel Corporation's role in the design and construction of the hotel was defined and limited by the way the machadato outlined the project to favor the Cuban government, and the architecture is testament to strategies of negotiating complex international relations.

The machadato-defined terms of the project created a relationship between the National Cuba Hotel Corporation and the Cuban government that was defined by compromise and negotiation. Although the corporation was responsible for the costs of constructing and operating the hotel, the government retained ownership of the land and would take over control of the hotel after a limited term.[64] The final contract stipulated that the corporation pay for the land owned by the Havana Automobile Company, an area of about thirty-five hundred square meters located in part of the zone where the hotel complex was to be built. This was not a purchase of the land, however, but was referred to in the contract as a lease payment. The machadato then used this $141,940 lease payment to buy the land from the Havana Automobile Company.[65] These terms ensured the Cuban government's clear ownership of the plot of land. A close reading of the preliminary draft and the final version of the contract demonstrates how the machadato forcefully negotiated for—and ultimately obtained—a contract that clearly demonstrated their ownership of the land and the National Cuba Hotel Corporation's temporally limited role in the hotel.

## *Negotiating Construction*

Documents in the McKim, Mead & White papers indicate that, despite the many restrictions laid out in their contract, the firm sought agency in the project through their vigilant monitoring of building and design changes and careful attention to the budget. Correspondence chronicles the architects' strategic response to addressing the limited budget, such as their opinion that the project should be exempt from local building codes because it was a national building, a status they perhaps felt would allow for more efficient and economic designs and construction.[66]

Charged with maintaining the preapproved budget for the construction of the hotel, the architectural firm was invested in carefully monitoring all costs; the contract stipulated that the National Cuba Hotel Corporation had to cover all overages, and correspondence that circulated within the corporation specifies that overages were to come out of McKim, Mead & White's commission.[67] The architects did not unthinkingly accept alterations to the design when it affected the budget, even if the alterations came directly from the Cuban government. A letter from Purdy & Henderson reported the architects' responsibility to pay additional costs to the four-thousand-dollar estimate given by the Secretaría de Obras Públicas for running water and sewage pipes from the hotel to the street. The correspondence suggests the contractors knew the architects would balk at the cost overage and push back against this commonplace form of institutionalized extortion. In a letter to the architectural firm, Purdy & Henderson suggested that these suspicious estimate overages were simply the cost of doing business in Cuba. The example of this letter—and the one it was responding to, in which the architects contested the overages—demonstrates the architects' attempt to exert agency in the environment of government authority.

The task of procuring materials and products for this project fell to the contractors, Purdy & Henderson; the request for bids specified that "materials and products coming from the soil and from the industry of Cuba" must be used whenever possible.[68] Lists produced throughout the construction process and located in the McKim, Mead & White papers chronicle how Purdy & Henderson, in turn, subcontracted work on the Hotel Nacional to an extensive list of providers and vendors located in Cuba and the United States. One list of subcontractors written toward the end of the construction period named sixty-three companies, of which forty were based in Cuba. Although the contract required the employment of as many Cuban businesses and materials as possible, a closer look reveals how much Cuban and US business interests were already intermingled. For example, Purdy

& Henderson contracted themselves to construct the swimming pool, but they subcontracted a Cuban company, Gerard Jansen y Compañia, to install the filtering and sterilizing equipment. Although subcontracting Gerard Jansen y Compañia satisfied contract terms to use Cuban companies whenever possible, the equipment to be installed included pumps and an Ozonator that came from the United States Ozone Company of America, located in Scottdale, Pennsylvania. Gerard Jansen y Compañia provided the labor and received the profits for this contract, but upon closer examination the intertwining of Cuban and US business is clear. Examples such as this reveal how complex and enmeshed Cuban and US markets and economies were and that classifications of companies as "Cuban" or "US" were often nominal at best.

Purdy & Henderson subcontracted two types of US companies. One type was a company located in the United States that sent people, materials, or products to Cuba for the express purpose of the hotel project. This type included companies such as the John Van Range Company of Cincinnati, which provided much of the kitchen equipment for the hotel, or Robert E. Locher of New York, which provided artistic paintings that decorated the hotel. The other type was a US business that had satellite offices or shops or subsidiaries in Cuba, such as the Otis Elevator Company, the Crane Company of Cuba, the General Electric Company of Cuba, the American Steel Company of Cuba, and of course, Purdy & Henderson. Oftentimes the materials or products supplied by these entities ultimately came from the United States as well. The largest differences between the two types of companies were the legalities and financial implications of being either a foreign or a local business. US businesses based in their home country had their own set of customs concerns when exporting their goods to Cuba for the project, and perhaps work visa issues as well, while businesses that were ensconced in the local setting perhaps had an easier time importing products they would sell but had a host of different local and national tax concerns to consider.

In fact, relationships between McKim, Mead & White, Purdy & Henderson, and the Cuban government become all the more of a gray area upon examination of the 90 percent Cuban ownership of Purdy & Henderson. Although originally derived from a US company, the local iteration of Purdy & Henderson may quite plausibly have been acting in the best interest of its Cuban owners and not of the National Cuba Hotel Corporation. As historians such as Rosalie Schwartz and Louis A. Pérez have shown, government and business were practically one and the same in the republican period.[69] Successful Cuban businessmen often simultaneously held government positions, and elected politicians often used their privileged position to enter into business deals so as to fill their pockets. The sector of choice was anything related to building and urban development, from bay dredging to real estate speculation to concessions for newly built entertainment venues. This broader environment helps contextualize the Hotel Nacional de Cuba, and the specifics of the contract terms and the construction of the building show that power relations between the United States and Cuba were not unilateral.

## *Site of Conflict*

The grand opening of this modern luxury hotel—seemingly a triumph for the Machado government on the one hand and of US interests in Cuba on the other—was set against the backdrop of political unrest that permeated all sectors of Cuban society. Despite its position on the lofty promontory and its relative separation from the surrounding neighborhood, the Hotel Nacional de Cuba became a key site in the Revolution of 1933, which ultimately resulted in significant changes to political and military leadership, the abrogation of the Platt Amendment (1901 legislation that limited Cuban sovereignty and permitted US involvement in Cuban affairs whenever deemed necessary), and a new Cuban constitution, which was eventually ratified in 1940.[70] The hotel's role in the Revolution of 1933 further underscores the way the hotel (along with building and urban development under the machadato) was a significant area of concern related to larger civil unrest in the 1920s and early 1930s.

The roots of the siege of the Hotel Nacional are tied to civil discontent with the machadato's cooperativismo and its failure to deliver promised reform and increased sovereignty.[71] Many Cubans felt the cooperativismo type of approach, with its emphasis on foreign investment, did not fulfill the goals of the Cuban wars for independence or speak to the average Cuban. This period witnessed the rise of a number of popular activist and revolutionary groups led by various workers, students, and intellectuals, who agitated against the political status quo as well as against the poor wages and low quality of life experienced by the majority of citizens.

Machado used the army to repress groups and individuals who were either proved or suspected to be lacking in support of the machadato; in the 1920s, army officials found that, as the enforcer of the government's authoritarian policies, the army had become an enemy of the people.[72] The general public looked with fear and disgust at the military, whom they held responsible for countless missing, murdered, and imprisoned citizens. Recognizing their precarious position and the growing influence of civilian radicalization, and with the persuasive encouragement of US ambassador Sumner Welles, army leaders decided to lead a coup against President Machado on August 12, 1933.[73] However, the political instability that defined the period after the coup and President Machado's subsequent escape to the Bahamas supported an open public acceptance of opposition to the military. The armed forces found themselves the target of revenge killings and mob violence. Many of these attacks were devised as strategic maneuvers to position specific groups in power during this tumultuous period or to realize a real revolution, rather than to settle for what many saw as little more than a palace coup.[74]

On September 9, 1933, several hundred deposed and vulnerable military officers sought refuge in the Hotel Nacional de Cuba. For some, the hotel stood as a bastion of safety. Surely, they believed, these rebel groups would not attack the building where Ambassador Sumner Welles and other US visitors were lodged, and even if they did, the presence of US government officials and citizens would guarantee US intervention should the conflict escalate.[75] The Hotel Nacional was the site of nonviolent confrontation for almost a month, with members of the activist groups Pro Ley y Justicia (Pro Law and Justice), Ejercito del Caribe (Army of the Caribbean) and ABC Radical maintaining a stronghold outside the hotel in an effort to cut off the flow of supplies to the hotel.[76] These three groups were united in their insistence on the immediate abrogation of the Platt Amendment, as well as their opposition to the US government's coordination of mediations in July 1933 between the machadato and opposition groups, and the subsequent interference of the US government in the selection of Cuban government officials in the wake of Machado's departure.[77]

Initially, the standoff was not much more than symbolic, with hotel business running normally and the ex-officers and supplies coming and going without interference. This ended abruptly in the early morning of October 2, when activist groups violently confronted deposed military leaders who were seeking refuge in the hotel. Rifle, machine-gun, and cannon fire rained upon the hotel and continued until the besieged officers surrendered in the evening.[78]

The projectiles ripped through the building, giving a pockmarked appearance to the massive edifice (figure 2.10). Blasting through walls, ceilings, and doors and destroying furniture and bathroom fixtures, the cannon fire also inflicted significant damage to some of the guest rooms (figure 2.11). A series of photographs chronicling the damage are disturbing portrayals of the calm after the violent exchange. The hotel appears eerily still, the spaces devoid of the usual activity that defines a busy modern hotel. In contrast to the impression produced by these photographs, however, the Hotel Nacional became all the more populated by visitors after the attack. The *New York Times* reported that in one day, six days after the

Figure 2.10. Photo of the exterior of the Hotel Nacional after the October 1933 bombardment. McKim, Mead & White Architectural Records Collection, Department of Prints, Photographs and Architectural Collections, New-York Historical Society Museum & Library, New York City.

attack, around five thousand people visited the Hotel Nacional to view the damage. As a response to the onslaught of visitors, the US hotel management established daily sightseeing hours in the afternoons as a means to profit from this demonstration of political instability.[79]

The chain of events points to the dissonance between the hotel as tourist space and the hotel as national symbol. This dual role would have perhaps been easier to negotiate in the nineteenth century when hotels functioned as more openly public spaces for visitors and locals alike.[80] Despite the government's emphasis on

Figure 2.11. Photo of the interior of the Hotel Nacional after the October 1933 bombardment. McKim, Mead & White Architectural Records Collection, Department of Prints, Photographs and Architectural Collections, New-York Historical Society Museum & Library, New York City.

the hotel's public function as a symbol of Cuban pride, however, the hotel's design and everyday use were much in line with the general shift toward the privatization of hotel public spaces that was occurring in the early twentieth century. The repositioning of hotel public spaces as being for guests only—or for those who could pay for drinks or food—highlighted the separate spheres of Cuban locals and the privileged US tourists.[81] Its precarious position as both architecture of the nation (though increasingly inaccessible to the average Cuban citizen) and architecture of tourism rendered the Hotel Nacional de Cuba an object and space of conflict.

## *Contested Meanings of the Hotel*

The insurgent groups certainly saw a natural relationship between the deposed officers and the Hotel Nacional de Cuba. With the military officers seeking refuge in this place of US imperialism, the insurgents saw the hotel as an architectural product of the machadato's corruption and pandering to US interests.[82] The groups' attack on a building laden with this meaning illustrates their rejection of the machadato's definition of nationalism and system of cooperativismo. It is not hard to imagine that the rebel groups saw the Cuban flag flying over the hotel—and the various visual markers of nation such as coats of arms, flags, and stars incorporated into the architectural ornamentation—as a concept of nation co-opted and perverted by those in power. For many Cubans, particularly those actively contesting the Machado regime, the national symbolism of the Hotel Nacional actually represented a dream deferred. This was not the free democracy that reflected the long struggle of the nineteenth century to renounce the authority of the Spanish crown and form a sovereign nation. Indeed, as historians of this period have persuasively demonstrated, activists of the twentieth century imagined themselves continuing the fight that was started in the wars for independence but which had been thwarted because of US imposition of limited sovereignty.[83]

The activists likely saw the shield of the Cuban nation that decorates the porte-cochère and main entrance of the hotel as a symbol of the country they were trying to retrieve in order to finally accomplish what was started in the previous century.[84] Despite the fact that machadato leaders, as part of their effort to create a national hotel, carefully negotiated a hotel project that set limits on a foreign conglomerate's economic ambitions, activists and other citizens nevertheless saw the Hotel Nacional as a prime example of the country's subjection to US economic influence, which was often tied to larger imperialist ambitions. In this case, national development through urban design was connected to a broader past and present in which many Cubans felt the United States had simply replaced the Spanish and that Cuba continued to be subjected to colonialism.

In the context of the Revolution of 1933, the Hotel Nacional de Cuba shifted from hotel to fortress in meaning and discourse; it represented two competing visions of Cuban nationalism before and after the uprising. Various news articles and personal accounts described the Hotel Nacional as a fortress—referencing the site's past as a military fortification protecting against pirate invaders and, subsequently, as the site of a Spanish arms battery, later converted to US military barracks.[85] Borrowing from the history of the site, the popular press imagined the structure not as a tourist hotel but as a "fortress," which activist groups were trying to force military officers to surrender.[86] Writing to McKim, Mead & White in New York to report that the attack yielded no significant damage, Will Taylor, manager of the hotel, reported that the Hotel Nacional "certainly proved to be a Second Santa Clara Battery and the building certainly did its part to withstand the onslaught."[87] Whether Taylor was conscious of it or not, he was reinforcing an idea that the Revolution of 1933 was the culmination of the long fight for independence, a struggle that was almost achieved in 1898, when the site was home to the Santa Clara Battery, a Spanish stronghold.[88] Thus, the attack on the "fortress" could be seen by anti-Machado Cuban nationalists as a move against occupiers, the US interference perhaps conflated with a plundering pirate attack, or perhaps the machadato was seen as a foreign body, similar to Spanish rule, that needed to be expelled from the land. For anti-Machado nationalists, the attack on the hotel was a symbolic act of retaking the nation, by the people and for the people. The attackers were not only retaking the nation from the machadato; in opposing the privileging of US visitors and business over locals, they were also taking back their nation from US imperialism.

In the popular Cuban imagination, the Hotel Nacional de Cuba was linked with the Machado government's larger, self-congratulatory building program. It was also an expansive private building associated with corrupt relationships between the government and national and foreign businesses.[89] The Capitolio was built around the same time as the Hotel Nacional, and although two different types of buildings, they were both part of a comprehensive political program the machadato wished to manifest in built form (figure 2.12). Arguably the grandest building project undertaken by the machadato, and undeniably the most costly, the Capitolio's construction was finalized between 1925 and 1929.[90] Many Cubans were critical of the Capitolio and in its construction saw the problems of the Machado government.[91] The celebrated first official historian of the city of Havana during the republic, Emilio Roig de Leuchsenring lambasted the Capitolio, calling it a "display of exaggerated magnificence, a foolish waste" in a country filled with poverty, illiteracy, sickness, and hunger.[92] Roig was particularly devoted to the built environment of the city, but even a devotee of urban architecture and member of the elite such as he could not overlook the pomposity and cost of Machado's projects in the face of the suffering of so many Cubans.[93] Thus, while Cuban government officials surely meant for projects such as the Capitolio and the Hotel Nacional to convey the greatness of the Republic of Cuba, for many Cubans these buildings seemed like a slap in the face, disturbing reminders that the Machado government was

Figure 2.12. The Capitolio, by architects Raúl Otero, Govantes y Cabarrocas, Eugenio Rayneri Piedra, José María Bens Arrarte, and others, completed in 1929. From *Album fotográfico ... por el General Gerardo Machado y Morales*. The Mitchell Wolfson Jr. Collection, Wolfsonian-Florida International University, Miami Beach, Florida.

not committed to improving the lives of Cubans as a whole. They saw colonialism under the Spanish replaced with coloniality, managed by a small set of powerful Cubans and the United States, that reinforced racial, class, and gender hierarchies.

The building projects of the machadato such as the Hotel Nacional de Cuba and the Capitolio were physical manifestations of the problems many Cubans saw plaguing the country at this time. Many felt that Cuban sovereignty, constricted by the Platt Amendment, was further undermined by government leaders who embraced corruption and privileged the few over the many and often the foreign over the local.[94] The reformed government and political system that many Cubans were agitating for would mean different relationships between government officials and citizens and between Cuba and the United States.

### *National Symbol or Government Failure*

Perhaps no better building existed to symbolically echo the conditions that activist groups were fighting to change than the Hotel Nacional de Cuba. If the attack had happened at the Capitolio, a straightforward example of government architecture, it would have carried a different significance. The Hotel Nacional de Cuba manifested and expressed a multitude of different interests. The hotel was meant to be a national monument but was also imagined as a business venture for profit that revolved around foreigners, specifically US visitors. The Capitolio has more obvious visual references that can be tied to US-Cuban entanglements, such as its similarity to the US Capitol, but the Hotel Nacional presents a more accurate parallel to the contested conditions of Cuba in the early 1930s. Even if it is not completely apparent at first glance, the hotel is a visual and physical manifestation of US-Cuban entanglements.

Immediately after the 1933 attack, the hotel became a popular tourist destination for a brief time, but business quickly returned to normal. The renovations for an additional pool and dance pavilion that were undertaken the same year, among other updates, helped ensure the hotel stayed relevant. Despite the ebb and flow of tourism in the subsequent decades, the Hotel Nacional remains one of the most well-known and most reputable hotels in Havana.

The hotel was one of the chief architectural works that reflected and shaped the complexity of US-Cuban economic, geopolitical, and cultural relations. Its position within larger projects of building and urban planning in this period has proved a lasting influence on the landscape of Havana and has shaped subsequent understandings and actions regarding the relationship between architecture, international relations, and national identity. The hotel illustrates how, despite the realities of US imposition on Cuba, the machadato leaders found ways to work within the imperial system in order to exert some agency in defining their own nation. But this is not a simple story of the underdog winning, as the machadato did not represent the interests of all Cubans and was ultimately an oppressive regime. The machadato used architecture to visualize national accomplishment through the erection of monumental buildings such as the Hotel Nacional de Cuba, the Capitolio, and commemorative monuments, which it highlighted through careful positioning within an urban master plan for Havana. The machadato privileged this type of building and was not concerned with architecture that might more directly improve the lives of everyday Cubans, such as better housing, schools, or hospitals, especially in rural areas. The Hotel Nacional de Cuba demonstrates how architecture and US-Cuban relations were not zero-sum games of winners or losers but, rather, reveals the precarious positions of power that were negotiated. Although the machadato manipulated a US conglomerate to create a hotel that was meant to be a national symbol, to many Cuban citizens this very architectural project came to represent the failure of the government.

Plate 1. Joiri Minaya, *I can wear tropical print now series*. 2018. Found used shirt, found fabric, paint, 40 x 32 x 3 in. each. Image courtesy of Red Bull House of Art.

Plate 2. Cover for a Grand Condado Vanderbilt promotional brochure published by the hotel. Archivo General de Puerto Rico.

Plate 3. Proposal for the Grand Condado Vanderbilt Hotel and grounds by Warren & Wetmore. Condado Vanderbilt Hotel.

Plate 4. Postcard of the lobby of the Grand Condado Vanderbilt. Author's collection.

Plate 5. Watercolor depiction of a guest-room suite from the Grand Condado Vanderbilt. "Porto Rico: The Island of Enchantment." Archivo General de Puerto Rico.

# CONDADO — VANDERBILT

|  | Miles |
|---|---|
| Mayaguez to Aguadilla | 30 |

(Passing through little town of Aguada where there is a monument erected to Christopher Columbus, his first landing place). Aguadilla noted for embroidery industry—restaurant at R. R. Station.

| Aguadilla to Arecibo | 32 |
|---|---|

(Passing through Quebradillas and Hatillo—Hotel Baleares at Arecibo).

| Arecibo to San Juan | 50 |
|---|---|

**TRIP NO. 3.**

| San Juan to Ponce by the Military Road | 7 |
|---|---|

Pass through Rio Piedras where the University of Porto Rico is located.

| Caguas (Tobacco industry) | 15 |
|---|---|

Pass through the town, climbing the hill of La Cruses; many sugar plantations to

| Cayey (Wireless station and soldiers' barracks) | 16 |
|---|---|

From Cayey over the long hill of La Plata, the largest tobacco plantation. Hotel Jiminez on main street. Down the hill (La Assomonta) coffee plantation to

| Coamo | 10 |
|---|---|

Just past the village and to the left and reach

| Coamo Springs | 4 |
|---|---|

(Coamo Springs Hotel with famous sulphur springs.) Back to the main road, passing

| Juana Diaz | 13 |
|---|---|
| To Ponce (Hotels Melia and Frances) | 9 |

(Second city of importance on the island).

| Adjuntas | 18 |
|---|---|

(From the top of the hill a fine view of the Caribbean Sea is obtained. Coffee and banana plantations.)

| Utuardo | 13 |
|---|---|
| Arecibo (Hotel Baleares) | 20 |
| Manati (Hotel Comercio) | 19 |
| Vega Baja | 8 |
| Vega Alta | 7 |
| Bayamon | 14 |
| San Juan | 5 |

## Short Trips

**TRIP NO. 4.**
San Juan to Trujillo Alto.

Take the Carretera Central town at the left in Rio Piedras, and after riding for two miles on the Carolina road, meet the Trujillo Alto Road on the right. Fruit and sugar cultivation. Trip covers 14 miles one way.

**TRIP NO. 5.**

| San Juan to Naranjito (New Road) | 18 |
|---|---|

Pass through Bayamon and take the Comerio Road. Pass the Plata Bridge and take the Naranjito road.

| Naranjito to Corozal | 7 |
|---|---|
| Corozal to Toa Alta | 9 |
| Toa Alta to San Juan | 14 |

**TRIP NO. 6**
San Juan to Guaynabo.

Take the new road to Bayamon. Cross the San Juan Bay. Keep to the left to Guaynabo. Trip covers ten miles one way.

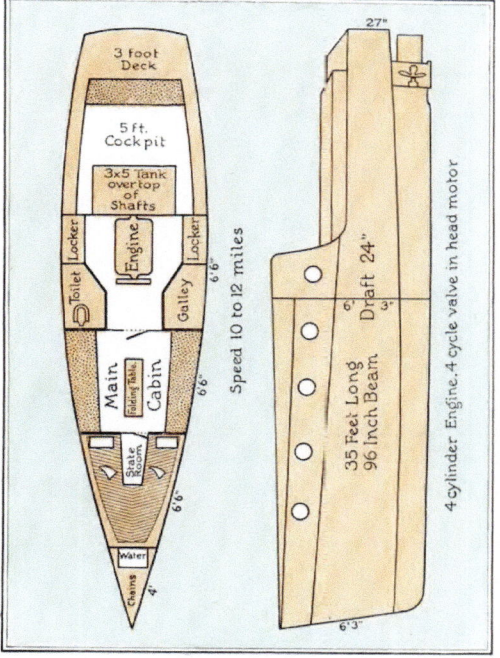

**MOTOR BOAT**

Above are reproduced plans of a type of motor boat popular and convenient for use in the waters about Porto Rico.

Plate 6. Header graphic from the Grand Condado Vanderbilt brochure "Porto Rico: 'The Switzerland of the Tropics.'" Archivo General de Puerto Rico.

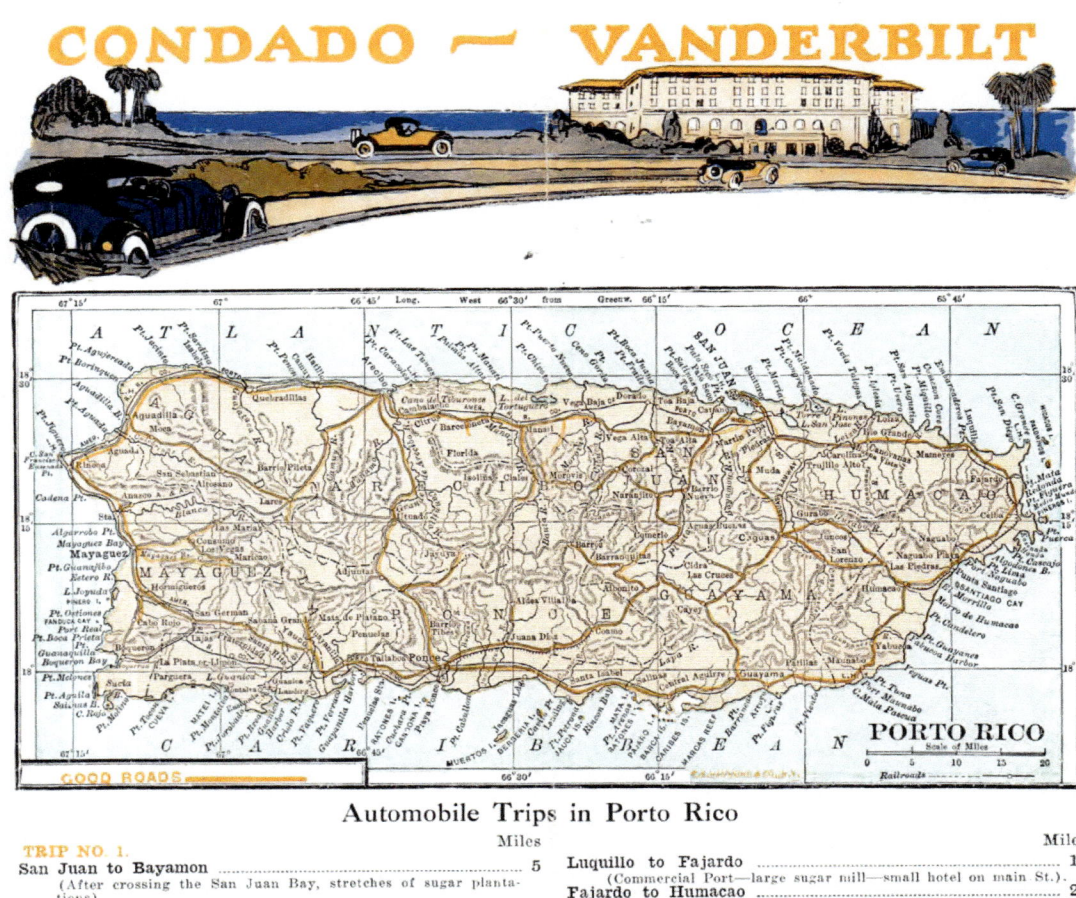

## Automobile Trips in Porto Rico

**TRIP NO. 1.**

San Juan to Bayamon ............................................................. 5
(After crossing the San Juan Bay, stretches of sugar plantations).

Bayamon to Comerio ............................................................ 18
(Mountain road which meets Comerio Falls—source of great water power).

Comerio to Barranquitas
(Splendid mountain scenery—one of the coolest places on the island and has many summer homes).

Barranquitas to Aibonito.
(A down grade until the Military Road is met).

Returning via Cayey, Caguas and Rio Piedras to San Juan 50

**TRIP No. 2.**

San Juan to Carolina ............................................................ 14
(Level road—sugar plantations).

Carolina to Luquillo ............................................................. 15
(Along the coast—cocoanut trees and sugar plantations).

Luquillo to Fajardo ............................................................. 10
(Commercial Port—large sugar mill—small hotel on main St.).

Fajardo to Humacao ............................................................ 24

Humacao to Yabucoa ............................................................. 6
(On top of a mountain which commands a fine view of the town and sea).

Yabucoa to Maunabo and Patillas to Guayama ................. 23
(A square in the centre of town with fountain—also some old churches here and a hotel).

Straight level road to Ponce .................................................. 40
(Sugar mills and sugar plantations all along the way).

Ponce to Yauco .................................................................... 18
(Large coffee plantations over the mountains).

Yauco to San German ........................................................... 9
(One of the oldest towns of Porto Rico and contains one of the best Professional Schools).

San German to Mayaguez .................................................... 30
(Half destroyed by earthquake of 1919, Hotel Palmer and Imperial here).

Plate 7. Road map with header graphic of cars in front of the hotel. From the brochure "Porto Rico: 'The Switzerland of the Tropics.'" Archivo General de Puerto Rico.

Plate 8. Watercolor depiction of the Coamo Springs Hotel from the Grand Condado Vanderbilt promotional brochure "Porto Rico: The Island of Enchantment." Archivo General de Puerto Rico.

Plate 9. Ceramic ashtray, ca. 1950. Author's collection.

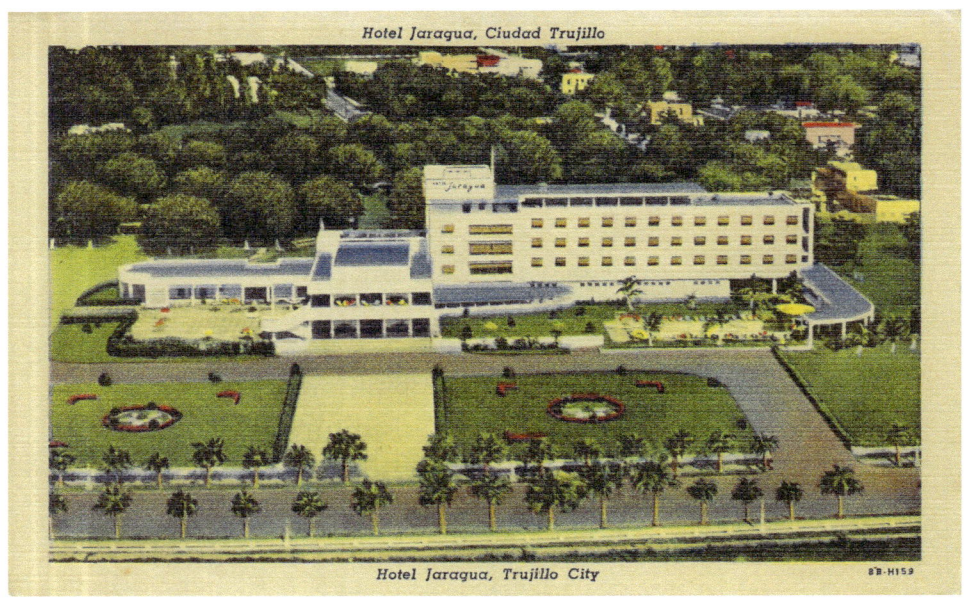

Plate 10. Postcard of the Hotel Jaragua in its original configuration. Author's collection.

Plate 11. Postcard of the Hotel Jaragua's swimming pool. Author's collection.

Plate 12. Promotional poster for Puerto Rico designed under the NYC Arts Project, Works Project Administration, 1940. Silkscreen by Frank S. Nicholson, artist. LC-USZC2-5643, WPA Poster Collection, Prints & Photographs Division, Library of Congress.

Plate 13. Promotional poster for Puerto Rico designed under the NYC Arts Project, Works Project Administration, 1940. Silkscreen by Frank S. Nicholson, artist. LC-USZC2-847, WPA Poster Collection, Prints & Photographs Division, Library of Congress.

# 3

# The Hotel Jaragua

### Race and Nation Building in the Dominican Republic

**Water forcefully shot high toward the sky from the grand fountain marking one** of the ceremonial centers of the 1955 Free World's Fair of Peace and Confraternity in Ciudad Trujillo. The fountain served as a focal point around which fairgoers circulated and parades marched. The design of the fair provided opportunities for these parades, which leveraged the public nature of the demonstrations to project the Trujillo regime leaders' idea of who Dominicans were and what they looked like.

Comprised of seventy-one buildings across almost six and a half acres, the fair marked President Rafael Leónidas Trujillo Molina's twenty-fifth year as dictator of the Dominican Republic and celebrated his accomplishments in building a modern nation. Building the urban landscape of this fair was no small feat, and the Trujillo regime relied on one of its trusted architects, Guillermo González Sánchez, to create impressive well-planned spaces and structures. González employed a modernist idiom in his designs for the fair to reinforce notions of modernity. With expansive grounds abutting the Caribbean Sea, the fair was defined by wide streets, which reinforced a sense of monumentality in the space and the buildings, and the intersections strategically highlighted the fair's seaside location. The aim of the fair was to provide an experience largely shaped by spatial and architectural engagement that served to reinforce the Trujillo regime's conception of the Dominican nation.

The Hotel Embajador was visible from the monumental fountain. Designed by US architect Roy France as part of the fair's total design and opened in 1956, the modernist hotel began welcoming hordes of US tourists who were taking advantage of economical airfares from places such as New York. Often referred to as the Dominican Republic's first modern luxury hotel, the Hotel Embajador offered guest rooms with balconies looking out over the Caribbean Sea; live entertainment and gambling drew tourists and the local elite alike.

While the hotel was certainly significant when it opened, an overly narrow focus on this narrative belittles the history of another important hotel, the Hotel Jaragua, which was inaugurated in 1942 by President Trujillo (plate 10). Designed by Guillermo González Sánchez and though smaller than the Hotel Embajador, the Hotel Jaragua reflected equally grandiose ambitions of the Trujillo regime. It was directly tied to regime efforts to construct a new Dominican modernity in the wake of the 1930 Ciclón de San Zenón (Hurricane San Zenón) through attention to the intersection of urban design and architecture, rural development, and race-based notions of Dominican identity. Indeed, the Hotel Jaragua was a key project in defining Trujillan modernity and nationhood after the hurricane, and the hotel's design reinforced the regime's vision that the modern Dominican Republic was a white Catholic patriarchy.

The 1955 Free World's Fair of Peace and Confraternity, as Jennifer Baez astutely points out, "constructed the idea of a Dominican nation by defining a cultural and spatial geography that was described by a solid partition in the geopolitical border with Haiti, and a fluid marine threshold for tourists along the coastline."[1] Dark-skinned Haitians were not welcome, but light-skinned tourists were. In this chapter, I trace these concepts even further back in time to reevaluate the Hotel Jaragua project as bound to the larger agenda of nation building undertaken by Trujillo in the 1930s and the 1940s, which followed the same logic and practices as articulated by Baez. More specifically, I triangulate the Hotel Jaragua via the aftermath of the Ciclón de San Zenón, the 1937 genocide of Haitians and dark-skinned Dominicans by the trujillato, and the fluidity of the marine threshold not just with tourists but with the US Marines and US imperialism that extended both before and after Trujillo's government.

In calling out the Hotel Jaragua as demonstrative of González's skill in rotation when using a modernist idiom, Omar Rancier indirectly points to function as a key concern in the planning of the hotel.[2] Although capable of designing with a Beaux Arts approach, the architect leaves behind the types of planning used for the Grand Condado Vanderbilt in Puerto Rico and the Hotel Nacional de Cuba (and indeed, in most grand hotel construction in general up to this point) in favor of an architectural modernism that was quite avant-garde for hotel design. In this case, the hotel design indicates studied attention to the careful arrangement of volumes to create a visual complexity for a design that programmatically differentiates various functions of the hotel into different zones.

The hotel's main drive, which culminates in a loop in front of the main entrance, boasts a double-height volume, indicative of the soaring ceilings of the impressive lobby area. From this central zone other massing juts off—lower volumes indicate public spaces for entertainment and dining, and a larger rectangular volume is dedicated to the guest rooms. Looking at the structure from the ocean, one can clearly see how, devoid of ornamentation and rendered in clean white surfaces, the hotel's visual vibrancy comes from architectural details that facilitate function and movement. For example, a portico wraps around the Spanish Courtyard, the main outdoor space for music and dancing; in doing so, the portico creates interstitial zones connecting indoors and out. One of the most visually engaging aspects from this vista is the spiral staircase that leads up from the courtyard to galleries up above, highlighting passages visitors might use to stroll around that part of the structure. The piloti-like columns in the portico below are echoed above in the roof terrace that caps the rectangular slab of guest rooms. Not only does the repetition call out the use of these spaces as public and social spaces, as opposed to the more closed volume of the guest-room area, but it also works to pull the design together into one cohesive work from one side to the other and from top to bottom. Not only does this provide balance to an otherwise sprawling design, but the columns, along with the galleries and the staccato punctures of fenestration on the guest-room block, are the details that bring dynamism to this modernist design.

The Hotel Jaragua has been cited as the first modernist hotel in the Americas, but its architectural merits have not earned it a position in the canon of architectural history. Despite this, what is most compelling about this project is arguably not its modernist design. One reason for its lack of renown may be because it never enjoyed the international reach of the other hotels under study in this book. Indeed, the hotel never functioned primarily as a destination for foreign visitors; rather, it was a social space for the Dominican elite. The emphasis on public spaces, where Dominicans could dine, dance, drink, and enjoy entertainment, was key to this design. The hotel provided the spatial guidelines for Dominicans to perform Dominican identity, creating a spectacle that reinforced Trujillo's narrow definition of modernity and national identity.

Figure 3.1. Images of the Villa Francisca neighborhood in Santo Domingo before and after the Ciclón de San Zenón. Before photograph by Luis Mañon, ca. 1930. Archivo General de la Nación, Santo Domingo, Dominican Republic.

## *A Nation-Building Opportunity*

Santo Domingo was largely destroyed during the hurricane; winds of up to 150 miles per hour tossed about the hallmark zinc roofs and wooden pieces that defined the buildings from the early twentieth century and which characterized the urban landscape (figure 3.1). The city's Río Ozama overflowed, washing away all these building fragments, as well as bridges and port facilities. The loss of life was in the thousands, and even more were left homeless and without food. El Ciclón de San Zenón showed no mercy when it hit in September 1930, only weeks after Rafael Trujillo took control of the government.

Although undoubtedly a challenge, Trujillo also saw this as an opportunity to justify his rule and to shape a new, modern Dominican Republic.[3] His military background served him well in organizing the relief efforts in an efficient manner, and in following years Trujillo and his regime used this response to legitimize his rule and to shape a specific narrative of history. Mark Anderson argues that Trujillo's actions in the aftermath of the hurricane, such as renaming the capital Ciudad Trujillo in 1936, should not be written off as symptoms of megalomania but should be recognized as a project of rewriting Dominican past and future, both in the physical landscape and in the ideology of what was meant by the term "Dominican."[4]

Trujillo took control of a nation that had been plagued by US imperialism and interference since the republic won independence from Haiti in 1844. Although the Civil War in the United States put an end to US competition for the island nation, and Spain reannexed the republic in 1861, US businesses and government maintained an eye looking south to the Caribbean. US government officials understood the strategic location of the Dominican Republic, especially in relation to the isthmian canal projects they were pursuing. As a result, they acquired a naval base, or "coaling station," at Samaná Bay in 1854 as a precaution against a possible war. Eric Roorda notes that, although presented as coaling stations, these projects were often just a pretext for establishing a military presence.[5] In 1865, the Dominicans forced the Spanish out of the island and claimed sovereignty for themselves.

In what ended as a dictatorship, the leadership of Ulises Heureaux (1883–1899) succeeded in putting the Dominican Republic in deep debt to European countries, while a consortium of US businessman called the San Domingo Improvement Company bought out the failed Dutch bank Westendorp, taking over its railroad contracts and European bondholders. After seeing European powers bring warships into the Caribbean and threaten bombing in order to extract debt payments, the US government under President Theodore Roosevelt extended the 1823 Monroe doctrine, which claimed security for Latin American countries against European imperialism. The Roosevelt Corollary, as it was named, was based on Roosevelt's interpretation of the Monroe Doctrine, stating that it was the US government's responsibility to step in and police, in an international sense, when European powers threatened US neighbors to the south. Although seemingly altruistic—and certainly paternalistic—the Roosevelt Corollary and the Monroe Doctrine were primarily about protecting US interests and power in the Western Hemisphere. Roosevelt used this new legislation as pretext to use executive power to take control of Dominican finances in 1905, which was formalized as legislation in 1907.[6]

Under this arrangement the Dominican Republic was put into receivership with the General Receivership of Dominican Customs, overseen by the US Bureau of Insular Affairs of the War Department, extracting 55 percent of duties paid on imports to apply to debt. Moreover, a twenty-million-dollar loan organized by the US government and administered by the National City Bank of New York helped pay off the bonds held in Europe and then floated new US bonds. This was the beginning of the evolution of US dollar diplomacy in the Caribbean. When this was threatened for any number of reasons, US warships were sent to "protect" and exert a "moral effect" through enforcement of the dictates of the US government. These visits were invasive at times; Roorda points out that Presidents William Howard Taft and Woodrow Wilson dispatched warships that resulted in "the removal of two presidents, the cutoff of government revenues by the general receiver, US supervision of a Dominican Election, and then a nationalist crisis."[7]

Economic, political, and military interests went hand in hand, and in 1916 the US Marines began an occupation of the Dominican Republic that lasted until 1924. Effectively running two competing leaders out of office and out of town, the United States then set up a military governor who threatened democratic practices by imposing censorship on citizens and the press, cancelling elections, and suspending Congress. Even though there was to be a dual US-Dominican government, the Dominican president, Francisco Henríquez y Carvajal, and his cabinet resigned. Because of the circumstances of World War I, the United States succeeded in effectively removing all European competition from the Dominican Republic; having removed foreign and domestic political powers, the occupation government began to restructure many facets of the country.

Civil order in the countryside, which was found to be particularly lacking and unacceptable by the occupation government, was pursued alongside the increasing ownership of Dominican lands by US-owned sugar companies. One result of this was the displacement of peasants from the land, which is an important context for understanding Trujillo's success in earning the respect of many rural peasants. The US Marines also started training Dominican soldiers and ultimately formed the Dominican Guardia Nacional (Dominican National Guard, later renamed the Policía Nacional [National Police]), another key action of the US occupation that aided Trujillo's rise to power. According to Roorda, the occupation government's agenda was marked by infrastructural and organizational programs similar to colonial projects in Haiti and Veracruz, Mexico under President Wilson, and "defined a kind of Progressive imperialism concerned with much of the same reforms of Progressivism in the United States: public health, public works, education, fiscal management, and civil and military service."[8]

A "small village" is how architectural historian Omar Rancier describes the capital city in the early twentieth century, despite the fact that it was undergoing a period of rapid urbanization starting in the late nineteenth century.[9] Engineer and historian Eugenio Pérez Montás notes that the transformation of Santo Domingo was marked in particular by Calle Mayor (now Calle el Conde), a main thoroughfare in the colonial center, and that overall the city took on "the air of eclectic neoclassicism."[10] In 1910, urban growth, partly caused by new technologies such as the train, caused the city to expand beyond its colonial walls. Although the majority of buildings were fashioned of wood with tin roofs, the new garden-city-style district of Gazcue, comparable to the Condado neighborhood in San Juan, Puerto Rico, boasted detached homes in then fashionable neocolonial and Mediterranean Revival styles; the construction of some dwellings included portions fashioned of reinforced concrete, a construction method slowly gaining popularity in the republic.

Of note, numerous residences and civic buildings in Santo Domingo were built in the second and third decades of the twentieth century by famed San Juan–based architects Antonín Nechodoma and Pedro Adolfo de Castro. Nechodoma, a Czech, came to Puerto Rico via the United States, where he became deeply engaged with Frank Lloyd Wright's Prairie Style. Once in San Juan, he developed what has been referred to as the "Prairie School in the Caribbean."[11] De Castro brought what has been described as a "Spanish-Moorish" style to the residences he designed in Santo Domingo. As Pérez Montás outlines, "the frequent and intense relationship with Puerto Rico determined a flow of authors" in this period just before the Trujillo regime.[12]

Although inflected by the occupation of US military forces from 1916 to 1924, the first decades of the twentieth century were marked by economic stability, partly because of agreements with the United States. This environment allowed for the launch of an ambitious program of public works throughout the country, including the building of roads, a postal system, hospitals, and schools, designed by engineers and architects both Dominican and foreign. In Santo Domingo, rain and wastewater were disposed of in colonial systems that met the standards of US technological systems.[13]

All of this is to say that even if Santo Domingo was not a metropolis comparable to, say, Havana at this time, it was not a stagnant backwater, either. However, even though modernity was making its mark on the urban landscape, there lacked a narrator to shape the story in a powerful way. This changed with Trujillo, who aimed to capitalize on the opportunities of rebuilding in the wake of the Ciclón de San Zenón as a means (one of many) to equate his rise to power with the coming of modernity to the Dominican Republic.

The dire situation faced by the country in the wake of the hurricane provided the perfect opportunity to practice a form of authoritarianism, painted as humanitarianism. With thousands hungry and homeless and disease sweeping the city, there was little protest at Trujillo's autocratic leadership; citizens saw his actions as a necessary response to the post-hurricane emergency. As Lisa Blackmore notes, this meant, "cladding the landscape and social body alike in modern materials," with concrete as the main building material and a new law that required wearing shoes in Santo Domingo.[14] Trujillo viewed both the city and the body as landscapes over which to exert control and enact his programs for modernity.

Trujillo came to power by taking advantage of the Dominican Revolution of 1930. He used his position as the leader of the Ejército Nacional Dominicano (Dominican National Army, formerly the Policía Nacional) to supply arms to a rebel group, enabling their subsequent actions against the then-present government. In the wake of this upset of power, Trujillo positioned himself as a candidate for election in May 1930. Through intimidation and his own form of martial law, Trujillo and his troops commandeered the election. The US minister Charles Curtis tried to curtail Trujillo's moves, but the policy of nonintervention coupled with the large US-trained Dominican standing army, led by none other than Trujillo himself, left Curtis with little recourse. Trujillo had trained in the Guardia Nacional starting in 1918 at the age of twenty-seven. Three years later he was part of the first class of officers to graduate from the US-Marine-led Military Academy in Haina. With a rank of second lieutenant, he received further training by the US military and was seen as a promising leader by his US supervisors.[15] President Horatio Vásquez (ousted by rebels armed by Trujillo) promoted him to commander, and then he gained the rank of brigadier general in 1927. It was Trujillo who pushed to change the military body from "police" to "army" in name, and who effectively shifted the Ejército Nacional Dominicano from a US-Marine offshoot to an agent of Dominican nationalism.[16]

Although Trujillo was intent on creating a new future for the Dominican Republic, he did not erase the past. Instead, he rewrote pre-Trujillo history as a complete failure so as to legitimize his rule and elevate the perception of his accomplishments. One means to do this was by replacing the post-independence oligarchy with intellectuals and bureaucrats who would be faithful to him, calling upon them to fabricate and promulgate a new discourse of Trujillo's power that both justified and concealed his repressive rule.[17] Trujillo's actions were set against what was described as failure after failure to advance a true national culture. Achievement of this culture, as painted by Trujillo's intellectuals, was thwarted by the failures of previous governments to thwart Haiti, to squelch Yankee imperialism, and to modernize the country, among other shortcomings.

In articulating this notion of a national culture, the Trujillo regime laid bare the connection they were drawing between a particular type of national subject as the route to modernity. *La raza dominicana* (the Dominican race) was defined by intellectuals as heterosexual Catholic Hispanics, both *blancos* (whites) and *indios* (Indians).[18] Those of African descent (estimated to be 80–90 percent of the population) had no place in the new nation that Trujillo was building. As Ana-Maurine Lara points out, the creation of the possibility of Catholic Hispanic Indians was also a means to erase the possibility of Afro-Dominicans, or *negros* (Blacks).[19] In other words, the trujillato created a movement to erase any notion of blackness from Dominican identity; regardless of skin color or ancestry, Dominicans were defined according to the terms *blancos* and *indios*.[20] This racism within Dominican society was connected to anti-Haitianism, which was undergirded by racism as well as by anxieties of labor that could be traced back to the early twentieth century when Haitians came to the Dominican Republic to labor on sugar plantations. Both in how they fashioned their own ideal national subject and how they regarded their Haitian neighbors, trujillato officials worked to naturalize anti-blackness as a matter of national interest. It short, they firmly cemented blancos and indios as the only constituents of the raza dominicana.

## Urban Plus Rural, or a Wholistic Project of National Identity and Placemaking

Just as Trujillo utilized the Ciclón de San Zenón to shape urban development, he deployed agrarian reform to manage rural development, and works in both urban and rural areas were meant to articulate a national identity based in the privileging of certain genders and races. The fruits of the rural landscape and the labor taking place there are intimately connected to the wealth enjoyed in urban areas; they often finance construction in the urban built environment. In the Caribbean, it is easy to see how this can be understood as a parallel to the rural plantation system, which came to dominate and to funnel goods—and ultimately profits—to urban cores, whether on the same island or back in Madrid or in London. As Jennifer Jolly articulates in her study of Mexico under President Lázaro Cárdenas, the ways in which rural areas and their imaginaries play a vital role in defining a contradistinctive urban identity are often manipulated in national identity agendas.[21] Jolly reminds us that contrast was a way to bring identity into relief, which could happen through violent or symbiotic relationships. Thinking across the urban and the rural in Trujillo's Dominican Republic allows for a more comprehensive understanding of the spatial politics of the regime's ideology, especially as it related to race.

Trujillo's projects for rural areas were meant to promote economic development, increase national autonomy, and consolidate his regime through peasants' acceptance and support.[22] These were mutually constitutive goals. The Trujillo government enacted a program of agrarian reform, made possible in part because large amounts of uncleared territory and a lack of absolute land titles allowed the regime to expropriate large amounts of terrain. Coupled with projects that expanded infrastructure such as roads, bridges, and irrigation, the government created a new condition in which peasants were now reliant on the state for their subsistence. The state provided access to land and other types of assistance, but peasants had to change their habits and farm in a more stationary and intensive manner. The trujillato was able to more readily monitor and control the movement of Dominicans in rural areas. A clear practice developed whereby those who were deemed "men of work" were rewarded with aid and access of various types whereas vagrancy penalties were administered to those who fell outside the regime's expectations for work. Historian Richard Turits contends that this was a project of modernization that "served to pry open the countryside to state power."[23] With increased control in the rural areas, the regime was able to effectively promote a homogenous Dominican identity throughout the whole country.

The Trujillan project of modernity utilized infrastructure as a means to transform the rural and urban landscapes alike. Blackmore chronicles how water and waterworks were part of this project of modernity, which flowed throughout the whole nation. Urban monuments in the core used water as a spectacle for propaganda, extolling Trujillo's shaping and development of a modern capital while also building more than seventy irrigation canals to bring water to more than 320,000 acres of agricultural land.[24] Trujillo's intermingling of authoritarianism and dedication to a developmentalist attitude is exemplified in the Canal Presidente Trujillo in Santiago Province, a concrete waterwork raised on stilts. With Trujillo's name emblazoned on the side, the public infrastructure left no room for doubt that it was Trujillo who was bringing modernity to the people. The landscape was transformed through this monumental work, which signaled the control of water throughout the nation as a means of modernization. Trujillo's success in inscribing his name on the project of modernity through developmentalism is noted in particular in the work of Turits, who has chronicled how peasants who were forced to labor uncompensated on canal projects, in other words they built the canals for themselves, still credited Trujillo with giving them irrigated lands.[25]

It was laborers, and not the moneyed urbanites of Ciudad Trujillo, who were witness to some of the bloodiest aspects of the shaping of Trujillo's ideal Dominican society. Not only were rural peasants subject to forced labor projects, but those living near the border with Haiti were in peril of being deemed Haitian and being either deported or killed. The research of scholars of Hispañola such as Turits and Lauren Derby has shown that the border area in the decades leading up to Trujillo's rule was a rich vibrant cultural mixing of Haitian and Dominican society. Many people crossed the border multiple times a day, effectively living a full life in both

Haiti and the Dominican Republic. Dominicans and Haitians intermarried and formed families together, and as Turits and Derby have found through oral histories, folks in these areas acknowledged that there were more Dominican-Haitians than there were "pure Dominicans."[26]

Despite the ways in which transborder relations were both positive and symbiotic, the Trujillo regime saw the border area and its society as something to be brought under the control of the regime and modernized. This aligned with the project of modernity's reliance on coloniality and the way this was enacted through domination of groups based on the intersection of labor and race and gender. Although there were agrarian reform programs to do this, the most heinous path the Trujillo regime took to border control—which was bound to larger concerns of a unified nation and a specific historical narrative—was the massacre of an estimated fifteen thousand or more Haitians and dark-skinned Dominicans near the border with Haiti in the early days of October 1937.

At the beginning of the month, Trujillo commanded his army to kill all Haitians in parts of the Cibao region near the northwestern region of the Dominican Republic that borders on Haiti. A growing anti-Haitian rhetoric, spouted by Trullijan intellectuals in both national and racial terms, was used in part as justification for this action. However, as Turits cautions, while this was certainly an act of violence against Haitians, the 1937 Haitian Massacre was an act of violence of the Dominican state against rural Dominicans.[27] Trujillo's vision of la raza dominicana as a white Catholic Hispanic patriarchy was sought through absolute state control, which deployed the rhetoric and programs of modernization as a means of social control. Even before Trujillo, the state had sought ways to exert more political authority over this region. With so much natural landscape, such a dispersed population, and so little infrastructure, these regions were hard for the national government to regulate politically and economically. Anxiety also arose over this borderless frontier in terms of illegal commerce and the flow of goods and bodies, especially in terms of potential "revolutionaries" who could easily cross over to Haiti to organize and weaponize. We see this in contrast to the urban landscape of post-hurricane Ciudad Trujillo, especially in such spaces as the Hotel Jaragua, which regulated space and types of bodies present and how they acted within this space. The spectacle of Trujillo's project for modernity took place largely in the urban zones, but it was also substantially grounded in populist agrarian policies that would ideally win over the peasant base, enable agricultural self-sufficiency, and expand state control more fully throughout the nation, resulting in the possibility of a strong national border.[28]

There were a number of reasons for Trujillo's mandate for the genocide of all Haitians, but the subsequent deft employment of anti-Haitianism and anti-blackness allowed the trujillato to further reinscribe Dominican national identity, largely through what it was not.[29] Dominican identity was not defined by the biculturalism and bilingualism that characterized the border regions; the monoethnic nation proposed by the regime was inconceivable to those who lived in the frontier zone. However, this is not to say that the 1937 Haitian Massacre was an attempt at "whitening" the country, as many dark-skinned Dominicans in those areas were not targeted, nor was it a move against Haitian migration to the Dominican Republic. Anti-Haitianism and national identity rhetoric was deployed after the massacre in order to justify the event and further cement a Dominican monoculture.[30]

Although the genocide of thousands of ethnic Haitians in a region far from the capital city may seem disconnected from the Hotel Jaragua, the 1937 Haitian Massacre is key to understanding what kind of nation Trujillo was aiming to create and how he was doing it. The spectacle of the Hotel Jaragua and the Dominican society and foreign visitors who would enjoy it represented the ideal Dominican Republic that was inextricably bound to the rural peasantry who contributed to insular self-sufficiency. Urban and rural were distinct but were interconnected parts of a larger puzzle that made up this new Dominican nation under Trujillo. The spatial politics were significant as Trujillo utilized agrarian reform and public works and infrastructure projects to win over rural peasants while also instilling a sense of a homogenous modern Dominican identity. At the same time, he manipulated the urban development of the capital city in the wake of the hurricane as a means to provide spaces where Dominican identity would be on display, largely through the spectacle of Dominican society in spaces of entertainment and leisure. Monuments were constructed throughout the nation both to modernize the country and to reinscribe the role of Trujillo in doing this. The Canal Presidente Trujillo in Santiago Province, for example, was emblazoned with his name for the local peasants to see, and in Ciudad Trujillo public leisure spaces complemented urban infrastructural works.

## Monuments of a New Nation, Architect of a New Nation

As the Trujillo regime was attending to border regions and massacring thousands of Haitians, it was concurrently renaming Santo Domingo as Ciudad Trujillo and opening Parque Ramfis in 1936–1937 (figure 3.2). Blackmore has positioned Parque Ramfis, a public children's park on oceanfront land in Ciudad Trujillo, as material

Figure 3.2. Aerial view of Parque Ramfis, designed by Guillermo Gonález Sánchez, 1936–1937. Photograph by Kurt Schnitzer. Archivo General de la Nación, Santo Domingo, Dominican Republic.

manifestation of Trujillo's triumph over chaos, death, and disease, and "transformation of water-as-threat into water-as-relief."[31] Located on the site of a mass grave of victims of the 1930 hurricane, the park demonstrated the regime's use of the built environment to highlight a narrative of Trujillo as redeemer of the nation after the hurricane, a man who could control what was before the uncontrollable water of the storm.

The park was designed by Guillermo González Sánchez, who came to be one of the main architects of the Trujillo regime and the main architect of the 1955 World's Fair. González was a perfect candidate for the autocratic leader. Born in the capital city, he could represent Dominican identity, yet he had far-ranging training and worldly experiences. His father was a diplomat educated in the United States as a dentist, his mother was a Cuban from Holguín, and González spent time during his youth in other countries because of his father's diplomatic posting.[32] After some work doing drawings for an architectural firm, González enrolled at

Columbia University to study architecture and then transferred to Yale. While at Yale he won a competition and traveled for eight months in Europe, where the modernist movement that would be known as the International Style was in full swing. After graduation in 1930, he stayed in the United States for a few years and worked for architects Edward Durell Stone and Francis Keally, both of them known for embracing modernist approaches in architecture. González was a cosmopolitan Dominican who, as an architect, brought to his work a Beaux-Arts education and much experience in modernist architectural practices.

Upon his return to the Dominican Republic, González started working for the Trujillo government. One of his first projects, which he undertook with his brother Alfredo González, an engineer, was Rancho Cayuco, a residence for Trujillo's daughter Flor de Oro and her husband, Porfirio Rubirosa Ariza. Shortly thereafter González won a public contest sponsored by the state for the public park for children—Parque Ramfis. It was in this design, which projected Trujillo's leadership out to the public, that González helped secure his reputation as a designer capable of capturing the dictator's narrative in spatial terms. The park offered Dominicans a leisure space right next to the Caribbean Sea, inviting a new type of relationship with the water that was not defined by fear of pirates or invasion by US Marines or hurricanes but, rather, pleasurable consumption of the landscape. The concrete esplanade flowed down a number of graded steps toward the *malecón* (waterfront promenade). A large oval reflecting pool was the central anchor of the design, with benches, pavilions, and walkways enabling Dominicans to move around, relax, and socialize. In the southwest corner of the park González located a large obelisk, which subsequently served as a site for pro-Trujillo rallies.[33]

Rancho Cayuco gave González the opportunity to show off his skills in designing in a Mediterranean Revival style, and Parque Ramfis was an opportunity for him to flex design muscles in bigger spatial terms. Then, the Pavilion of the Dominican Republic for the New York 1939 World's Fair gave him the chance to show off his prowess in International Style modernist architecture, both to Trujillo and to the world. In the wake of the 1937 Haitian Massacre, which was known beyond the island of Hispaniola, Trujillo was eager to showcase how the Dominican Republic was engaged in programs of modernity so as to avoid attention being paid to other, more unsavory and heinous aspects of his rule. The Pavilion of the Dominican Republic in New York showcased those programs of modernity through its cubic forms and large sections of factory-like windows, which marked it as architecture of the moment. Inside the pavilion, the theme was "The land that Columbus loved the most," deployed to legitimize Trujillo's rule and the regime's agenda. The focus was on the richness of Dominican culture through a display divided into three sections: Yesterday, Today, and Tomorrow. Narratives of the past aligned with the Trujillo regime's agenda for the present and future. Spanish—that is, European—roots were highlighted, underscoring Trujillan notions of a Dominican society of white Hispanic Catholics. Any doubt of the attention to race fell away when the large text on the wall introducing "Santo Domingo, now Trujillo city" described the capital as "the oldest White settlement in the New World." Reference in this sentence to the renaming of the capital city after Trujillo reinforces the connection between the leader and notions of this long-standing white society. Present and future were represented in such objects as the plans for the Columbus Lighthouse that was in progress, a project that was meant to position the Dominican Republic as a beacon of the Americas.[34] Moreover, the Columbus Lighthouse circled back and aimed to legitimize the theme "The land that Columbus loved the most," reinforcing European heritage and presenting the Dominican Republic as the chosen land.

## *A Project of Dubious Circumstances*

The Hotel Jaragua was part of nascent attempts to develop tourism in Ciudad Trujillo, although these first gestures were not part of more comprehensively thought-out programs of tourism infrastructure. In the early 1940s, tourism was based upon the patterns of visitors already coming to the island and attention to nationwide tourism would not come until later. Perhaps looking to other examples such as the Grand Condado Vanderbilt (or the Hotel Nacional de Cuba, which shared parallels in the autocratic approach to governing and tourist development), the Trujillo regime turned its attention to first building a landmark hotel that would make a statement to potential visitors about Dominican culture and society.

In the years preceding the Hotel Jaragua project, tourism to the Dominican Republic was primarily composed of visitors who came to the island by ship, particularly ocean liners heading south from the United States and west from Barcelona. Robust commercial air service to the Dominican Republic took longer to develop than in other Caribbean destinations. This was probably for several reasons, including the fact that other locations had more developed tourism infrastructure (such as Cuba), were seen as more culturally intriguing (such as Haiti), or did not have such recent international bad press regarding human rights (1937 Haitian Massacre).

The Trujillo regime was behind on tourism development compared to other countries such as Cuba, Mexico, and Jamaica, but the aim was to develop a form of tourism to highlight the urban works in Ciudad Trujillo that came out of the Ciclón de San Zenón, in particular by promoting Ciudad Trujillo as modern infrastructure supporting a colonial core rich with history and culture. Connection between the colonial center and the rest of the city for the purposes of the visitor was a focus of a publication from 1940, *Guia de Ciudad Trujillo República Dominicana: la ciudad más antigua de Ámerica* (Guide to Ciudad Trujillo, Dominican Republic, the most ancient city in America), which framed tourist experience around a Trujillo-driven narrative.[35]

The guidebook, published by the Dirección Nacional de Turismo (National Bureau of Tourism), presents a narrative of the modern Dominican Republic based on history structured around two major destructions to the capital city. The first was the chaos wrought by the hurricane on July 2, 1502, which provided a space for the rebuilding of Santo Domingo under Governor Fray Nicolás de Ovando. This is what created "the first city constructed by Europeans in the New World and for this [it] is of [the] highest historic merit in America."[36] The guidebook locates this first American city as the launching point of famed European men who went on to conquer various parts of the Americas and "discover" the Pacific Ocean. Santo Domingo is also praised as the city with the first monuments constructed by Europeans on the "new continent," and this list with descriptions is comprised of structures utilized to exert Catholic-driven Spanish colonial control over the land. Black and Indigenous groups are absent from the narrative. The colonial zone is romantically described as "silent witness of that remote era, evocative of the splendor and magnificence of the strong conquerors of the American lands." In a declarative statement meant to set Ciudad Trujillo apart from all other cities in the Americas, the guidebook author states with prideful tone that "no city in the New World preserves the footprint of European colonization like Ciudad Trujillo."[37] Echoing the messaging of the Dominican Pavilion at the 1939 New York World's Fair, this colonial history and the legacy it imparts on present Dominican society is defined by Spanish heritage.

The second destruction was caused by the Ciclón of San Zenón in 1930. Creating a parallel between the two hurricanes and subsequent urban building, the guide compares Trujillo's work on the city with the construction of that unmatched colonial city. Trujillo's city shines as brightly as Santo Domingo did as the most exceptional of colonial cities. The guidebook differentiates a Ciudad Trujillo Antigua, which comprises the colonial zone, and a Ciudad Trujillo Moderna, which defines the post-hurricane civic center of the city, divided into two sections of the book. The Trujillo regime's post-hurricane work is what brought modernity to the city, according to the guidebook, and helped support the colonial zone for tourist enjoyment. While modern works, such as hospitals and the malecón are mentioned, the modernity of Ciudad Trujillo is embedded in the guidebook structure that lists modern amenities the city has to offer, such as telephones and telegraphs, multiple and frequent access by a variety of steamship lines, and accommodations, including an announcement of the upcoming opening of the Hotel Jaragua.

The new Hotel Jaragua would be the built symbol of modernity in contradistinction to monuments in the colonial zone such as the Alcázar de Colón and the Catedral de Santa María la Menor. According to Alex Martínez Suárez and Rab Messina, much of the impulse and inspiration for building a flagship hotel to mark this new emphasis on tourism came from Trujillo's visit to the 1939 World's Fair and his stay in the Waldorf Astoria.[38] A new hotel could help solve the complaints coming from US politicians that Ciudad Trujillo did not offer comfortable lodging; it spoke to a 1934 proposal Trujillo had received from the manager of the Grand Condado Vanderbilt offering to leave that establishment and come to Ciudad Trujillo to run a grand state hotel built by the Trujillan government. In this missive, among other descriptions of this impressive hotel, the author insists on the importance of an oceanfront location.[39]

An investigation into the history of the land on which the Hotel Jaragua was built reveals some of the suspect ways in which Trujillo both implemented projects and profited from them. It is estimated that Trujillo, like most dictators, amassed a fortune while in power. Before any idea of a hotel project existed, Trujillo's second wife, María Martínez, had already bought a plot of land along the newly forming malecón. Later, in 1937 and 1940, she acquired two adjacent plots of land, the latter purchase most likely made with the hotel project in mind. In 1942, the land was officially purchased by the government from British subject Hallet Neville Hansard, who was known to be a frontman for Trujillo's private interests.[40]

The funding for the hotel suggests equally dubious circumstances. Money for the hotel came from a large loan negotiated by the Domincan ambassador to the United States, Andrés Pastoriza. Loan negotiations were started in 1940 with the Export-Import Bank of Washington, the official credit agency of the US federal government. Established under President Franklin Delano Roosevelt as a body to facilitate exports and imports between other nations and the United States, the bank was initially focused on making loans to the USSR and Latin America.[41] The majority of the three-million-dollar loan that was finally approved in 1941 was to be used for public projects—namely, dredging for a future port and purchasing refrigeration for a local slaughterhouse, but four hundred thousand dollars was earmarked for the hotel. Research by Suárez and Messina

Figure 3.3. Aerial view of the Hotel Jaragua showing its relationship to the malecón and Caribbean Sea, 1939–1941. Photograph by Kurt Schnitzer. Archivo General de la Nación, Santo Domingo, Dominican Republic.

raises questions as to how loan funds for the hotel were used, and although exact numbers may never be known, it is clear that Trujillo used Hansard to profit handsomely from this loan as funds disbursed do not match records of funds spent on the project.[42]

The hotel's location on the malecón, then called Avenida Presidente Trujillo, reinforced this practice of ocean-facing architecture and urban works started in the post-hurricane years with projects such as the malecón and Parque Ramfis (figure 3.3). Started in 1931, the project of an oceanfront drive that doubled as a promenade space was led by engineer José Ramón Báez López-Penha. The project involved taking down the old city walls and San Gil Fort, as well as requiring the people owning plots along the water to donate the first thirty-five meters of land to the project, which for many was more than 10 percent of their plot size. Completed in 1936, the malecón provided those in the city with several kilometers of oceanfront drive that invited engagement with the Caribbean Sea.

Figure 3.4. Hotel Jaragua, Ciudad Trujillo, Dominican Republic, 1942. Photograph by Guillermo González Sánchez. Archivo General de la Nación, Santo Domingo, Dominican Republic.

## *Spaces of Spectacle for Trujillo's Raza Dominicana*

Suggesting an ocean liner docked on the shore of Ciudad Trujillo, the Hotel Jaragua could not be missed; its bright white form surrounded by careful landscaping demanded the attention of all within sight (figure 3.4). Round cutouts in the white structure suggest the portholes of a liner, and the rectangular slab of guest rooms suggest the main body of the vessel where cruisers would enjoy comparable accommodations. Notions of leisure and the good life expanding across land and sea are captured in the hotel's design.

A beacon of modernity, marker of Trujillo's rule, and testament to the new spatial order and building techniques that grew out of a post–San Zenón context, the hotel was much more than simply a place for temporary lodging. Overnight stays seem almost secondary to the predominant use of the hotel as a space of social interaction and leisure entertainment; the hotel's design dedicated more space to public areas than to guest rooms. Moreover, the leisure and entertainment offered at the hotel were predominantly enjoyed by Dominicans, not by foreign visitors. The Hotel Jaragua served as a space of spectacle for Dominican society—more specifically, the Dominican society that Trujillo was fashioning as a white Hispanic Catholic patriarchy.

The spectacle and drama of the Hotel Jaragua started immediately upon arrival at the complex. The main entrance was a palm-lined drive oriented south off

Figure 3.5. The Spanish Courtyard at the Hotel Jaragua, 1941. Photograph by Kurt Schnitzer. Archivo General de la Nación, Santo Domingo, Dominican Republic.

Avenida Independencia, which led to the north side of the structure, leaving the south-facing side of the hotel open to unobstructed views of the malecón (Avenida Presidente Trujillo) and the Caribbean Sea. Funneled down the main drive that culminated in a sweeping circle in front of the main entryway, visitors to the hotel would then step through the doors of a floor-to-ceiling glass wall. Although the expansive glass was impressive in its own right, there was still a feeling of opening up as one moved through the threshold into a space with a double-height ceiling. The guest's dramatic experience of arriving at the hotel culminated in front of a bust of Trujillo, a gesture meant to leave no doubt in the visitor's mind as to who was responsible for this truly modern space and experience.

Guests could take advantage of the lobby as the central point from which radiated a diverse array of public spaces. Movement to the west offered guests opportunities to spend their money in either the gift shop, the beauty parlor, or the casino. To the east, the dining hall and private dining areas awaited, coupled

Figure 3.6. Outdoor galleries and balconies encouraged looking down on social spaces such as the swimming pool area, 1941. Photograph by Kurt Schnitzer. Archivo General de la Nación, Santo Domingo, Dominican Republic.

with spaces of service, such as the kitchen, laundry, boiler room, repair rooms, and storage. Back to the north, toward Avenida Independencia, was the Spanish Courtyard and a terrace with garden views (figure 3.5). To the south visitors would find a banquet hall with a gallery around the perimeter and also gardens and the pool surrounded by an open-air terrace (plate 11).

An outdoor staircase spiraling upward as it wrapped around a flagpole proudly displaying the national flag brought guests up to the second level, defined by balconies and terraces. The upper-level spaces reinscribed the public areas as spaces of spectacle, and visitors were encouraged to climb up and look down below on others partaking in the leisure activities offered by the Jaragua (figure 3.6). There was no doubt that the purpose was to see and be seen in this spatial arrangement. Indeed, the sixty-six guest rooms, singles and doubles flanking a central hall, were finely appointed with amenities such as private baths, cedar-lined closets, phones, fans, and radios, but these accoutrements seem secondary given the amount of space dedicated

Figure 3.7. The rooftop had covering to provide shade and an open plan that made the space flexible for different uses, 1941. Photograph by Kurt Schnitzer. Archivo General de la Nación, Santo Domingo, Dominican Republic.

to and attention given to areas for social engagement. The emphasis on public spaces reached from the ground floor to the rooftop, designed as a sun terrace and gardens with a bar and a dining area. It was a multipurpose space that provided views of the forests to the north and the sparkling Caribbean Sea to the south (figure 3.7). The rooftop sun garden offered the predominantly Dominican clientele an opportunity to visually own the landscape around them and to connect the landscape of the Dominican Republic—both natural and constructed—with Dominican identity.

Upon opening, the Jaragua Hotel became one of the most popular spots for nightlife in Ciudad Trujillo, less for US visitors than for Dominican society. Local Dominican bands were the most prominent on the calendar, along with visiting musicians, and they brought the terrace to life with their sounds and the couples they inspired to take to the dance floor. Other parts of the hotel offered different types of entertainment, including Broadway-style shows, rendering it as much—if not more—a space of entertainment as of temporary lodging. Yet, the Hotel

Figure 3.8. Photograph of the Hotel Jaragua under construction, revealing the racial politics of labor and Dominican society at large, ca. 1939–1941. Photograph by Kurt Schnitzer. Archivo General de la Nación, Santo Domingo, Dominican Republic.

Jaragua was not accessible to Dominicans of all economic levels (never mind race); it required a certain level of financial means to gain entry or to partake in the entertainment. Although there may have been some variety of economic classes that could afford day passes to the pool or some of the nighttime entertainment, photos of the Jaragua from its early years reveal that the guests were predominantly light-skinned. This is brought into sharp relief in photos showing musicians, service staff, and revelers together, as the musicians and hospitality workers were often darker-skinned. The images lay bare how the hotel was a space that actively reinscribed Trujillo's racial politics.

Other images of the hotel disclose how the hotel project contributed to the racial organization of Dominican society under Trujillo. Images taken during the hotel's construction show white Dominican men in handsome suits overseeing the construction of the hotel (figures 3.8, 3.9). These are the social and political elite—men close to Trujillo who also functioned to express the ideal Dominican society.

Figure 3.9. Photograph of the construction of the Hotel Jaragua showing lighter-skinned statesmen or businessmen in the foreground and darker-skinned laborers in the background, ca. 1939–1941. Photograph by Kurt Schnitzer. Archivo General de la Nación, Santo Domingo, Dominican Republic.

They clearly take ownership of the hotel project, as if they are more responsible for building it than the Dominican laborers captured in the background. These workers are not given prominence in the composition, though they serve as evidence of the human energy and toil that went into building Ciudad Trujillo. Like the musicians in the photos of nighttime entertainment, these construction workers are also notably darker-skinned than their besuited counterparts. This formula echoes that of the colonial Caribbean and asserts the coloniality/modernity project's continued use of racism as it intersects with labor; more cerebral and intellectual work is associated with lighter-skinned society, while physical and manual work is associated with darker-skinned groups. We are reminded yet again of structures that revolve around oppressed labor. The photographs at once reveal the way in which race contributed to social and work hierarchy in Trujillo's Dominican Republic and belie proclamations and programs for a homogenous Dominican social body. Whether the dictator was okay with it or not, the reality was that Black Dominicans and others considered to be undesirably dark played a significant role in building Trujillo's Dominican Republic.

## *Trujillo's Big Dreams beyond the Jaragua*

Presumably pleased with the types of amenities and entertainment offered at the Hotel Jaragua, government leaders decided to build fourteen more hotels throughout the country at a cost of twelve million pesos.[43] Like the Jaragua, the majority, if not all, of these hotels were meant to cater to the Dominican elite and placed more emphasis on social spaces and leisure activities than they did on guest rooms. For example, the Hotel Hamaca, built in Boca Chica, sported a casino, a bar, a restaurant, a saltwater pool, and open-air leisure spaces, while containing only twenty-eight guest rooms (figure 3.10).

Guillermo González Sánchez designed the Hotel Hamaca as well as others of the fourteen new hotels located throughout the country. While the Hotel Jaragua resembled a grounded ocean liner, the Hotel Hamaca seemed more of the sea than of the land. Gone are the curves that suggest Streamline Moderne in favor of a long, horizontal, boxy form underscored by ribbon windows and a rectangular mass that juts out over the water and rests upon piers anchored in the water below. Clearly aiming to connect the structure to the water, González was highlighting the location as well as one of the main attractions of this hotel—sun, sand, and surf.[44]

Not all of these new hotels were centered on the beach; there was also a decided interest in mountain vacations during this period as Dominicans were drawn to the cool air and natural beauty of waterfalls and forests.[45] González designed the Hotel Nueva Suiza in Costanza and the Hotel Montaña in Jarabacoa, both located in forested areas. The Hotel Nueva Suiza boasts a boxy rectilinear modernism similar to that of the Hotel Hamaca and offers views outward. But it is decidedly focused inward as well, its square footprint is focused around the pool and patio area in the large interior courtyard. The spectacle of these social spaces is underscored by the outdoor galleries that run around the interior perimeter of the structure, allowing visitors to look onto the scene in the courtyard as they move into or out of their guest room. Like the Hotel Hamaca, Hotel Nueva Suiza had few rooms—only thirty—compared to the space dedicated to the casino, the restaurant, and several leisure halls. In the Hotel Montaña, though it is modernist at its core, González reasserted his ability to work in more than one idiom. He engaged with the hotel's rural, mountainous location by using natural materials such as stone, dark wood, and tile shingles. Likewise, he highlighted the landscape by orienting guest rooms

Figure 3.10. Guillermo González Sánchez, Hotel Hamaca, Boca Chica, Dominican Republic. Archivo General de la Nación, Santo Domingo, Dominican Republic.

so that they entertain views of the valley of the Cordillera Central. Both hotels boast names that invoke the landscape, whether of Switzerland and its impressive alps or the more evocative mountains.

It is useful to think of these hotels in relation to the trujillato's programs of agricultural reform in order to draw out a larger picture of how regime leaders imagined they were bringing modernity to the nation through domination of the landscape. Through development, the natural world was being artificially cultivated, as modernity was about mastery of the natural environment. In this case, the projects of agricultural works and supporting infrastructure as well as rural hotels were imagined to allow the nation to control food production and views of its own landscape; both the agricultural works and the supporting infrastructure can be seen as constituent parts of a bigger project, but they also served as important counterpoints to each other. As the natural world was understood to disappear through cultivation of the land, the rural hotels, developed as places to enjoy nature, were seen as an antidote to the enervating effects of modernity and as contributing to the quest to locate a romanticized "nature."

While Trujillo was using this group of hotels to expand and support tourism throughout the country, he also kept an eye on the hotels in Ciudad Trujillo. In 1946 González was commissioned to add a fifty-seven-room annex on the Hotel Jaragua. Along with more guest rooms, this expansion project included a new pavilion for entertainment, a bigger casino that could accommodate 250 people, and an enlarged space for the dining hall. The last part of the project was a collaboration between González and William Reid Cabral—five bungalows that were meant to provide more privacy and comfort to those who opted for them. They were a decided step up from the guest rooms as they were composed of two bedrooms, two bathrooms, a living room, and a terrace that offered views of both the ocean and the gardens. This design does suggest a consideration of catering to international visitors by offering a spacious and well-equipped home away from home.

As Trujillo moved decidedly toward placing more attention on the image of the Dominican Republic in the world, González was once again called upon to expand the hotel, less than ten years later, in anticipation of the opening of the 1955 Free World's Fair of Peace and Confraternity. As well as overseeing the design of the entire fairgrounds and the structures in Ciudad Trujillo, González designed a one-hundred-room annex on the northwestern side of the hotel that included a generously sized bar for breakfast and light food, a terrace lounge area, and an inner courtyard. It was clearly a move focused on expanding the number of guest rooms at the hotel for the estimated high number of visitors anticipated to attend the fair in Ciudad Trujillo.

According to estimates put out by the government, around half a million visitors, many of them foreigners, would come to the fair. It did not take much math to come to the conclusion that Ciudad Trujillo did not have enough guest rooms. To help ease anticipated lodging stress, two hotels were incorporated into the designs for the fair. Hotel Paz, designed by Guillermo González Sánchez and José Antonio Caro, was located closer to the oceanfront, overlooking the sea, while the Hotel Embajador, designed by US architect Roy France, was set further back north of Avenida Independencia, though its guest-room balconies still enjoyed ocean views. The Hotel Embajador opened in 1956 after a construction cost of five million pesos.[46]

With eight floors and 310 guest rooms, the Hotel Embajador was a much larger structure; it could provide much more lodging than the Jaragua, even with its two extensions. Although the location further from the sea may have seemed less desirable, it was easier to obtain a larger plot of land in this part of the city. As a result, the Hotel Embajador offered guest access to expansive grounds filled with a variety of leisure opportunities, including a golf course, several tennis courts, and a polo field. The hotel also included the requisite casino, nightclub, pool, Spanish courtyard, and bandstand that seemed to be expected at all fine hotels in the Dominican Republic. The Hotel Embajador overshadowed the Jaragua in size and social spaces and quickly took over as the most popular site for Dominican society.[47] Dominican high society moved their patronage to the Embajador's Embassy Club, furthering the financial stresses facing the Jaragua.

The Free World's Fair of Peace and Confraternity did not bring anywhere near the number of visitors government officials had estimated. Despite this, the fair was resplendent with pomp and circumstance. Different countries hosted their own pavilions, and important figures were brought in to demonstrate their nation's recognition of the fair. Although many countries did not wholeheartedly embrace the trujillato and its actions, their participation in the fair effectively functioned as recognition of Trujillo, his autocratic leadership, and his regime's agenda for the country. The fair reinforced notions of a Dominican Republic moving toward modernity, which was defined in tandem with a very circumscribed description of what constituted Dominican society. Trujillo's modern Dominicans of the present, as celebrated in social spaces like the Jaragua, as well as of those of the future were the blancos or indios that were certainly Catholic and who reinscribed patriarchal norms in their social behavior.

Perhaps one could say Trujillo was anticipating the problems recognized today in the overreliance on tourism by not devoting so much of the country's economy to tourism, or perhaps it was Trujillo himself who was getting in his own way of developing mass tourism in the Dominican Republic. The country would not see a significant growth in tourism until the 1960s under President Joaquín Balaguer, and this ultimately developed into resort tourism. After it opened in 1942, the Jaragua passed through more than a dozen operators before the civil war in 1965. At that point, it was temporarily used as a processing center for the thousands of US citizens who were being evacuated from the country in the midst of the conflict. US intervention called the Hotel Jaragua home, too, through the aegis of the Organization of American States that set up operations in the hotel, which resulted in the Inter-American Peace Force occupation of the Dominican Republic from

Figure 3.11. Model of the Hotel Jaragua with a portrait of President Rafael Trujillo above. Photograph by Kurt Schnitzer, ca. 1939–1941. Archivo General de la Nación, Santo Domingo, Dominican Republic.

1965 to 1967. Trujillo leveraged a history of US imperialism and interference in the Dominican Republic to help rise to power, and once stripped of that, the repurposing of the Hotel Jaragua suggests a circling back to an imperial environment.

Judging the Hotel Jaragua in terms of financial profits or losses leaves us with little to gain. Rather, the significance and impact of the Hotel Jaragua becomes clear within the larger context of Trujillo's nation-building agenda (figure 3.11). Not only was the modernist architecture heralded around the globe as a first, in such publications as *Interiors* and *Architectural Forum*, but the hotel was effectively harnessed as a space to enact the spectacle of Trujillan-defined Dominican identity. The dancing, socializing, and dining of a white Hispanic Catholic body in this urban hotel was intimately connected to the 1937 Haitian Massacre and subsequent rise of anti-Haitianism and anti-blackness racism. The display of ideal society in this modernist design was tied to the desire to lock down national borders and develop a rural population devoted to the regime as part of an agricultural revolution. These were all interlocking pieces of Trujillo's project of modernity.

Figure 4.1. Toro, Ferrer y Torregrosa, Caribe Hilton, San Juan, Puerto Rico (1949). Hospitality Industry Archives, Conrad Hilton College, University of Houston.

# 4

## The Caribe Hilton

### Redefining Puerto Rico through Operación Manos a la Obra

**When the Caribe Hilton opened in 1949,** *Architectural Forum* celebrated its innovative design: "This is the kind of hotel which should be built in Florida and California, but never has been."[1] One review of the hotel went so far as to claim, "it is so modern that it makes Frank Lloyd Wright's grandest architectural projects look like mid-Victorian monuments."[2] At this point, seaside high-rise hotels for the most part were still being built in Art Deco and Streamline Moderne styles, but developers and architects in Florida, the Caribbean, and other parts of the world heeded the *Architectural Forum*'s call and looked to the Caribe Hilton for inspiration (figure 4.1). New hotel architecture in Florida and the Caribbean increasingly called upon the Caribe Hilton's iteration of modernism, which presented a particular vision of tropical modernism that relied on an attention to nature and climate as well as to functional efficiency. Reviews of the Caribe Hilton in architectural journals and hotel trade publications extolled the virtues of urban resort hotels that offered "functional luxury"—meaning economically efficient design that successfully addressed the guest's desire for an unforgettable experience of an unfamiliar place, without resorting to kitsch design.

The Caribe Hilton offered guests the most up-to-date in hotel amenities: convertible furniture, which meant that rooms were living areas by day and sleeping

Figure 4.2. The Caribe Hilton's balconies were celebrated as a novel design that offered every guest room an ocean view. Photograph by Ezra Stoller, ca. 1949. TFA/0040/F0068, Collection Toro Ferrer Architects, Archivo de Arquitectura y Construcción de la Universidad de Puerto Rico.

spaces at night; a private balcony with a view of the ocean for every single room; and individual, guest-controlled air-conditioning units in each room (figure 4.2). Caribe Hilton promoters boasted that it was the first in the world to offer the latter two features. Other innovations remained unseen by guests, such as a kitchen on the same floor as the dining room filled with the latest in commercial kitchen equipment. These design details were meant to ensure that guests received their food at the proper temperature and were part of the overall program to create an unforgettable guest experience.

Along with design that presented certain imaginings of the tropical environment, these amenities were part of the Puerto Rican government's conception of the Caribe Hilton as a project not only to increase industry and tourism on the island, and thus promote the insular project of modernization, but also to serve as a symbol of national identity within the island and to the rest of the world. Puerto Rican government officials, guided by modernization theory, believed that development was the key to insular prosperity. This idea was contextualized within a recent reconfiguration of the globe into first, second, and third world countries at the 1944 Bretton Woods Conference. With this new hierarchical system in place, the goal of many second and third world countries was to use modernization theory and development to advance their country to a higher status. While the framework of first, second, and third worlds offered a particular lens or system, questions of modernization and development had long been a topic in Puerto Rico (see chapter 1).

Despite government leaders' intentions, diverse views of the hotel emerged. This was partly a result of how the project had to attend to both local and tourist expectations, which were not always aligned. For example, the architectural firm Toro, Ferrer y Torregrosa wanted a locally inspired modernist design for the hotel project, but the young architects had to create an innovative design that fit within the contours of tourist expectations. They worked with the latest in modern technology and theories of efficient planning and strived to satisfy US desires for tropical ambiance. Much of their design fused modernist design with the tropics, but there was no guaranteeing how people would understand the tropical modernist design.

Upon opening, the Caribe Hilton was hailed as a great example of tropical modernism.[3] But "tropical modernism" was—and still is—a loaded term with conflicted meanings that, in many ways, represent the multiple faces of the Caribe Hilton itself. The most basic definition of the term is the use of modernism to create a design that sensitively addresses local climate and conditions.[4] In this sense, tropical modernism was part of a larger discourse of regional modernism, which adapted modernist design to meet local conditions and needs—social, cultural, and economic, as well as climatic.[5] Architectural modernism was not new to the Caribbean, or even to hotel design therein, but compared to the modernist Hotel Jaragua in Ciudad Trujillo, the Caribe Hilton was much more declarative in its statement about tropical modernism.

There are many instances across Latin America and the world where states adopted modernist designs that were sensitive to local conditions as a means to embrace the new and the modern, often as part of a program of development, in a way that respectfully considered the unique situation of that particular nation. Indeed, we can see a connection between the way the trujillato used modernist design in the Hotel Jaragua and the more elaborated engagement of modernist design after World War II that we see in the Caribe Hilton. What I propose as one of the major differences between the two is the emphasis on the tropical as a defining feature of the Caribe's design. Rationalism and functionalism were highlighted in postwar modernist design as indicative of human control over the natural environment, symbolically representing mastery over the backward and the continued march of progress. Rationalism and functionalism were considered necessary components in thinking about design in tropical locations given conceptions of what "tropical" meant. By extension, using rationalism and functionalism in design signified the government's commitment to responsibly building a modern state in the broader sense, and therefore many of these projects connected to the social welfare of the populace.

The adoption of modernist design in relation to local contexts in Puerto Rico was more complex, as the island was a colony of the United States until 1952. Its subsequent status based on the Commonwealth Agreement has been described as everything from a de facto colony to being engaged in the politics of coloniality. I like to consider Puerto Rico and the Caribe Hilton through both lenses. In very real ways, the muñocian government officials were limited in what they could do because of US interference and power. However, there was also the reality of the politics of coloniality within the island, as officials embraced development and the project of modernity as being ideal for their island. So, even though Puerto Ricans could elect their own governor starting in 1948 rather than a governor appointed by the US president, the system itself, based on US democratic capitalism, was one that systematically exploited and subalternized its own people.[6] Luz Marie Rodríguez offers a compelling reading of the Caribe Hilton and ultimately concludes that it was not a representation of Puerto Rican identity but, rather, a "fictional reference in a context of non-confrontational colonial negotiations."[7] This is a convincing way to understand the project, but my aim in this chapter is to dig deeper and expose layers of complexity suggesting there were many different voices making claims to the identity of the Caribe Hilton.

### *Operación Manos a la Obra*

The Puerto Rican government leaders conceived of the Caribe Hilton project as the showpiece of Operación Manos a la Obra (Operation Bootstrap). This program of modernization and industrialization was meant to serve as a catalyst to launch Puerto Rico into first world status. With its connotations of US gumption and self-sufficiency, the name referred to the program overseen by Fomento, a division of the Puerto Rican government dedicated to promoting industries on the island, which was supported by the Puerto Rico Government Bank and the Puerto Rican Industrial Development Company (PRIDCO).[8]

In the 1940s, the ruling Partido Popular Democrático endeavored to establish industrial development and economic independence through government owned and operated factories. This unsuccessful initiative was followed by a decisive shift in the second half of the decade toward abandoning political independence in favor of cultivating economic growth through the development of US factories on the island. Although this change in policy meant that Puerto Rico became increasingly dependent on the United States, Puerto Rican government leaders fashioned a public image of Operación Manos a la Obra as representing the island's independence and self-sufficiency.[9] When Luis Muñoz Marín became the first democratically elected Puerto Rican governor of Puerto Rico in 1948, he placed great emphasis on using Operación Manos a la Obra as a means to define and encourage a new understanding of *puertorriqueñidad* (Puerto Rican–ness).

Leading Fomento throughout the 1940s and 1950s was Teodoro Moscoso, who guided the agency in establishing over five hundred manufacturing plants on the island.[10] After witnessing the failure of early initiatives of state-owned factories, Moscoso shifted toward private business. He privatized the state-owned factories and looked to US companies to invest in building and operating factories in Puerto Rico. The vast majority of these new plants were built and run by contiguous-US firms that Moscoso had lured to Puerto Rico with incentives such as lower wages and tax exemptions for between eight and twelve years, which made manufacturing in Puerto Rico particularly lucrative.[11]

Notably, Moscoso and other influential program leaders envisioned tourism development as a necessary and beneficial complement to increased manufacturing and industrial production on the island. A controlled increase in foreign tourism, they wagered, was one aspect of their plan for American-style modernization and promised to be profitable, increasing island revenues and serving to project the image of a modern Puerto Rico.[12] Leadership of tourism fell under the jurisdiction of the head administrator of Fomento, thus squarely tying tourism to Operación Manos a la Obra. Moscoso saw great opportunity to expand the tourism industry in Puerto Rico and he extolled tourism development as necessary for the cultivation of other industries on the island.[13]

The Caribe Hilton project was part of a larger program for carefully controlled tourism growth, with the government designing specific limits on transportation and accommodation infrastructure so as to manipulate growth. Businessmen needed adequate accommodations when they traveled to Puerto Rico, Moscoso argued, a sentiment that was echoed in the US press as well.[14] He maintained that San Juan needed a world-class luxury hotel in order to attract industrial development, and in the mid-1940s he proposed a government-sponsored hotel.[15] In an effort to position the project as being in the service of the local population, Moscoso articulated that public housing does not build hotels, but hotels offer the potential for continuous profits for long-standing public housing construction. This framework was to define the hotel project, as two-thirds of the profits from the hotel would go to the Puerto Rican government. Although the hotel was not the first edifice built by Fomento, it was the first hotel, and it promised to be its most important government building project as it would be the physical manifestation of Operación Manos a la Obra that was most experienced by visitors and that undoubtedly would be influential in introducing them to the new, modern Puerto Rico.

Government leaders recognized that the new hotel offered an opportunity to cultivate an image of Puerto Rico as an exotic, tropical vacation land made safe and enjoyable through modernization. To encourage more tourism, promoters were conscious they had to erase or at least diminish any negative associations potential visitors may have of Puerto Rico and its people. This is apparent in the many brochures directed toward potential contiguous-US visitors. The brochures take different tacks and one approach worth noting is the explicit discussion of stereotypes of Puerto Rico, which were then replaced with claims of what Puerto Rico truly was, according to promoters. Operación Manos a la Obra and the modern buildings it financed such as the Caribe Hilton were deployed as evidence that the Puerto Rico of the past had given way to a bright future made possible through industrialization and American-style modernization. The post–World War II push for tourism was grounded in previous approaches promoting positive representations of Puerto Rico, which often highlighted Puerto Rico's picturesque colonial past, its enticing tropical climate, and its unique geographical and political relationship with the United States—all of which was framed within an image of Puerto Rico as progressive and modern.[16]

This type of tourist literature stressed the Puerto Rican landscape as defined primarily by the historic and the tropical, tropes that date back to the arrival of colonialism on the island. Two promotional posters produced under the Works Progress Administrations in the late 1930s demonstrate the exact approach that was continued in the postwar period (plates 12, 13). One poster presents a view of San Juan from the vantage point of San Felipe del Morro Castle, giving the viewer a vision of the island's Spanish colonial past. Besides conjuring images of cannon fire from an attacking English fleet or pirate ships full of gnarly peg-legged troublemakers, reference to the Spanish colonial past was also intended to stress the Europeanness of Puerto Rico. Tourism promoters used Puerto Rico's Spanish heritage and San Juan's long history as a colonial port city to align the island with European culture and history and to promote the island as a closer, cheaper travel alternative to Europe for contiguous-US tourists. The other poster boasts a giant century plant (*Agave americana*) as the focal point of the image, flanked by palms, signifying the tropics to the targeted audience.[17] In this case, vegetation signifies escape from the quotidian to the exotic, romantic, and foreign.

These posters present Puerto Rico as both outside the United States and a part of it, a common approach used to appeal to contiguous-US tourists. The "USA" is a comforting reminder that one is still in the realm of US sovereignty, connected to the modernity of the United States, while the phrase "where the Americas meet" suggests Puerto Rico as a place on the border of, or just outside, the United States—offering enticement through the suggestion of the foreign. This also echoes the definition of Puerto Rico in *Downes v. Bidwell* (1901) as "foreign in a domestic sense" (see chapter 1). Just as the Supreme Court case defined Puerto Rico as both not part of the United States and not *not* part of it, so too do these posters suggest the liminal limbo of Puerto Rico both geographically and politically. Puerto Rico could be interpreted as a place of both adventure and safety.

Histories of Caribbean tourism have recounted that after World War II the combination of postwar prosperity, advancements in air travel, and the growing Cold War climate meant that more contiguous-US citizens were traveling, especially to promoted destinations.[18] A general increase in expendable income for contiguous-US citizens made vacations accessible and routine for many.[19] Many vacationers certainly chose to take their vacations within the confines of the contiguous United States, but advances in air travel spurred an explosion of international travel. After World War II, commercial air travel was faster and more affordable, making it feasible for a greater number of contiguous-US citizens to travel by plane.[20]

Before the onset of jet travel in the later years of the 1950s, Europe still remained rather distant, not to mention war-torn, and the Caribbean was promoted as a close yet still international destination. With the introduction of daily nonstop flights between New York and San Juan in 1946, a getaway to Puerto Rico was now only six hours away. This travel time was further reduced in the 1950s when jet airliners were introduced into commercial aviation. In 1948, Pan Am reduced their fares, offering tickets for as low as seventy-five dollars each way.[21] Further regulation of airline monopolies in 1951 effectively spurred competitive airfare pricing, allowing a Puerto Rican vacation to become accessible to a wider economic base. The breakup of Pan Am's monopoly seems to have been undertaken in an effort to achieve two results: to get more tourists to Puerto Rico by appealing to a wider economic base and to promote Puerto Rico as a symbol of the greatness of the Point Four Program in the face of communism. To accomplish the latter, US government leaders needed lower poverty and unemployment rates on the island. To address this, they encouraged the poorer sectors of Puerto Rico to emigrate to the contiguous United States. Lower airfares encouraged this mass migration, and the flow of contiguous-US visitors to Puerto Rico and of Puerto Ricans to the contiguous states sets into relief imperial politics and power relations.[22]

The Puerto Rican government had a committed program of tourism development, and the US federal government was also invested in promoting travel to Puerto Rico for its own reasons related to imperialism and international relations. The US government enhanced the allure of Puerto Rico through its active promotion of leisure travel to countries that were committed to capitalism as a means of development.[23] The US government encouraged US citizens to view the development and modernization of Puerto Rico as a direct reflection of the power and greatness of American-style capitalism and consumption, typical of the developing Cold War rhetoric of the period.[24] Traveling to Puerto Rico was promoted as a means for average contiguous-US citizens to help fight communism; by injecting their dollars into the local economy, they were investing in the democratic future of the island, setting an example for other developing nations whose leaders might be flirting with the idea of communism.

Thus, Puerto Rico was promoted as the "crossroads of the Americas."[25] Puerto Rico was at the same time both part of the United States and outside of it, and geographically it tied together the northern and southern portions of the Western Hemisphere, which seemed to be rapidly shrinking in the age of air travel and in a period of US interest in Pan-Americanism.[26] It was an exotic new frontier for contiguous-US tourists, rendered safe through US involvement in the island and its status as a US territory. By mid-century, the island was increasingly seen as a place where Latin American traditions and history met American-style modernity, a reputation firmly established through Operación Manos a la Obra and its leaders' efforts to tackle tourism development and industrialization as part of the same project.

## *Creating a Symbol for Operación Manos a la Obra*

Puerto Rican government officials likely felt that as a relatively public space experienced by foreigners and locals alike, a hotel was an effective way to symbolize the new image they wished to convey. Moreover, a new construction was vital for conveying the image of the modern Puerto Rico that Operación Manos a la Obra was meant to express. In the postwar period, the two extant grand hotels in the city—the Condado Beach Hotel (formerly Grand Condado Vanderbilt) and the Hotel Normandie—were no longer particularly contemporary. Both these private projects were funded by wealthy men and were operated as private businesses; neither offered a vision of the modern Puerto Rico that government leaders wanted to project. The styles of the hotels pointed to the past; the Spanish Revival theme of the Condado Beach Hotel held connotations of Puerto Rico's colonial past and contentious issues of the Spanish Revival as representative of US imperialism; the cruise liner reference and the opulent interiors of the Art Deco Hotel Normandie flaunted the inappropriate excesses of a previous time. Practically, the new hotel would address what market research determined was needed—a three-hundred-room hotel to accommodate the businessmen and their families who were expected to come to San Juan. The Puerto Rican government recognized the variety of opportunities presented by the hotel project.[27]

Moreover, lawmakers realized that the new project offered the chance to define advantageous terms that could benefit the local population. To this end, Moscoso designed the terms of the hotel project in 1946 so that the hotel would be entirely financed, built, and owned by the Puerto Rican government. Its monetary investment in building the hotel was a show of good faith and demonstrated the government's commitment to tourism. The project would cost a significant amount up front, but it promised substantial long-term returns of two-thirds of the hotel profits. To attract a contiguous-US hotel company to run the establishment, the legislature passed a measure that officially declared tourism an industry, making the tax exemption law applicable to hotel investments.[28] Governor Muñoz then sent letters to seven different hotel companies inviting them to run the government-sponsored hotel.

Conrad Hilton jumped at the opportunity when he received the letter from Muñoz. Undoubtedly, the proposition that Fomento sent him seemed like a small risk compared to building a hotel entirely on his own. Hilton had built a hotel empire in the United States, largely by acquiring existing hotels and renovating and remodeling them to extract maximum profit. He also had some experience in operating a hotel outside of the United States.[29] To minimize risk to the established chain, the board of the Hilton Corporation approved the creation of a separate company, Hilton Hotels International, specifically for the purposes of this business venture.[30] According to the proposition put forth by the Puerto Rican government, Hilton was to be responsible for staffing and covering all of the operating costs, a relatively small financial investment that made this venture an attractive first step for Hilton into the world of international hotels.[31] For the Puerto Rican government, Hilton was bringing his established name and operational expertise to the project.

Given the lawmakers' commitment to publicly promoting the hotel as a state project (supported by private business), it is no surprise that the design of the hotel was given priority and was carefully considered. While it is important to acknowledge that the Caribe Hilton was fundamental in shaping the nature of subsequent Hilton Hotels International chain hotels, it is imperative to look at the Caribe Hilton less as a Hilton hotel and more as a project of the Puerto Rican government's negotiation of relations at once local, global, and imperial/colonial. When we consider the design of the hotel, it is essential to understand how the state was utilizing modern architecture to visually fashion the new identity of Puerto Rico.

The Caribe Hilton boasts a striking and unequivocally modernist design. Located on a fairly empty tract of land that jutted out into the ocean, the hotel's relatively simplified form was rendered in abstract, rectilinear shapes. The major division of spaces by function—public spaces versus private guest areas—was visually apparent in the cubic forms of a horizontal pedestal and a vertical tower. The two lower floors, which contained public areas such as lobbies, bars, restaurants, and casino, were spread out horizontally, sprawling out across the land perpendicular to the guest rooms. A large rectangular slab containing the three hundred guest rooms—the surface of which was broken up by the angled balconies and windows that covered both sides—topped the transparent, open ground level. Boasting materials associated with architectural modernism such as plate glass, steel, and concrete, the hotel marked a new style of building on the island. Indeed, Fomento's new commitment to architectural modernism marked a pivotal shift not only in architecture in Puerto Rico but also in hotel design around the globe.

Decisions surrounding the design of the hotel reveal how much stock Puerto Rican leaders put into design as a vehicle for defining and projecting Puerto Rican identity. While the Puerto Rican government allowed input from Hilton Hotels International in the location and design of the hotel in some respects, local leaders were uncompromising in others, especially when it came to the architectural style of the hotel. Fomento invited five architectural firms to submit proposals in a competition to determine the design of the hotel and used this competition as another opportunity to make a statement about the new modern Puerto Rico being built through Operación Manos a la Obra. Hilton contacted two firms based in Florida and asked them to submit proposals to the competition. These architectural firms were were Frederick Seelman from Palm Beach and Robert Swartburg from Miami Beach. Both firms submitted designs that employed Beaux Arts–informed floor plans and eclectic styles influenced by the Spanish Revival. Hilton preferred to use one of these designs for the hotel. The other three submissions were by local Puerto Rican firms, and the two not selected were from Schimmelpfennig, Ruz and González and The Office of Henry Klumb. The Puerto Rican administrators favored the young firm of Toro, Ferrer y Torregrosa's design proposal, which they convinced Hilton to accept.[32]

Toro, Ferrer y Torregrosa was established and led by Puerto Rican architects Osvaldo Toro and Miguel Ferrer and a structural engineer, Luis Torregrosa. All three went to the United States for their education and returned to Puerto Rico to adapt what they had learned to the climate, culture, and politics of their native Puerto Rico. Architectural education abroad was still a necessity in this period as the Escuela de Arquitectura (School of Architecture) was not established at the Universidad de Puerto Rico until 1966. In the twentieth century, colleges and universities in the contiguous states were the most popular destination for Puerto Rican architectural students. Toro studied architecture at Columbia University and Ferrer received his degree in architecture from Cornell University. After their studies, they worked for seven years in a number of local and federal government agencies in Puerto Rico before establishing a firm in San Juan with Torregrosa in 1945.[33]

Hilton's original preference for a Mediterranean Revival style speaks to the tradition of employing historical styles to appeal to romantic notions of Puerto Rico as a place of the exotic past. The Spanish Revival style found in Puerto Rico was developed in the United States and then exported to places in the Hispanic Caribbean, and for many Puerto Ricans it symbolized US imperialism. In addition, the Puerto Rican officials' insistence on modernism indicated their unwillingness to engage with and perpetuate representations of Puerto Rico as a place of the past, as the Spanish Revival style was no longer considered a modern style. Modernism was a means to change perceptions and demonstrate to the world that Puerto Rico was progressive and forward-looking.

Puerto Rican leaders considered their rejection of historical styles in favor of this new ahistorical idiom a vital step in defining their nation and culture on their own terms.[34] Their selection of Puerto Rican architects reinforced the idea of national self-definition, and the modernist vocabulary was evidence of the architects' training and understanding of avant-garde architectural practices. Promoters advertised the fact that the architects had been educated in the United States, presumably to tap into the prestige associated with US education, but they also highlighted the fact that the architects were native Puerto Ricans, which emphasized that Puerto Ricans could self-sufficiently shape cultural identity and reinforced the idea that local architects were somehow more attuned to address local conditions than architects from other countries.[35]

Presented as the face of the modern Puerto Rican state, the modernist design approach championed functionality and efficiency. It was understood as a tool that could be used not just to tame the tropical environment but also to enhance its positive characteristics. During this period, politicians, businessmen, and academics advocated modernism through much of Latin America as a way to shed the colonial past and firmly announce a commitment to progress.[36] The proponents of a modern, industrialized Puerto Rico echoed the voices coming from other places in Latin America that situated modernism as not simply a style of architecture but also a powerful symbol of the movement toward premier status and participation in the global marketplace.[37]

## *Negotiating Criticism*

The expression of Operación Manos a la Obra and its vision of modernity through modernist design were not without critics. Despite the government leaders' firm belief that modernization was the key to the island's success, other Puerto Ricans questioned the good that would come out of Operación Manos a la Obra. Critics saw the program as an elite government project that compromised the island by positioning the island as a place ripe for US plunder through numerous tax incentives and thus promoting a new form of colonialism.[38] They were also critical of the emphasis on manufacturing and tourism and the lack of attention to failed agrarian reforms, which resulted in the mass exodus of Puerto Ricans from rural areas to cities in Puerto Rico and to the contiguous United States in search of work.[39] Although the Caribe Hilton project certainly created jobs and paid good wages, as did the new factories, many Puerto Ricans, especially those who were formerly involved in agriculture, had little say in determining their livelihood; they had to take whatever job they could find and wherever they could find it. As a result, many found it difficult to relate to or support the top-down Operación Manos a la Obra program, especially given its visual distinction through modernist design and the visible emphasis on tourism from the contiguous states, which smacked of imperial relationships.

Moscoso's commitment to tourism caused many Puerto Ricans to further question the future of Puerto Rican agency and the preservation of Puerto Rican culture. Not only were government officials encouraging contiguous-US businesses to come to the island, businesses whose presence would undoubtedly hold sway in future policymaking, but many saw the growth of the tourist sector as a threat to Puerto Rican culture. To them, tourism meant pandering to visitors—from serving them in hotels and restaurants to having to compromise and adapt cultural traditions in order to meet contiguous-US expectations.[40] Puerto Ricans looked to the gambling and prostitution that had come to define tourism in Havana and feared this would end up their fate as well. The fear of the effects of casinos and gambling was produced by the proposal of a casino for the Caribe Hilton. In order to lessen the negative view many Puerto Ricans had of tourist-oriented casinos, Moscoso drafted laws that stipulated strict guidelines for opening and operating casinos, ensuring that the government would be able to exert substantial control over them and profit from them, the proceedings of which were to be funneled into social programs for Puerto Ricans.[41] Despite Moscoso's efforts, however, critics dubbed the hotel, with its boxy modern design, "Moscoso's white elephant" and "Moscoso's folly." For them, the modern architecture of the Caribe Hilton, meant to represent the new Puerto Rico being built by Operación Manos a la Obra, was ultimately not to benefit Puerto Ricans in a meaningful way.[42] The conflicting identities attached to the Caribe Hilton indicate the role the hotel played in negotiating notions of place and identity not only between locals and foreign visitors but also among Puerto Ricans, who certainly did not all share the same ideas or opinions about what Puerto Rico was or should be.

Articles in the Puerto Rican press and promotional materials published by the Puerto Rican government attempted to establish the Caribe Hilton as the face of a modern Puerto Rico—it was made by Puerto Ricans of modern materials and goods produced in Puerto Rico.[43] For example, goods used in the hotel were produced in factories on the island, such as those of Crane China Company and General Electric, and the general contractor was the Puerto Rican division of the George A. Fuller Company. However, many reports and commentaries generated in the contiguous United States questioned the very Puerto Rican–ness of the hotel, arguing that it was a US hotel, full of objects and materials made by contiguous-US companies and operated by a contiguous-US business. Underscoring this perspective of the hotel, *Architectural Forum* praises the hotel but notes that the visitor will be disappointed with the lack of "local flavor" and highlights the contiguous-US businesses and products that contributed to the construction and outfitting of the hotel.[44] This position was grounded in the fact that Crane China Company, General Electric, and the George A. Fuller Company were all businesses with main offices in the contiguous states. Articles in newspapers and trade publications also stressed the role of the contiguous-US design firm Warner-Leeds in the design of the hotel and were quick to point to Toro's and Ferrer's educations at universities in the contiguous states. These critics associated the modern aspects of the hotel, and by extension the modern attributes of Puerto Rico, with the contiguous United States, reinforcing the paternalistic position that the United States was responsible for the progress and modernity that had come to Puerto Rico.

Commentary produced in the contiguous United States did not use the Caribe Hilton to paint the same uniform picture of Puerto Rico. Some commentary cast the positive modernist qualities of the design as an importation from the contiguous states, rather than something authentically Puerto Rican. Others used the same qualities to point to the Puerto Ricans' efficacy in embracing progress and development, thanks to US colonialism. The two approaches were not mutually exclusive, and different aspects of the hotel project and its design were employed to construct various images of Puerto Rico for a contiguous-US audience, suggesting varying levels of autonomy and self-direction on the part of Puerto Rico in order to create different arguments about the relationship between democracy, capitalism, and development.

To a great extent, Puerto Rican leaders tried to avoid conversations with too much focus on the juridical complexities between the island and the United States. The political identity of Puerto Rico was a complicated one that was also tied to economy and development. And with the island becoming more dependent upon the contiguous states (both businesses and the federal government) throughout Operación Manos a la Obra rather than becoming more independent, government officials tried to downplay or avoid what many found to be troubling topics regarding sovereignty and autonomy. Therefore, there was a move away from attention to national identity in favor of an emphasis on fashioning a cultural identity that would define the island and its people.

## *The Historic as Foil*

Muñocian government leaders encouraged the conflation of the positive aspects of Operación Manos a la Obra with Puerto Rican identity, suggesting that Puerto Ricans, by virtue of the modernization program, were a particularly modern people.

Visual examples such as the Caribe Hilton served as symbols of this identity that were also didactic in expressing to Puerto Ricans how they should understand this cultural identity. One way to help underscore the difference between modernity and the historic was to divorce the past from this modern cultural identity. Therefore, references to Spain, provincialism, and Catholicism—deemed part of a historic past—were partitioned off from references to the modern aspect of Puerto Ricanness.

To avoid definition through political terms, tropicality, cast as both apolitical and timeless, was promoted as the main qualifier for the modern identity, conveyed in modernist design that eschewed reference to historical styles and that highlighted the tropical environment. The climate was no longer referenced through historical styles pointing to the temperate Mediterranean; rather, this modernist design exploited weather and climate to propose new fusions of elements associated with tropicality and modern design. However, modern architecture's emphasis on a lack of historical reference necessitated a different relationship with the idea of the historic. Signifiers of the historic were necessary tools of comparison to further underscore the modernity of the Caribe Hilton. As historian Phoebe Kropp discusses in her work on the role of culture and memory in modern placemaking, past and present may be positioned in opposition but they often work in concert. Nostalgia for a historic past is not simply the expression of a fear of or disdain for modernity and progress. As Kropp posits, the impulse for history and nostalgia was an integral part of modernity itself.[45] In the context of the tourist industry, Puerto Rican leaders harnessed the historic as a tourist attraction, while championing the modern as defining the infrastructure and the tropical as shaping another aspect of the experience of Puerto Rico.

The Caribe Hilton was a key element in the juxtaposition of historic and modern, old and new. Comparison to historic sites served to reinforce the striking quality of tropical modernism and was connected to larger debates about Puerto Rico's history and its physical manifestation in San Juan. Not only did the historic underscore the modernity of the hotel, but the modern qualities of the hotel in turn emphasized the age of the city, particularly the area of San Juan Viejo. For tourists, Puerto Rico's past was defined by the Spanish colonial project. The historic was a tool used by the Puerto Rican government to clearly delineate contemporary Puerto Rico as decidedly modern and liberated from the past in order to appease critics who believed modernity meant the death of Puerto Rican culture and to provide visitors with the opportunity to experience the old, colonial culture of San Juan. This clear separation between the modern and the historic, whether the Spanish colonial historic center or the Hispanic Revival indicative of US imperialism, was a way for the muñocian government to further underscore the notion that Puerto Rico was experiencing a new level of autonomy and self-sufficiency.

The Puerto Rican government was not the first government in Latin America to address the concept of the historic within larger programs of modernization employing modernist design. The modern urban form of Ciudad Trujillo, for example, was juxtaposed against a renewed effort to consider the colonial core. In the 1930s, the Brazilian president Getúlio Vargas's government undertook a program of national identity construction that revolved around notions of Brazil as modern, but officials were also concerned with preserving the country's colonial heritage.[46]

In 1933, the Brazilian government issued a decree to preserve the colonial mining town of Ouro Preto as a national monument, and shortly thereafter the newly created federal agency Serviço do Patrimônio Histórico e Artístico Nacional (SPHAN, the National Historic and Artistic Heritage Service) was charged with overseeing historic preservation.[47] As scholar Leonardo Castriota reveals, SPHAN initially supported the construction of new modernist structures in historic areas because its directors held a negative opinion of copying past styles and maintained that, besides the architecture of the mining period of the eighteenth century, the only other authentic Brazilian architecture was that of the contemporary moment.[48]

As a result, the historic preservation efforts in Ouro Preto, which involved readying the town for tourists, included the construction of Oscar Niemeyer's modernist Grande Hotel. The SPHAN directors' attitude, as scholar Hugo Segawa notes, permitted the organization to create a context in which "new" could occur inside of the "old," allowing the new structures to exist in a way that encouraged the acknowledgment of the authenticity of historic architecture.[49] This was also the case in Puerto Rico, where the muñocian government's distaste for revival styles was based on a belief that those styles were inauthentic through their "imitation" of older architecture. While the Beaux Arts architects who created revival style buildings would not have described them in pejorative terms of imitation, modernist thinking generally subscribed to this viewpoint.

Unlike in the case of the Grande Hotel in Ouro Preto, Puerto Rican leaders did not locate the Caribe Hilton within the historic center but just outside it, where it was visually and geographically coupled with a colonial fortification. Whether the Hilton executive who nominated the spot of land for the hotel realized it or not, the site was strategic for the success of the hotel and for reinforcing the notion of a tropical modern identity through contrast with the historic. The windswept plot of land on which the hotel was situated was only a short distance from historic San Juan, which was actively forming its identity as San Juan Viejo under the charge of J. Stanton Robbins, a man with a long career in the travel industry and in Latin American foreign policy who came to Puerto Rico to work in restoration and tourism development. Robbins had also worked on the reconstruction of Virginia's Colonial Williamsburg, and when he started his new job in San Juan in 1948, he quickly realized that the historic center of San Juan was one of the island's greatest resources for tourism.[50]

In the postwar years, the historic city center was filled with run-down buildings, some of them abandoned with others, meant to house only two or three families at most, crowded with ten or more families. Robbins invited a group of colleagues from Colonial Williamsburg to examine the potential for restoration in the historic center. Characterized by the blue cobblestones that paved its narrow streets, which had come from Europe to Puerto Rico as ship's ballast, and delineated by the fortresses and defensive walls surrounding much of it, the historic area offered a discrete workable area for restoration. Robbins organized his ideas into a proposal for restoration that would turn the walled area of the city into a clean, safe historic zone for the enjoyment of locals and tourists alike. The proposal helped him get the local government to pass a law declaring San Juan Viejo an "ancient and historic zone."[51]

Although conceived in the late 1940s, the restoration project did not move forward significantly until the 1955 formation of the Instituto de Cultura Puertorriqueña (ICP, Institute of Puerto Rican Culture), which was a government-organized entity intended to demonstrate government commitment to the preservation and continuance of Puerto Rican culture. Endowed with a small budget and employing a team of restoration architects, the program was fairly limited and primarily involved restoration architects advising property owners on how to fix up their structures. Many of these projects could become quite expensive, so Fomento offered tax incentives and convinced the government bank to issue loans to encourage private individuals to undertake the costly restoration projects. Not only did the ICP oversee the restoration project in San Juan Viejo, but under the leadership of Ricardo Alegría the organization also started a movement to recover and preserve the history and traditions of the Indigenous Taíno, who had been decimated during Spanish colonization of the island and whose culture was in danger of disappearing. Colonial architecture and "primitive" Indigenous culture were thus lumped together and fashioned as markers of tradition and the historic past of Puerto Rico, considered aspects that needed to be preserved for prosperity rather than being vital and relevant to the present.

The Caribe Hilton's location in relationship to San Juan Viejo reinforced the conceptual dichotomy of the modern and the historic. Even if the restoration project had not yet commenced, the colonial buildings and fortifications were already long-established points of interest on every tourist's itinerary. Travelers could stay at the hotel and enjoy its modern amenities and take a quick trip into San Juan Viejo during the day to experience its historic charm. Movement between the two areas served to reinforce the idea of a Puerto Rico of the past (where Puerto Rico came from) and the modern Puerto Rico of the contemporary moment. This was certainly in lawmakers' minds as they as they took on the restoration of San Juan Viejo.

The most prominent contrast between the modern and the historic was the hotel's location next to the colonial Fortín de San Gerónimo (plate 14). The fourteen-acre piece of land on which the hotel was situated included this fort, which was built by the Spanish in the seventeenth century as part of San Juan's line of defense against attacks and invasions. Thus, a little piece of Puerto Rican colonial history was conveniently located a mere stone's throw from the hotel. Guests could enjoy historic San Juan without having to venture too far from the hotel. In fact, many guests did not even need to leave their air-conditioned enclave, as the colonial structure was visible from many rooms.

Photos from the time—printed in the architectural and popular presses, in marketing materials, and as postcards—consistently boasted compositions that treated the hotel and the fort as a unified entity. This marked comparison highlights the tourist's experience of the historic and the modern. Indeed, the hotel's modern design was most likely striking to the typical contiguous-US tourist. Compositions were also often carefully arranged so as to cut out an extant small hotel located close to the Caribe Hotel, the Pan American Guest House.[52] The exclusion of this hotel and the inclusion of Fortín de San Gerónimo in images worked to locate the Caribe Hilton as the most important hotel on the island, discounting the existence of other accommodations and highlighting tourism to San Juan as a truly modern act through contrast to historic aspects of the setting.

After the construction of the Caribe Hilton and other subsequent modern hotels, many brochures included a section presenting the modern accommodations available in San Juan.[53] These brochures highlighted the historic and the tropical, an established marketing approach, but also presented the reader with images and text highlighting the cutting-edge accommodations in Puerto Rico. The presentation of the Caribe Hilton as symbolic of the modern, set in contrast with other historic areas, helped establish the concept of a dual experience for tourists, foregrounded a multifaceted and complex identity for Puerto Ricans, and supported the packaging of historic Puerto Rico for tourist consumption.

## *Fusing the Modern and the Tropical*

Not only was the association of tropicality with the modern a useful way to depoliticize Puerto Rican identity, but combining the two aspects was also effective in expressing the concept of the taming of nature, which is integral to the project of modernity and development. The Caribe Hilton's use of the tropical as a theme that could express a cohesive national identity shared among all Puerto Ricans promoted new understandings of tropicality, and thus Puerto Rican–ness. For contiguous-US tourists, the experience of San Juan was defined in large part through notions of tropicality. Although the Caribe Hilton's design stressed tropicality, it also complicated traditional notions of this idea. Out of necessity, parts of the hotel's design did reinforce traditional understandings of the tropics. However, although the concepts of tropicality and modernity were traditionally at odds, much of the design in the Caribe Hilton redefined these notions by blending the two in a manner that was incorporated into the cultural identity campaign.

Tropicality at the Caribe Hilton was largely visualized through architectural framing, which transformed the natural landscape into a spectacle to be consumed by guests at every turn. Tropicality was constructed in all aspects of the hotel, from the landscaping and architecture to the guest services and the decoration of the guest rooms. A review of the Caribe Hilton in the *New York Times* suggests the role of the hotel in producing a vision of the tropics for guests:

> Throughout the hotel there is a sense of making the most of the natural drama of the sea and of the view of old Spanish forts and walls, green coastal strip and spiny, blue-hazed fertile mountains. There are constantly and surprisingly new architecturally framed vistas of the spectacle—you see one as you walk in, before you turn by a bamboo-screen wall to the registration desk; another as you walk to the long cocktail terrace; another as you mount the stairs to the dining room, and, when you enter the dining room, the whole magnificent panorama is spread before you.[54]

The Caribe Hilton's modernist design composed picturesque assemblages of nature as both built into the design through materials and form and outside it, through the framing of views beyond whether of the hotel grounds or of more distant landscapes. Local landscape architect Hunter Randolph designed the grounds to offer guests an enjoyable tropical environment. Photographs of the hotel taken shortly after completion show coconut palms dotting the lawn, planted to add a tropical flavor to the grounds immediately surrounding the dining room

Figure 4.3. Photograph of the main pool at the Caribe Hilton, ca. 1949. TFA/0040/F0257, Collection Toro Ferrer Architects, Archivo de Arquitectura y Construcción de la Universidad de Puerto Rico.

projecting from the south façade of the building.[55] The highlight of the grounds was an area dubbed the "Garden of Eden," which contained native plants as well as many non-native plants such as yellow hibiscus trees, breadfruit, and almond trees, undoubtedly incorporated for their tropical associations.[56] The name of this area highlights the tendency to conflate tropical environments and vegetation with the primeval past and adding, in this case, biblical overtones. The name was part of a discourse that considered tropical environments to be untouched by time, representing a lack of civilization and progress.[57] Of course, these "timeless" landscapes were actually the products of global exploration and trade and were, in fact, very unnatural in their representing endemic flora. Since the late fifteenth century, different flora have been transplanted around the globe. By the twentieth century, many of the species of vegetation considered characteristic of the island actually had been imported from some other part of the world.

Although palms and other tropical vegetation were potent visual markers of the tropics, the warm ocean water of the Caribbean was also incorporated into the hotel landscape for guests to enjoy as a characteristic tropical attraction. An inviting beach, completely man-made, capped the "natural" landscape of the grounds; it was blasted out of a coral reef and filled with imported sand guaranteed not to stick to clothing. The seemingly natural landscape of the beach and the artificial nature of the sand point to the construction of tropicality as mediated by the desire for comfort. A free-form pool was carved into the coral rock, its organic shape meant to blend

Figure 4.4. Photograph of a courtyard at the Caribe Hilton, ca. 1949. TFA/0040/F0275, Collection Toro Ferrer Architects, Archivo de Arquitectura y Construcción de la Universidad de Puerto Rico.

more naturally into the outdoor landscape, and it was filled with salt water that was pumped in fresh every four hours (figure 4.3). The guests were meant to feel they were plopped into a natural tropical paradise, but it was, in reality, anything but.

The openness of the architecture of the Caribe Hilton emphasized tropicality in the interiors through a design that seamlessly blended indoor and outdoor spaces through transparency, visible flexibility of space, and the incorporation of nature into the design, all of which shaped the guests' experience as they moved through the hotel's public spaces. Guests alighted from their cars and followed a covered walkway to the lobby, with no clear transition moment from outdoors to the interior of the building. The entry was enhanced by thin columns and a minimal concrete roof, which maintained the experience of the outdoors. The connection to the outdoors was further underscored by the path's alignment with openings on the other side of the building, which allowed guests to see straight through to the pool area and the sea on the other side.

The design's emphasis on outdoor connection while inside the building presents the tropical climate as ideal.[58] The designers accomplished this through the use of pilotis, large glass walls, the absence of doors, and other modern design elements, which created an open plan that dissolved any sense of interior and exterior separation (figure 4.4). The resulting design suggested that Puerto Rico had

Figure 4.5. Photograph of the lobby with the pool that crosses indoor and outdoor space, ca. 1949. Hospitality Industry Archives, Conrad Hilton College, University of Houston.

an ideal natural environment—that the temperature outside was perfect for the indoors, and thus the two spaces did not need to be separated from each other. This notion is perhaps no more successfully expressed than through the incorporation of a pool that flowed easily between the interior and exterior underneath a divider (figure 4.5). Located near the grand staircase, this pool was carefully placed so that all visitors would come in contact with it. Complete with stepping-stones and a handrail, it invited guests to interact with nature even inside the hotel. An article from *Interiors* noted that the pool was meant to have an "authentic" feel; hotel staff made sure it was "kept scrupulously muddy and disreputable, in conformance with the outdoor world it represents," so that hotel guests could experience the tropical world without even having to go outside.[59] In effect, the architecture not only framed views of the tropical nature that was outdoors but also brought it indoors, signaling architectural modernism as an effective tool in taming nature for the guests' enjoyment.

Guest rooms were utilized as spaces to reinforce the notion that modernism and tropicality could be blended harmoniously. They were accented with elements meant to impart a local flavor to the space to remind guests they were in a foreign place. Potted plants were incorporated into the rooms to reinforce the notion of tropicality through exotic flora, continuing the trope established in the public

Figure 4.6. Photograph of a typical guest room, ca. 1949. Hospitality Industry Archives, Conrad Hilton College, University of Houston.

spaces. Chairs designed by Jens Risom, a Danish designer who had immigrated to the United States, boasted modern forms and fabric with strong geometric patterns and bright colors that contiguous-US tourists most likely associated with local folk traditions (see figure 4.6).[60] However, Risom's chair revealed the Scandinavian design values in which he was educated. The chairs were representative of a global trend in modern design toward simplicity and functionality, whose aesthetic projected sophistication and refinement, and a general interest among US and European designers in what they deemed "folk" design.[61] By incorporating this fabric, Risom's design demonstrated that traditional elements and progressive design were not mutually exclusive.

Perhaps no aspect of the guest rooms exhibited the adept fusion of notions of the modern and the tropical more than the bedside console. The console housed modern devices, a telephone and a radio, and had speakers covered with a rough, locally produced fabric meant to impart a native flavor to the piece. The fusion of details that were understood as local (however inaccurately) with modern designs or technologies challenged the notion of tropicality as primordial or timeless, instead pointing to the construction of tropicality as something that could be shaped and applied as desired. This is not to imply that these details were simply used as decoration or ornament, however; they were considered integral in designing new forms that were localized, while participating in globalized discourses of modernism.

The lobbies, lounges, bars, and restaurants were the true public face of the hotel, featured in promotional materials and articles that defined the Caribe as an innovative form of tropical modernism. Promotional material represented the interior decoration of the lobby, which was marked by comfortable modern furniture integrated with elements of nature incorporated into the hotel. One brochure for the hotel includes a drawing that contains Eero Saarinen's Womb Chair, which had only been on the market for a year, placed next to the little indoor-outdoor pond (plate 15). To counter narratives that modern life had alienated people from nature, images of the Caribe Hilton's interiors were a utopic vision that demonstrated how humankind had reconciled nature and modern life.

Although the majority of the furniture was imported from the contiguous United States, the designers prominently displayed chairs and benches by ARKLU in the public spaces of the hotel (figure 4.7).[62] ARKLU was a local furniture company founded in 1944 by the German émigré architect Henry Klumb and Stephen Arneson.[63] Initially drawn to Puerto Rico to run the Comité de Diseño de Obras Públicas (Committee on the Design of Public Works), Klumb and Arneson were driven by social consciousness to adapt the architectural concepts of European and US modernism to the particularities of Puerto Rican culture in order to contribute to the development of the island.[64] Their modern furniture referenced global trends, but they used local materials and techniques uniquely Puerto Rican to create furniture that could be placed anywhere, which demonstrated their interest in blurring the lines between interior and exterior, a common practice in design in tropical climates.[65]

The ARKLU furniture certainly did not go unnoticed in the Caribe Hilton, and its incorporation in the hotel helped it gain recognition in other parts of the world. ARKLU received a number of commissions as a result of the strong impression the

Figure 4.7. View of a bench designed by ARKLU in one of the Caribe Hilton's elevator banks. Photograph by Ezra Stoller, ca. 1949. TFA/0040/F0093, Collection Toro Ferrer Architects, Archivo de Arquitectura y Construcción de la Universidad de Puerto Rico.

furniture left on people who experienced it at the hotel. Unfortunately, because of insufficient raw materials and labor, the company was unable to fill many of these orders and it folded in 1948, but the failure of ARKLU does not diminish the importance of its role in promoting modern Puerto Rican design, which advanced the government's goal of an island identity based on modernity and tropicality. An advertisement for ARKLU furniture printed in the United States announced that "designed with striking simplicity, these pieces reflect the timeless beauty of simple, uncomplicated living."[66] ARKLU furniture underscored the important distinction between simplistic and simplicity. Rejecting notions that to be tropical was to be simplistic or unsophisticated, ARKLU furniture suggested that the tropical could be a valuable tool to guide the design world toward simplicity and functionality.

Guests were encouraged to consume the tropical during their stay using all of their senses. Besides the visual representations, the sounds of the ocean and the local music, and the feel of the tropical heat, guests quite literally consumed the tropics upon arrival at the hotel, where they were met with the Caribe Hilton's welcoming drink—a concoction of coconut water, coconut milk, rum, lime juice, sugar, and an apricot brandy floater, all served in a fresh coconut. Attention to tropical tastes continued as a priority at the hotel. According to popular history, in 1954, the hotel manager enlisted bartender Ramón Marrero to invent a new cocktail that would satisfy the US thirst for tropical drinks.[67] The result was the piña colada, a particular blend of Puerto Rican rum, the local invention Coco López (cream of coconut), and pineapple juice.

Guests were also encouraged to buy locally produced goods at the hotel. In the hotel gift shop, they could buy souvenir versions of the lampshades and place mats made of native natural fibers found throughout the hotel. These souvenirs allowed guests to bring a little bit of Puerto Rico back home, a material trace of their vacation that authenticated and domesticated the experience.[68] In this case, tropicality is embodied in such objects as woven grass souvenir place mats, which tourists would have then incorporated and displayed in their homes to substantiate the travel experience and remind them of the bountiful tropics they experienced at the hotel. From drinks to souvenirs, from vistas to the strong Caribbean sun, the guest experience was about consumption. Here we see in practice Ian Gregory Strachan's notion of consumption and its relationship to extraction, which he locates as a through line from the plantation system to the tourist system.

The notion of the tropical was a paradox in the context of the Caribe Hilton and the role of tropicality as a symbol of Puerto Rican identity. On one hand the tropical was promoted as a positive facet of local identity, but on the other it was something that could be easily manipulated for tourist consumption in a way that essentialized local culture or reverted to conceptions that carried connotations of primitiveness. In the case of the Caribe Hilton, however, aspects of its design fusing tropicality and the modern invited a reexamination of some traditional stereotypes and proposed new possibilities for defining a modern cultural identity.

## Driving Development in Puerto Rico and Beyond

December 9, 1949, marked the kickoff of a weekend-long opening ceremony for the Caribe Hilton personally hosted by Conrad Hilton himself, which exemplified many of the influences the Caribe Hilton would have on the future of tourism in

Puerto Rico and the Caribbean. Hilton chartered four Eastern Airlines planes to transport celebrities and key figures in business and politics to the Caribe Hilton for the opening celebration, guaranteeing media attention and coverage of the event in the contiguous states. Activities and performances during the weekend presented specific visions of the island and encouraged appropriate tourist behaviors. For example, a troupe of "pirates" revealed a treasure chest full of Puerto Rican rum on the hotel's beach, and a party of beautiful bikini-clad young women were enlisted to frolic in the ocean and demonstrate the proper way to have fun—by swimming up to the floating bar and ordering a drink. In short, the highly publicized opening of the Caribe Hilton taught future guests near and far how to understand Puerto Rico and how to act when visiting.[69]

Without a doubt, reports of the inaugural fanfare helped with the immediate success of the Caribe Hilton. Newspapers, magazines, and radio programs in Puerto Rico and the contiguous United States furnished glowing reviews of the hotel. The establishment of a luxury hotel that bore the Hilton name along with the promotional efforts of the Puerto Rican office of tourism all helped increase tourism to Puerto Rico; the number of tourists and tourist dollars coming to Puerto Rico grew steadily throughout the decade following the opening of the Caribe Hilton.[70] Puerto Rican government promotional pamphlets from the late 1950s boasted that 85,000 tourists came to Puerto Rico in 1950, and by 1955 that number had jumped to 150,000.

The Caribe Hilton alone could not accommodate the influx of tourists to the island, and a number of other hotels cashed in on the growing industry. East of the Caribe Hilton, on Condado Beach, was the Condado Beach Hotel (formerly the Grand Condado Vanderbilt). The Caribe Hilton was connected to Condado by the Puente Dos Hermanos, which crossed the lagoon separating the two pieces of land. The Caribe Hilton effectively worked as a node to connect Condado and San Juan Viejo in the network of the city, enticing passersby to stop to play in the hotel's casino or enjoy a meal or a drink at one of the hotel's bars and restaurants. Additionally, the location of the Caribe Hilton between San Juan Viejo and Condado supported the spread of tourism infrastructure outward, ensuring that the Condado beachfront area to the east would develop through the stronger connection to San Juan Viejo via the Caribe Hilton. The two extant luxury hotels in San Juan— the Normandie and the Condado Beach Hotel—were remodeled and updated in an effort to meet current tourist expectations.[71] The owners of the Condado Beach Hotel invested one million dollars in a new eighty-eight-room annex, a new lobby, a cabana club, and air-conditioning. In addition, they commissioned Spanish artist

Figure 4.8. View of La Concha Hotel from the Ashford Avenue side. Designed by Toro y Ferrer, the hotel opened in the Condado area of San Juan in 1958. TFA/0060/F0071, Collection Toro Ferrer Architects, Archivo de Arquitectura y Construcción de la Universidad de Puerto Rico.

Hipólito Hidalgo de Caviedes to paint a mural in the hotel, a commission that may have helped him secure a mural project in the Havana Riviera (see chapter 5). The Hotel Normandie management also undertook extensive renovations and constructed a sixty-four-room annex. Owners of each hotel endeavored to modernize their establishments by offering modern amenities, even if these did not physically alter the appearances of the edifices to anything more modernist.

The success of the Caribe Hilton and the growing popularity of San Juan as a vacation destination spurred the construction of hotels that addressed a diverse array of budgets, from the expensive La Concha to hotels and motels for more budget-conscious travelers. La Concha was one of the architectural highlights of the spate of new hotels that opened along Condado Beach in the wake of the Caribe Hilton (figure 4.8). Like the Caribe Hilton, the hotel was designed by Toro, Ferrer y Torregrosa and was funded by PRIDCO. San Juan's La Concha was, in many ways, a continuation of hotel building that was inaugurated with the Caribe Hilton in 1949. Like the Caribe Hilton, La Concha was defined by the insular government's heavy involvement in developing, controlling, and benefiting from tourism. Similar to the financial scheme behind the Caribe Hilton, La Concha was a project built and owned by the government but operated by a private company. Like the Caribe Hilton, La Concha through its modernist design was intended to promote a new identity of Puerto Rico as a place of progress and modernity. La Concha magnified—quite literally—the focus on the tropical to a new level with its giant shell-shaped dome structure located on the beach side of the resort. Not a literal representation of a shell, the structure utilized parabolic shell construction to suggest its form. Here, guests were ensconced in a giant abstracted shell form while they dined. On a more personal scale, tropical vegetation and water elements abounded in the lobby area—much more so than at the Caribe Hilton.

Besides La Concha and other new hotels offering more hotel rooms in San Juan, in 1956, the Caribe Hilton announced an expansion to the hotel to help support the massive influx of tourists to Puerto Rico in the 1950s. The new airport in Isla Grande made this number of visitors possible. Located to the east of the city and completed in 1955, the fifteen-million-dollar airport could accommodate around five hundred flights a day, and longer runways ensured that large jet planes could land in Puerto Rico.[72] The large number of tourists that the airport now served could find lodging in other new hotels such as the San Juan, El Imperial, the Puerto Rico Sheraton, or the Dorado Beach Hotel and Golf Club.[73]

By this time, critics were bemoaning the massive growth of the tourist industry and its effects on San Juan in general and Condado in particular. They started to compare San Juan to Miami in order to convey their concerns that what they saw as a modern urbanity, empty of meaning, was killing Puerto Rican culture.[74] Despite the criticism of these hotel projects and the development of infrastructure to support tourism, the Puerto Rican government stayed true to its commitment to limit the tourist industry on the island, largely by exerting control over the number of hotel rooms on the island, ensuring that tourism never accounted for more than 10 percent of the gross domestic product—a striking figure considering that tourism accounts for as much as 85 percent of the gross domestic product in other Caribbean islands.[75]

The impact of the Caribe Hilton reverberated well beyond the shores of Puerto Rico, in part because it gave Conrad Hilton the confidence to take on an international chain of hotels. Almost all other Hilton International hotels built in the next ten years used the Caribe Hilton as a model, despite Hilton's initial preference for a revival style hotel. The Caribe Hilton convinced him of architectural modernism, and subsequent hotels were designed in this idiom, effectively using modernist design as a weapon in the Cold War. Hilton believed—as he elucidated in many speeches and publications, including his 1957 memoir *Be My Guest*—that the war against communism could be fought and won through international trade and travel. According to his memoir, after World War II he felt personally called upon to develop a chain of international hotels as a way to use trade and tourism to spread peace throughout the world. He equated peace with the triumph of capitalistic democracy over communism, and he felt he was making an important contribution to the Cold War through the expansion of his international hotel chain.[76]

The modernist design of Hilton International hotels was meant to symbolize US capitalist and anti-communist values. As art historian Annabel Jane Wharton persuasively argues in her study of the Hilton International architecture, the modernism of these hotels was intended to convey the progress of the city and the country in which they were located, and the hotels' architecture suggested that modernization and technological advancement were key to this social and economic progress. In addition, one could understand the modern aesthetic as a symbol of the efficiency and modern amenities of the hotel—no matter where they were in the world, guests could expect a certain level of comfort at Hilton hotels.[77] What I want to underscore here is the fact that the Caribe Hilton was the pioneer and the testing ground for the international chain; its significance—in terms of architecture and design, financing, and operations—should be acknowledged. Although there is scholarship on Hilton International hotels, very little attention has been paid to the significance of the Caribe Hilton. This may be because it is in Puerto Rico, and Puerto Rico has not been incorporated into dominant narratives of influential players in Cold War geopolitics.

Not only did the Caribe Hilton establish the preference for modernist design in Hilton International hotels in general, but its configuration of a monolithic slab of guest rooms placed over an open ground level proved an efficient design that was then employed in Hilton hotels around the globe—including those built in Latin America such as the Continental Hilton in Mexico City, the Havana Hilton, and the Trinidad Hilton in Port of Spain.[78] They are similar and yet also fostered the localization of modernism in various countries and offered an opportunity for governments to shape local and national identity. Although officials of the local or national government may have seen a Hilton hotel determining the nation's reputation as a modern place and society, to critics the countless Hiltons that soon dotted the globe represented growing US cultural, political, and economic dominance throughout the world.

The Caribe Hilton also helped frame the Hilton International company's unified approach to creating unique, locale-appropriate interiors, rather than trying to establish a uniform interior design scheme across the brand. In all Hilton International hotels there was a concerted effort to evoke the local culture and environment in the interior decoration, often through murals executed by local artists and the use of local materials in architectural details and furniture.[79] Like the Caribe Hilton, both the Havana Hilton and the Trinidad Hilton boasted modern abstract murals by local artists depicting local traditions or history. For many guests, especially the business travelers who may not have had time for sightseeing, the representation of local culture inside the hotel, whether authentic or not, was important in shaping their understanding of the foreign place in which they found themselves.

Moreover, the financial terms of the Caribe Hilton fundamentally shaped Hilton's approach to financing his international chain. In subsequent Hilton International projects, the government or a government-approved entity financed the construction of the hotel and the Hilton Corporation covered the operating costs.[80] Thus, in many countries the modern architecture of the Hilton was also meant to reflect the hard work of the government in building a modern state since the hotel projects were often, and very publicly, co-sponsored by the state. Moreover, they were often tied to a larger program of development and modernization, just as in Puerto Rico. The Caribe Hilton demonstrated to other countries how building a Hilton was a means to define national identity.

This type of financial arrangement was attractive to Conrad Hilton because it required relatively little investment and therefore relatively little loss if he had to pull out, which is no better illustrated than in the case of the Havana Hilton. Financed by the pension fund of the local food workers union, the hotel had been open for less than a year when it became headquarters for Fidel Castro's revolution in January 1959. When Hilton Hotels International pulled out of the Havana Hilton in June 1960, the company lost only the operating costs, not the construction costs.[81] The Hilton system of developing international hotels required little investment in terms of time as well as money. Hilton did not have to concern himself with learning the inner workings of state and municipal departments in order to learn codes, obtain permits, and ascertain the best contractors. Thus, the Caribe Hilton spurred the development of a hotel chain that was at once both uniform and varied—with a similar financial scheme and an architectural modernist design across the board, Hilton projects were also seen by respective state governments as a unique opportunity to shape a particular local identity.

The Caribe Hilton influenced shifts in the world of hotel design and architectural discourse writ large, extending well beyond the immediate sphere of Hilton hotels. Revolutionary in its use of modernist design, the Caribe Hilton was perhaps rivaled only by Edward Durell Stone's El Panama Hotel in Panama City, which opened around the same time (it appears as though the Caribe Hilton was designed first); but chronology aside, what is more significant is that the Caribe had a bigger presence and greater influence in the architectural world than El Panama. Shortly after the completion of the Caribe Hilton, hotel and motel construction boomed in Miami and many buildings were designed in a fashion similar to the Caribe Hilton. Many of these mimicked the open-plan ground floors of the Caribe Hilton whose modernist design blurred the distinction between indoors and outdoors. However, none of these was a government project in the same way as the Caribe Hilton. Therefore, those funding hotel projects were concerned less with the message that modernist design could convey in terms of identity politics; they were concerned more with creating a design to attract the masses, often through the adoption of popular themes or ornament.

One such example is Morris Lapidus's Fontainebleau Hotel (1954) in Miami Beach. At the funder's directive to create a luxurious hotel that would draw crowds, Lapidus decorated the architectural modernism of the hotel with baroque ornaments and details. Florida did not offer the same foreign or exotic quality as destinations outside the United States. Given this context, many hotel funders often relied on contrived themes such as pirates or tiki culture to define their complexes. Even the more sophisticated designs such as Morris Lapidus's Americana Hotel in Bal Harbour relied on a thematic narrative to impart a sense of character to the space and experience.

The rhetoric of modernist design's equation with hotel efficiency was also a principal factor in the Caribe Hilton's influence on subsequent hotel design. The Caribe Hilton encouraged hotel designers to embrace the idea that luxury could be found in functionality and simplicity, not excessive ornamentation. The adoption of this idea is especially notable in other modern hotels in the Caribbean, such as Lapidus's Aruba Caribbean Hotel (1955), the Hilton Trinidad (1962), and various hotels in Cuba such as the Havana Riviera (1957), the Hotel Capri (1957), the Havana Hilton (1958), and the Hotel Rosita de Hornedo (1955). Similar to the Caribe Hilton, many of these hotels utilized straightforward, uncomplicated designs to underscore a connection with the outdoors and to showcase nature as the primary decorative element. The Aruba Caribbean Hotel is a good example, with guest rooms located in a rectangular slab raised off the ground by pilotis, which allowed warm breezes to pass through the ground-level public spaces (plate 16). Like the Caribe Hilton, the ground level spread out horizontally, and architectural planes created spaces that were both indoors and outdoors. Also inspired by the Caribe Hilton's groundbreaking use of angled balconies, Lapidus provided each guest room with an angled balcony that delivered both privacy and spectacular views.

## *Unfixed Meanings*

Although the unwillingness or inability of some to reconcile notions of modernity with tropicality does not diminish the importance of the Caribe Hilton as an object and a space that fostered the negotiation and contestation of identities, it points to the failure to discard the colonialist mentality so entrenched in a contiguous-US culture that relegated Puerto Rico to an undeveloped, unsophisticated place. Even the author of the *Architectural Forum* article who offered a glowing review of the Caribe Hilton seemed unable to shed stereotypes completely. The author claimed that many would be disappointed by the lack of "local flavor" in the hotel, save for some Spanish colonial style tiles. Although the author does not expound upon what this local flavor could be, the reader is left with the feeling that, for the author, "local flavor" is that which references the Spanish colonial past and is decidedly not modern. This reveals a failure to accept a new paradigm in which Puerto Rican culture did not have to be historicized and fixed but could be considered evolving and dynamic.

The debates point to the very real challenge facing Puerto Rican government officials as they tried to express a sense of the Puerto Rican nation, which, through the 1940s and 1950s, had become increasingly dependent on contiguous-US businesses and the federal government to define its economy. The Caribe Hilton demonstrates how hotels are so much more than merely places for tourists to sleep. The hotel's history reveals the ways in which various agents, from Puerto Rican government officials to contiguous-US tourists, understood this as well. Promoted as the symbol of Operación Manos a la Obra, the Caribe Hilton—both as a project and through its design—was meant to embody the features of the new Puerto Rico that the local government was trying to advance. The very advantages of using a hotel to do this, a contact zone where foreigners are introduced to the local conditions of San Juan, also presented disadvantages as well. The Caribe Hilton did not convey a fixed identity to all who experienced it, whether visitors or locals. Especially in relation to the tropes of the modern, the historic, and the tropical, the Caribe Hilton points to the powerful role that the touristic landscape plays in allowing notions of nation, self, and other to be constantly contested and negotiated.

Figure 5.1. Entrance of the Havana Riviera Hotel, with sculpture in the front by Florencio Gelabert, 1957. Photograph by Bill Mark, 8 x 10 inches. 1986-222-304, Igor B. Polevitzky Photographs Collection, HistoryMiami Museum.

# The Havana Riviera

### Cultural Capital and *Cubanidad* in 1950s Havana

**While San Juan was still developing as a novel destination for US tourists, in the** postwar period Havana built upon its already established reputation as a popular vacation spot to further urban development and lure more tourists. A short flight from Miami, Havana was a popular choice for a weekend getaway. One option for vacationers was the Tropicana Special. Started in 1956, this promotion included round-trip airfare from Miami, the dinner show at the Tropicana Cabaret, a night in a Havana hotel, and breakfast before the return flight—all for only $68.80. This was no ordinary flight to Havana, however. Operated by Cubana Airlines, the aircraft was dubbed the Tropicana Special, and the Tropicana logo was emblazoned upon the headrests and the curtains. Eight seats had been removed from the aircraft to make room for a stage. After takeoff, passengers were treated to a glimpse of what they would experience at the Tropicana showroom. Roderico "Rodney" Neyra, the Tropicana's main choreographer, and performer Ana Gloria Varona, backed by a band and a small acrobatic dance team from the nightclub, entertained guests with an abbreviated show. Passengers even participated in the singing and dancing on this flight, which no doubt helped prime them for the show at the Tropicana and the carefree good times Havana promised US tourists. The Tropicana Special functioned as a general entrée into the world of tourism that US travelers would experience in Havana and as a specific sample of the experience they would have at the Tropicana. These shows titillated and amazed, fulfilling the image of Cuba in the US imagination as a place of sensuous rhythms and sensual, carefree people.

That the Tropicana, other cabarets, and hotels built in the 1950s followed already established trends in Cuban tourism does not detract from the unique trajectory of the growing tourism industry in the post–World War II period, which shaped the urban landscape of Havana. The dictator President Fulgencio Batista and his government were concerned with developing Havana into a modern international destination, although greed and corruption defined their approach to development and, consequently, the city was subject to US business interests and tourist desires for the sake of bringing more money into the country and ultimately into the pockets of Batista and his cronies.[1] The consequence of building codes enacted by Batista in order to ensure handsome personal profits from the tourism and gambling industries, designs such as the Tropicana and the Havana Riviera shaped tourism practices and the understanding of Cuban culture.

In order to lure more tourists, Cuba needed to offer a better version of Miami, Jamaica, Puerto Rico, and other competitors, which meant offering guests all the luxuries they could find in these other places, and then more, if it wanted to gain a competitive edge. Thus, as a means to compete with other destinations, the tourism landscape that emerged in Cuba in the 1950s was marked by development intended to fashion Havana as a modern international destination marked by a unique local identity. I will explore that history through an examination of the Havana Riviera, a modernist high-rise hotel located on the famed oceanfront Malecón that was marked by interiors filled with Cuban modern art and design.[2] The marked internationalism of the hotel's modern architecture, designed by a foreign firm known for their skill in designing for the tropical climate, was balanced with interiors where the focus was on expressing a notion of *cubanidad* or Cuban-ness, and attention to this design provides the means to explore the politics of the design of tourist spaces in the postwar period (figure 5.1).

Meaning was never fixed or static and was contingent upon the attitudes and experiences of the people who visited the building and shaped the images of it, but we can still identify these multiple meanings despite the fluid identity of the hotel. As with the other buildings studied in this book, I consider the Havana Riviera's design within the broader context of building in Cuba, Latin America, and the Western Hemisphere in order to examine two distinct but interconnected phenomena. The first is the employment of certain design approaches that were labeled uniquely Cuban or that supported the idea of a unique Cuban identity. The display of some version of local identity was important—both as an earnest attempt to assert cultural and national independence and as a way to cater to tourist expectations. The second phenomenon is the pointed presentation of Cuba as thoroughly knowledgeable in and engaged with a larger global discourse of modern design.

Many Cuban designers sought to project the notion of Cuba as a place defined by a unique cubanidad informed by the island's sociocultural traditions shaped over centuries and by the more recent global exchanges that indicated participation in the modern world. More specifically, I propose the notion of "cosmopolitan cubanidad" as a term that describes a mode of thinking and being in this period. This is not a term that was used at the time, but one I have coined based on the work of other scholars who are also thinking through questions of nationalism, creolization, and cosmopolitanism.[3] Françoise Lionnet's work has been particularly useful in identifying the connections between creolization and cosmopolitanism, despite the persistent tendency to disconnect the two. Pointing to the connctations that each term has accumulated, Lionnet proposes the ways we can think of "creolization as the cosmopolitanism of the subaltern and cosmopolitanism as the creolization of the elites."[4] Lionnet's formulation provides a useful path for dismantling the connotations of creolization that invoke otherness and deficiency in order to focus on particularity and locality as positive attributes of creolization that are in sync with cosmopolitanism. In this case, cosmopolitanism is not limited by the elitist rationalist connotations that Lionnet as well as María Fernández break down but, rather, exhibits universal tendencies that exist in concert with possibilities of the particular and the local.[5] To clarify even further, I maintain that cubanidad is not equivalent to creolization or territorial nationalism but, instead, is a concept of and an identity that considers the local and national while also being attuned to a position within a global context. Cosmopolitan cubanidad was an attitude—practiced or believed—that was prevalent in the 1950s and that defined the dominant approach to design in this period.

The history of the post–World War II years has undergone much revision in the wake of the Cuban Revolution in 1959. Although atrocities against Cubans and the mismanagement of the government and money were brought to light in subsequent decades, political ideologies and agendas have colored interpretations of tourism in the 1950s. When historians or regimes paint other regimes in a negative light, it is quite difficult to assess any part of this culture, and in this case the result has been a negative effect on the appreciation of the design of tourist spaces. Through an examination of the Havana Riviera hotel, I aim to recover a part of the history that has been distorted or lost. I do not mean to suggest that the ugly realities of Batista's promotion of unchecked US tourism are pardonable, but I do wish to recuperate the positive and innovative aspects of Cuban tourism design in the postwar period. Most significantly, the design of tourism spaces promoted modern Cuban architecture, design, and art in public spaces for all to see, which allowed architects, designers, and artists to continue the established tradition of redefining and promoting notions of cubanidad through these cultural objects.

## *Icon of the Hotel Boom*

The Havana Riviera hotel can serve as both agent and example of the hotel boom in the late 1950s. The hotels built during this boom were—and still are—contested spaces. Elite private interests, handpicked by a corrupt Cuban government, made them possible but also made them controversial from their inception. However, building under Batista's authoritarian system allowed for certain rules and regulations to be skirted or overlooked and projects to be fast-tracked, ultimately resulting in a significant amount of completed projects. However corrupt the system was, it made Cubans feel justified and proud to claim their country's status as a truly modern metropolis.

Tourism development in Havana in the 1950s was both directly responsible for urban growth and a product of it. Through a series of new laws and initiatives in urban infrastructure and construction, the city spread further out and up. There was no need to demolish buildings in the old part of the city because Batista was buildings roads, bridges, and tunnels to better connect the outskirts of Havana to the city center, continuing a practice of many of his predecessors.[6] Notably, President Ramón Grau San Martín (1944–1948) made impressive improvements to city infrastructure as part of the largest urban planning project carried out by the Cuban state in the first half of the twentieth century.[7] During Batista's dictatorship, skyscrapers proliferated, thanks in part to the 1952 Ley de Propriedad Horizontal (Condominium Law), which allowed buildings taller than six stories to be built along the Malecón, the wide drive that ran along the shore from the bay to the Río Almendares.[8] Most of the new hotels raised Havana's skyline and were focused in the area known as La Rampa, along the Malecón in the Vedado district, and further west in Miramar. The urban form of Vedado, especially near the Malecón, was drastically altered by the towering height of these hotels, which transformed the city's skyline and stifled the Antillean breezes that cooled the city.[9] The new modern hotels were clearly separated from the historic city center, reinforcing the notion that the modern was where US visitors stayed, was the world they lived in, while the historic was something to be visited and consumed on a day trip.[10] In fact, it was because so many of the new hotels were built in Vedado that it became the preeminent tourist district in the 1950s.[11]

A highlight of these new, ultramodern skyscraper hotels, the Havana Riviera was perhaps rivaled only by the 1958 Havana Hilton, a building that has been studied more than the Havana Riviera. In my opinion, the understudied Havana Riviera is more representative of hotel building in Havana in this period than the Havana Hilton, which adhered to an investment, design, and operational scheme that was more specific to Hilton Hotels International policies than to Havana tourism trends. Conrad Hilton dreamed of a Hilton in Havana in 1950 based on the immediate and great success of the Caribe Hilton, though the Cuban project was not realized until the end of the decade. The Havana Hilton opened in October 1958, and in the early days of January 1959 it became headquarters of Fidel Castro and the revolutionary troops in Havana, further dampening US desires to lodge there. Because the Havana Riviera was a project tied to US mobsters (Meyer Lansky, in particular), the project moved forward quickly. It opened in 1957 and had operated for more than a year before the 1959 Cuban Revolution disrupted tourism.

Although the architecture of the Havana Riviera has often been overlooked or dismissed because the architect was not Cuban and US mobsters funded the building, in my analysis I present a new appraisal of the Havana Riviera as a complex yet significant example of modern Cuban design. In my examination of the architecture and interiors I illustrate a concern for promoting a sense of Cuban identity that was both modern and traditional, and which, at the very core, presented modern design as desirable. Although a Cuban desire to be modern and to make Havana a modern city had existed for some time, in the years after World War II the quest for modernity was uniquely defined by the larger postwar climate. Finally, I hope to resituate our understanding of the Havana Riviera—and persistent claims that its design was simply an imitation of thoughtless Miami kitsch—by considering the Havana Riviera in relation to modern hotels built in Miami in the 1950s.

## *Postwar Tourism in Havana*

Since the nineteenth century, Cuba had led the way among Latin American countries in modernizing transportation, communication, and infrastructure, which was partly because of the commitment to sugar production on the island and partly because of Spain's attention to modernizing Cuba as a statement of the benefits of colonialism and modernity.[12] Thanks to Spain and Cuba's attention to modernization during the colonial period, after Cuba's independence the island quickly became a destination for US tourists, which was supported by US imperial interests and intervention. The onset of Prohibition in the United States as well as other economic factors in both the United States and Cuba helped propel its rise as a tourist destination in the 1920s. The postwar period was marked by President Batista's efforts to increase tourism and to initiate a variety of modernization programs throughout the country. The arrangement that emerged was not something official like Puerto Rico's Operación Manos a la Obra but, rather, a series of deals between Batista and various US investors (including mob syndicates) that involved heavy payoffs to Batista and other officials in high positions. In effect, the agendas of those in power in this period were successful in projecting a modern Cuban identity, even if through questionable means, and although this seemed to be of benefit to many, it was still bound within structures that limited the sovereignty of Cuba and its people in notable ways.

The continued growth of the tourist industry in the post–World War II period, which was particularly robust from 1952 to 1959, was the result of a combination of factors. Like Puerto Rico in the postwar period, Cuba's tourism industry was not viewed independently of other business interests on the island; it was but one piece in a larger framework to develop Havana as a major metropolis of the Caribbean and the world. Just as it remains today, in this period the reputation of Havana was fundamental to the definition of Cuba, as the city and country became synonymous.[13] The capital city functioned as the test sample for ascertaining the country's progress and status. This was at times convenient for Cubans, especially politicians, who would reference the capital city as the definition of the country, when in fact most of the rest of Cuba lacked the level of wealth, technology, education, public health, and general standard of living that defined Havana. The constant international attention on the city meant that the government often concentrated in Havana new projects that they felt would convey a good image to the rest of the world.

The most powerful internal force in the tourist industry was President Batista, who wielded largely unchecked power as dictator and who was committed to increasing the profits Cuba could make from US tourists.[14] The initiatives he spearheaded, both those directly part of the tourism sector and broader programs related to urban development, public works, and foreign and domestic investment in the island, heavily favored the growth of tourism in Havana over any other place in the country. He imagined Cuba would be a leading global country through development in its capital. His suspension of the constitution allowed him the freedom to manipulate the government in whatever ways he saw fit. Shortly after taking power, he founded the Instituto del Turismo Cubano (ITC, Institute of Cuban Tourism) and tasked the agency with upgrading the island's tourist infrastructure, including hotels, casinos, roads, bridges, and more, rather than promoting the natural beauty of the island. In point of fact, the ITC vice president, Armando Maribona, had proposed that the agency focus more on promoting the natural beauty of Cuba's beaches, which would encourage tourism to the more rural areas, but his opinion fell on deaf ears.[15]

Reports generated by the ITC found that restaurants and hotels in Havana had grown shabby or had closed as a result of neglect during the Great Depression and World War II. During this period, hotel construction had all but ceased. Figures revealed that Caribbean neighbors were increasing in tourist numbers, causing Cuba to lose part of its share of the tourist market, which inspired the Batista government to commit to making Cuba the top Caribbean destination once again.[16] This was done largely through urban development in Havana. Batista offered tax breaks and other incentives for new hotel construction, and during his period as president (less than eight years), thirteen ultramodern hotels were built in Havana.

The type of tourism promoted under Batista and the image of Havana that was projected were largely based on tourism practices of the 1920s and 1930s. One of the main social driving forces in the development of tourism in Havana after World War I was Prohibition in the United States, which encouraged US citizens to travel abroad as a way to drink legally. US citizens could get to Cuba quickly and drink to their hearts' content, indelibly impacting the nature of tourism in Cuba. Travelers often also had easier access to drugs, prostitution, and gambling when in Cuba than at home. Havana became not just a place to drink but a place to escape the strictures of everyday life in the United States. This reputation continued in the post–World War II period. Therefore, we can see post–World War II tourism as not being drastically different, even though Prohibition had been repealed by this time, and we can consider World War II as simply a pause or an interlude in the growth of tourism in Havana.

Indeed, tourism in the 1950s was marked by a preponderance of US travelers who viewed Cuba as a place where anything goes. An exotic, mysterious, and romantic place, Havana was where vacationers could indulge in activities that were frowned upon in the United States. Christine Skwiot chronicles Batista's approach to reinvigorating the lagging tourist industry in the 1950s by cashing in on Havana's preexisting sex-and-sin reputation.[17] Promotional materials played to and reinforced the concept of Cuba as an irresistible, fun-loving temptress, as depicted in two images by Cuban graphic artist Conrado Walter Massagüer (plate

17, 18). In both these images, Cuba is personified as a beautiful alluring woman. In the postcard, Cuba is a curvy, vivacious, maracas-wielding woman who, through the movement conveyed in her pose, suggests the carefree dancing and partying that US tourists associated with Cuba. Her confident pose combined with a low-cut blouse project a sexual assertiveness that US citizens linked to Cuban society. The brochure produced by the ITC is even more explicit in its representation of Cuba as a destination for sex tourism. An attractive woman personifies Cuba, and she reaches out to kiss the male US visitor who has just reached her shores. Leaning toward the somewhat startled tourist, her unabashed reception of the man in the image conveys to the male tourist not just a willingness but even an eagerness of Cuban women to cater to the desires of US males.

A growing tourist economy was also possible because there were willing and able US tourists. Just like tourism to Puerto Rico in the postwar period, the tourism industry in Cuba profited from advances in air travel technology, lower airfares, and increased spending power and leisure time on the part of the US middle class. Daily direct flights from New York, Chicago, New Orleans, and Miami facilitated tourism, and Batista encouraged airlines to fly into Havana by more than quintupling the size of the main terminal of the Rancho Boyeros International Airport.[18] A variety of airlines offered a multitude of flights to Havana, including Cubana Airlines, Braniff International Airways, Pan American Airlines, Eastern Airlines, National Airlines, and Delta.

As in the case of Puerto Rico, where low airfares designed to encourage low-income Puerto Ricans to leave the island also had the effect of encouraging tourism to the island, travel between the United States and Cuba was not a one-way street. As Louis A. Pérez illustrates extensively, Cubans had long been traveling to the United States for a variety of reasons. Many middle- and upper-class Cubans had family in the United States, had their children educated at US institutions, vacationed in the United States, and shopped there. This trend continued in the 1950s, and flights to Miami were so affordable it was not uncommon for Cuban women to fly to Miami for the day.[19] By the middle of the decade, Pan American offered six daily flights to Miami for thirty-six dollars round-trip.[20]

The strong connection between Cuba and the United States was evident in Cuban culture and society. The strong economic ties between the two countries—namely, that Cuba was a major purchaser of US goods—undoubtedly encouraged the US government to be more tolerant of Batista despite rumors of the indignities and atrocities suffered by the Cuban people under his dictatorship. As Pérez outlines, twentieth-century Cuban culture was focused on a notion of modernity that was inspired by the United States, one that was defined by "a condition of material progress based on consumption, convenience, and comfort."[21] US businesses and goods flooded the marketplace in Cuba; in 1947 the United States was supplying Cuba with 84 percent of its imports, valued at $436 million, and by 1957 that amount reached $577 million annually.[22]

The symbiotic relationship between the United States and Cuba in regards to consumer society and culture defined and encouraged US tourism to Havana. The considerable influence of US culture and consumer goods made Havana familiar enough to US tourists. They could travel to Cuba in search of the exotic or the foreign while knowing they could also find comfort in the familiarity of a Coca-Cola and a hamburger. The presence of such familiar goods was reassuring and seemed to provide evidence of the positive effects of the United States as it sought to spread capitalist democracy, which was presented as synonymous with progress, throughout the world.

### *Postwar Hotel Building in Havana*

New, modern hotels and the area in which they were built were the direct result of Batista's approach to utilizing Havana as an outward visual representation of development in Cuba and of the urban planning project of Ramón Grau San Martín's government. President Grau's public works projects modernized the city, especially at the outskirts, by providing new roads, upgrading water and sewage systems, updating port facilities, creating parks and gardens, and building schools, hospitals, and residences. Despite all of the advances, the city retained much of its old appearance, and newly developed areas simply mimicked other visual characteristics of the city. A proliferation of styles in these new peripheral areas—such as Spanish-colonial, Art Deco, and proto-rationalist styles—echoed those in the center and continued the tradition of building heights limited to four stories.[23]

With Grau's urban development as a base, the Batista government issued $350 million in bonds to finance public works, including aqueducts, roads, industrial projects, and tunnels. Two major tunnel projects were meant to connect central Havana to areas further east and west. One was a tunnel under Havana Bay that connected the urban area to the relatively undeveloped area to the east, which the Batista government had plans for developing. The second project was comprised of two tunnels passing under the Río Almendares, effectively connecting the rapidly growing western residential municipalities of Playa, Marianao, and La Lisa, in particular via Quinta Avenida, a grand boulevard that ran through the Playa district and was flanked by the grand homes of Havana's wealthiest residents. In search of development and economic prosperity, Batista looked to elite private interests to invest in the island.[24] In particular, Batista needed an influx of foreign money as there was more Cuban money leaving the island than there was foreign currency coming in. The most obvious and lucrative source was tourism, and Batista set out to entice investors to buy into this industry.

Ley de Hoteles 2074 (Hotel Law 2074), adopted in 1953, did just that. It offered a range of tax breaks and incentives to encourage investment in large-scale hotel projects. It stipulated that if investors committed at least one million dollars to build a hotel or two hundred thousand dollars to construct a nightclub, they would also be allowed to include a casino as long as they paid the government twenty-five thousand dollars for the license, plus a monthly fee of two thousand dollars and a percentage of the take. Of these monthly fees, Batista declared that a portion would be used for charitable works, a move surely meant to reduce criticism of his decision to grow the gambling industry.[25]

Batista strongly encouraged investors who were interested in tourism projects to solicit funds from government lending entities such as the Banco de Fomento Agrícola e Industrial de Cuba (Banfaic, or the Bank of Agricultural and Industrial Development of Cuba). As its name indicates, this publicly funded entity was originally founded for agricultural and industrial development. Along with steering the extant Banfaic organization to fund tourism projects, Batista established the Financiera Nacional de Cuba (National Finance Company) in 1953 and the Banco de Desarrollo Económico y Social (Bandes, or the Bank of Economic and Social Development) in 1955. The Financiera Nacional de Cuba funded public and private ventures by taking out loans from other entities in order to issue bonds for those venture.[26] Those policies were overseen by Banco Nacional de Cuba (National Bank of Cuba) who owned a controlling share of the Financiera Nacional de Cuba. The president of the Banco Nacional de Cuba also managed Bandes, which was funded in part with government money; Banfaic was also a subsidy of the Banco Nacional de Cuba. Besides providing loans for such projects as building or improving railroad and airline facilities, Bandes also issued loans for hotel construction, most notably for the Havana Hilton and the Havana Riviera. Batista created and manipulated government organizations as he saw fit in order to promote tourism development, and his banks replaced the foreign National City Bank of New York as the major supplier of investment capital. During the 1950s, these Cuban entities loaned more than eighty million dollars in public loans to private companies who were building in the tourist sector.[27]

Batista's efforts to lure private interests to invest in Cuban tourism coincided with a move by US mob syndicates to set up more gambling operations outside the United States. Meyer Lansky and other major mob leaders were not strangers to Havana, but the incentives Batista was offering to set up operations there came at a particularly critical moment for them. In the United States, growing public awareness and concern about increased juvenile narcotic use, organized crime activity, and corruption among politicians and law enforcement officers, all of which was linked to the Mafia, propelled the US government to take action against mobsters. Hearings held from May 1950 to May 1951 by the Senate Crime Committee led to a heavy crackdown on mob-controlled gambling, which had the effect of pushing some mob-run gambling outside the United States.[28] The timing was fortuitous for Batista in his efforts to encourage tourism through hotel building and increased gambling.

In fact, for many, the arrival of the US mob in Cuba marked a positive turn in gambling in Cuba. Gaming in Cuba had become notorious for pushing illegal games that were fast-paced, impossible to win, and that quickly stripped US tourists (the unwitting targets of these games) of large amounts of money. When a well-connected and respected lawyer from California, Dana C. Smith, raised a commotion in 1953 in the United States about a game called razzle-dazzle, in which he had lost several thousand dollars in Cuba, Batista responded to the bad US publicity by immediately proclaiming razzle-dazzle illegal and ordering police to monitor casinos to make sure tourists were treated fairly.[29] This scandal undoubtedly also encouraged Batista to open his arms more widely to US gambling mobsters, who knew how to run a tight ship and who could come to Havana and operate establishments that tourists would respect.

Lansky, who was indicted on illegal gambling charges in Florida, seized this opportunity to invest more heavily in gambling in Cuba.[30] Lansky had a relationship with Batista dating back to the 1930s, and Cuba's president was eager to bring in someone with Lansky's reputation for running professional, reputable games in a classy atmosphere.[31] Lansky bought a share in the Montmartre Club in Vedado and set up a school that trained and screened casino workers. He became convinced of the potential of Havana and commenced upon a plan to build a large, impressive, modern resort hotel with a first-class casino.[32] The investors of the project provided eight million dollars to build the hotel and solicited a six-million-dollar loan from Bandes. Top Cuban officials spoke glowingly of the project and its role in increasing foreign exchange, supporting Cuban employment, and growing the tourist industry.[33] Lansky was committed to moving forward on the project at top speed, while still ensuring that his hotel—the new Riviera of the Americas—was one of the finest in Havana.

## *Modernism on the Malecón*

Trying to build new high-rise hotels in the historic center would have been a logistical nightmare and would have involved the demolition of an entire block or more of high-density structures. But the urban infrastructure projects completed under Presidents Grau and Batista meant that neighborhoods peripheral to the historic center were now easily accessible and navigable.[34] The neighborhood of Vedado was less developed than the older ones and boasted a large expanse of Havana's Malecón, the eight-kilometer oceanfront promenade along the sea wall.

Before the 1950s, most buildings in the neighborhood reached four stories or less, the most notable exception was Mira y Rosich's fourteen-story Art Deco López Serrano Building. The Havana Riviera is also the example par excellence of the desire to situate these new high-rise structures close to the ocean to achieve desirable views and to benefit from the ocean breezes (plate 19). Vedado was a booming area in the 1950s and home to the majority of new hotels: the Havana Riviera, the Havana Hilton, the Hotel Capri, the Flamingo, St. Johns, and the Hotel Vedado. The location of the Havana Riviera, near the western end of Vedado where the area meets the Río Almendares and turns into the Miramar neighborhood, served as a useful node to aid in the spread of tourism infrastructure from Habana Vieja to the outer edges of Vedado and out toward Miramar, consistent with the spread of the city to the west.

With the location of the hotel project determined in 1956, Lansky began looking for an architect to design a thoroughly modern resort hotel. His desire to start profiting from his investment as quickly as possible played no small part in the selection of the architect. Originally, Philip Johnson developed a design for this prime waterfront location. His proposal was for a tall rectangular tower with a profusion of plate glass windows and completely closed off from the outside. This design would have presented issues in terms of exorbitant air-conditioning cost to keep the interiors cool, but the disagreement the investors had with the project was rooted in the interior decoration. A widely disseminated anecdote about Philip Johnson's withdrawal from the project involves a meeting between the architect, Lansky, and some of Lansky's associates. As the story goes, Johnson finished pitching his design proposal, at which point one of Lansky's associates suggested that a large pair of dice should be painted on a ceiling. Johnson reportedly responded, "Gentlemen, let's not be crude," and walked out of the meeting.[35] What is noteworthy about this anecdote is that, despite the request for kitsch interior decoration (the kind that proliferated in Las Vegas and Miami gambling establishments), the project ultimately was more of the refined, high modernist type of design that

Johnson had originally proposed, although better suited to and representative of the climate and culture than Johnson's proposal.

After Wayne McAllister, a Los Angeles–based designer known for his Las Vegas hotels, reportedly declined the commission because of Lansky's insistence on a six-month completion schedule, Lansky solicited Polevitzky, Johnson and Associates.[36] The Miami-based firm was respected in the field for its regionally inspired modernism and for its hotel design abilities, a perfect combination for the project at hand. The firm already had a fair amount of experience in designing hotels and motels in the greater Miami area. Igor Polevitzky accepted the commission and began work on designing a hotel that respected the climate and the natural and man-made environment that surrounded it.[37]

A brief look at Polevitzky's previous projects reveal insight into the details of the Riviera's design. Polevitzky had been designing projects in the Miami area since he moved there in 1934, and by the 1940s he had developed a reputation for his innovations in tropical domestic architecture.[38] Most notably, through an understanding of architecture as volume rather than mass, he stripped down the white planar wall to little more than a light frame denoting the perimeters of the volume of the structure.[39] In doing so he was pushing his personal interest in developing architecture that was appropriate for the Florida climate, architecture in which he believed, the polarity between inside and outside could be mitigated.[40] As scholar Allan T. Shulman observes, the approach of integrating inside and outside "embodied the intertwining of modern and primitive and the progressive and traditional."[41]

The particularities of designing and building homes versus larger commercial and residential buildings meant that Polevitzky could be more experimental in his domestic architecture. For example, his hotels of the 1930s and 1940s such as the Albion (1939), the Shelborne (1940), the Center Hotel (1945, unbuilt), and the Golden Strand Hotel and Villas (1946), though modern for their time, did not allow Polevitzky to push the boundaries of indoor/outdoor living. However, Polevitzky had the opportunity to be innovative in other aspects of the hotel design. For example, scholars have also positioned Polevitzky's Shelborne hotel of 1940 as a "forecast [of] disengagement between tower and pedestal forms that would distinguish the modern resort hotel."[42] He did this by covering the pedestal in a curtain wall of mahogany and glass, revealing the multi-story lobby.

By the 1950s, Polevitzky was a recognized figure of regional modernism in the United States. His work was considered innovative and functional because, as Allan T. Shulman summarizes, "it addressed issues considered central to the modern movement in the United States: contextualism, a responsiveness to environmental

Figure 5.2. View of the Havana Riviera Hotel from the Malecón, 1957. Photograph by Bill Mark, 8 x 10 inches. 1986-222-291, Igor B. Polevitzky Photographs Collection. HistoryMiami Museum.

factors, and a creative use of materials and techniques."[43] The Havana Riviera is characteristic of Polevitzky's design approach in many ways, yet it also reveals compromises he had to make to accommodate the location and the owner.

For the design of the hotel, Polevitzky developed a twenty-one-story Y-shaped tower that, from certain angles, appears lifted up off the ground on spindly columns (figure 5.2). The Y-shaped form worked well with the plot of land Polevitzky had to work with. Surpassing the limitations of a simple rectangular slab, the Y-shape allowed two shorter wings to come off the building on one end, increasing the number of rooms, and in particular the number of end rooms, which had balconies.

The resulting form was dynamic; the curve of the front façade and back pool façade and the positioning of the façades in relation to the ocean suggest the smooth motion of ocean breezes across the surfaces of the building. Finally, in using the Y-shape, Polevitzky inserted a shaft in the intersection of the wings that is taller than the rest of the structure, highlighting the vertical thrust of the building and creating a space to prominently display the hotel's name.

The Havana Riviera's form is visually more open to the outside than Polevitzky's previous hotels, the result of floor slabs that extend the volume of the walls on all sides of the hotel, the scalloped edges of which lend a sculptural and organic feel to the two broad sides of the building. The walls are set back in the structure and are composed of large windows and a light turquoise infill, effectively conveying their nonstructural quality and lending a lightness to the structure. The columns on the ground floor allow for an open plan that can accommodate hotel facilities. Likewise, they create a sense of expansiveness to the ground level. Characteristic of the architect's concern with blurring the boundaries between indoor and outdoor, the open space of the ground level extends down to a lower level of public space level with the Malecón. Large plateglass windows opened views to the outside, while protecting people from the noise and pollution of passing automobile traffic.

Guests approached the main entry by passing under a large porte-cochère with a massive wall of sculpted concrete blocks on the left side. At the top of the stairs, beyond the glass doors, the space opened up and the view extended through to the pool and cabana deck on the other side of the building. After passing the hallway to the casino on the right, the guests experienced a space expanded into an area of floor-to-ceiling plate glass walls overlooking the Malecón and the ocean. Polevitzky created the gradation of space between inside and outside through the transparency of large amounts of plate glass and areas that are not physically, just visually, open to the next.[44] This arrangement accommodated Lansky's requirement that the hotel have central air-conditioning, as he was determined to build the first hotel with central air-conditioning; this was a compromise for Polevitzky, who did not like to utilize air-conditioning in his designs.

In the 1950s, no luxury resort hotel located in a warm climate was complete without a pool. All of the new high-quality hotels in Havana had them, even if a diminutive plot size meant they were located on the roof, such as at the Hotel Capri and the Havana Hilton. As Rocco Ceo and Allan T. Shulman discuss, the pool was seen, like air-conditioning, as a symbol of luxury—yet a necessary one—in postwar hotels. Hotel investors used details such as pools and air-conditioning to compete with Miami and other destinations in the Caribbean, such as Puerto Rico,

Mexico, and Jamaica. Polevitzky was not just familiar with the practice of including pools in his designs, he was swept up in the pool craze in the postwar period, as were many other architects. At the Havana Riviera, Polevitzky included a diving platform that sported a large observation deck intersected by a cantilevered arc.[45] Interestingly, this design was not new, he had proposed it for the Center Hotel, an unbuilt project from 1945.

While Polevitzky may have recycled the diving platform design, the rendering of the Center Hotel reveals just how far he had come in conveying volume over mass in his hotel designs and the sense of lightness and openness this could engender. This is further confirmed by a brief look at the Carlton Terrace Apartments in Bal Harbour, Florida, also started in 1956 (plate 20).[46] The Carlton Terrace Apartments were composed of two rectangular towers of equal dimensions that intersected at the ends at a right angle. The visual result is not unlike the Y-shape at the Havana Riviera. The curved façade on one side of the Carlton Terrace Apartments seems to be a scaled-down version of the sweeping curves of the front façade and pool façade of the Havana Riviera. Comparing the two structures underscores the visual lightness that Polevitzky achieved with the Havana Riviera by placing an emphasis on the floor slabs that extend out and by filling the space between them with large windows and infill panels, whose color makes them appear less structural than the white walls of the Carlton Terrace Apartments.

This effect of lightness and openness allowed US guests who saw and experienced the Havana Riviera to draw connections to the climate to aid them in defining the tropics. In this case, tropicality was not referenced by lush vegetation but, rather, through an attention to climate through transparency and lightness, whether the plate glass or the color of the exterior walls, which were also a traditional color for buildings in the Caribbean. A design that stressed connection and flow between interior and exterior would remind guests of their foreign environment, one markedly different from the environment at home, and the approach to architecture that the foreign world necessitated. As a forerunner of the modern postwar hotels in Havana, the Havana Riviera contributed to the highly developed nature of tourism design in the city and displayed to visitors the way Cuba embraced modernity via modern design as a means to achieve higher standards of living.

## *Displaying Modern Cubanidad*

The architecture was certainly impressive, and the interior design and decoration of the public areas on the main level conveyed the richness of modern Cuban art and design. The lobby was a veritable *gesamtkunstwerk* composed of Cuban artwork, furniture, and materials that unequivocally presented Cuba and its people as simultaneously engaged with their heritage and thoroughly modern.[47] References to global trends in design and assertions of a unique Cuban identity through materials—and even more strongly in the many works of avant-garde art displayed prominently in the public areas—expressed a Cuban cosmopolitanism and cultural nationalism. The hotel's lounges, bars, and restaurants encouraged guests to linger in spaces that explored the notion of cubanidad and offered the most luxurious and up-to-date in resort hotel experiences.

Artworks, from figural to abstract, engaged with themes of Cuban heritage and culture, from images of carnival to more abstract depictions of symbols related to the uniquely Cuban syncretic faiths of La Regla de Ocha-Ifá or La Regla de Lukumí (previously commonly referred to as Santería), Palo or Las Reglas de Congo, or the Abakuá society.[48] Just as all of the artworks had subject matter that dealt with cubanidad, they all expressed a clear engagement with global avant-garde trends. A number of the artworks warrant consideration in terms of their position within the historical framework of Cuban art and their function within the hotel setting.

Before entering the hotel, guests saw Florencio Gelabert's white marble sculpture outdoors in front of the porte-cochère (see figure 5.1). Displayed above a pool, *Danza* (Dance) is composed of intertwined abstract forms of a mermaid and a sea creature (variously described as a swordfish or a dolphin), suggesting associations of Cuba as a place of natural abundance intimately connected to the marine world. The sculpture brings this to the point of fantasy in its use of the mythical mermaid, a parallel and a reminder to guests of their passage from their everyday lives into the escapism of vacation.

Born just after the turn of the twentieth century, Gelabert was an established and respected sculptor by the time he received the commission for the various artworks he produced for the Havana Riviera. He had studied in Havana at the Academia Nacional de Bellas Artes San Alejandro (San Alejandro National Academy of Art) from 1928 to 1934 and traveled throughout Europe, including Paris, to study the famed masters. Upon his return to Havana, he continued his artistic practice and was consistently included in expositions and awarded prizes throughout his career. The outdoor sculpture *Danza* and other sculptures Gelabert created for the Havana Riviera are typical of his work: smooth and attenuated abstracted forms with an emphasis on curvilinearity and negative space to convey movement.

Another sculpture by Gelabert dominated the lobby. Cast in bronze, *Ritmo Cubano* (figure 5.3) depicts an abstracted male and female couple frozen in dance,

Figure 5.3. Lobby of the Havana Riviera Hotel, ca. 1957. Photograph by Rudi Rada, 8 x 10 inches. 1986-222-323, Igor B. Polevitzky Photographs Collection, HistoryMiami Museum.

twirling around and engaged with each other in a manner reminiscent of *Danza*. The subject engages with the famous legacy of dance in Cuba. Representations of dance have been popular in the art of Cuba dating far back. Foreigners represented this theme in their works. Frenchman Frédéric Miahle, for example, captured the various social and ethnic classes of Cuba in his series of lithographs that were then published in *Album pintoresco al redador de la isla de Cuba* in the mid-nineteenth century.[49] Miahle's project was one of colonialism as it worked to essentialize and objectify the people of Cuba into easily digestible types so as to project European superiority over the people of the Americas. In the much cited *El zapateado*, a lithograph included in the volume, Miahle depicted people from the rural countryside partaking in traditional peasant dances.

Dance was also an important subject for Cuban artists, especially the *vanguardia*, which made its appearance in 1927.[50] For many, dance was a reclamation of what had been otherized and exoticized when taken up by Europeans as subject matter. One of the most iconic works of the early vanguardia is Eduardo Abela's *El Triunfo de la Rumba*, painted around 1928. Content and iconography were a means for the vanguardia to position art as a means to convey and define Cuban identity. Vanguardia artists utilized explorations in form in order to underscore the theme or subject matter of the work. Such is the case with Abela's *El Triunfo de la Rumba*, where line is used to evoke the movement of Cuban dance, and color is used to reinforce notions of place—the pastels of blue, green, and bits of yellow and salmon depict the ocean, the tropical vegetation, the sun and warmth of the Caribbean island. The main focus of the painting is a mixed race woman dressed in white, flanked by drum players and other figures. As more recent scholarship has pointed out, the vanguardia artists' use of Afro-Cuban themes in their work is not unproblematic, as many of these mostly white artists were not considering racial politics as they co-opted Afro-Cuban expressions and claimed them as national identity.[51]

Nearly thirty years separate Abela's painting and Gelabert's sculpture, but they make a useful comparison. Abela's work focuses on Cuban rumba as part of the African heritage of Cuba, with background figures who are certainly laborers and could be either dancing or laboring, or perhaps referencing some romantic notion of dancing while working. All of this is framed by palm leaves, connecting the figures to nature, and more specifically to a tropical nature often associated with the primitive. The woman, as focal point of the image, points to the topic of race in Cuba and the complex and multiple significations of the *mulata*, established as a racial type in Cuban visual culture in the nineteenth century, as symbol of racial mixing in Cuba.[52] For many in the United States, the rumba reinforced popular stereotypes that there was something untamed or primitive in the Cuban soul when it came to dance—that Cubans were born with rhythm and they all lived for music and dance, especially forms of dance that were viewed as overtly sexual to more puritanical US norms. On the other hand, the sweeping curves that define Gelabert's sculpture render it less provocative than Abela's *mulata* who stares out in a confrontational invitation to the viewer.

The figures in Gelabert's work are raceless and could be dancing any one of a number of Cuban dances, such as mambo, son, cha-cha-chá, or guaguancó, as well as rumba. All of these dance forms were informed by African culture, but they were not as closely associated with African spiritual traditions as the rumba. Likewise, Gelabert's sculpture would not have been considered as avant-garde as

Abela's painting, at least not by art critics and historians, but it was easily legible to tourists. Gelabert's sculpture invites the viewer to contemplate these two figures who have become one, lost in the dance. His work projects the idea of escape, the way movement across a dance floor could transport one somewhere else, connotations all fitting for the sculpture's placement in the hotel lobby and as something to be viewed by guests who found themselves transported to a foreign place.[53]

Dance most often relies on music, and the fame of Cuba's dance was associated also with its musical production. Just as Gelabert's *Ritmo Cubano* brought a sense of movement to the lobby, Cundo Bermúdez's mural *Los Musicos* activated the space of the bar next to the casino. Stretching out on the walls on either side of the staid and sober semicircular bar, the murals, a series of paintings on Masonite panels, bring energy and life to the space. Black line drawings depict musicians in what may be historical garb—or what could be described as an idiosyncratic sartorial collection resulting in figures that, in some respect, read as figural archetypes. Although replete with decorative moments, there is an economy of line to these figures that evokes modernist art practices engaged with psychology, such as tapping into an unconscious. In this case, it is an unconsciousness of shared mythological types who suggest the intersecting roles of music and the spiritual. The sinuous lines of the figures convey a movement that is arrested by the implementation of color in these images. Overlayed geometric forms brought into relief with a dual color theme of varying gradients seem to freeze the figures in their location. While the color seems to fix the figures, the contrast lends its own type of rhythm to each panel, and the resulting effect alternately pulls the viewers in and pushes them out. We can imagine what this engagement, this movement in and out, might have felt like with contemporary cha-cha-chá music playing in the bar.

A juxtaposition of two works on the main floor, one to the right in the hallway to the casino and the other to the left in L'Aiglon Restaurant, also provides an illuminating display of ideas of Cuban identity. Perhaps the most narrative driven and representational pieces in the hotel are the painted murals by Hipólito Hidalgo de Caviedes gracing the walls of the hotel's formal dining restaurant. Set amid the splendor of eighteenth-century French Revival chandeliers, fittings, and settings, Hidalgo de Caviedes's paintings depict historic scenes of Cuban Carnival (plate 21). Trained primarily in Spain and Berlin, Hidalgo de Caviedes moved to Cuba in 1937 because of the Spanish Civil War; he worked in Cuba and other parts of the Caribbean.

For his murals in the Havana Riviera, Hidalgo de Caviedes adopted a simplified and stylized manner to depict the figures performing various activities from playing music, flying a kite, and engaging in general revelry to standing, poised, women and men in elaborate costumes, seemingly ready to commence parading (plate 22). The simplicity of the scenes is underscored by the backgrounds, which include the minimal amount of representation needed to convey setting and, in some areas, none at all. The subject matter reinforces the festive carefree aspect of Cuban culture. In the most positive light, they reference the rich cultural traditions of carnival, similar to those in Venice, Rio de Janeiro, or New Orleans. However, negative attributes of carnival—combined with stereotypes to which many US citizens subscribed—meant that, for many US guests, these images reinforced notions of Cuba as a site of debauchery and depravity. It was, of course, a double standard. These were the exact reasons that many US travelers flocked to Havana but also the source of the severe judgment of Cuban culture and society by some.

On the other hand, Rolando López Dirube's relief sculpture *Abstracción*, which runs along the left wall of the hallway to the casino, also references Cuban culture but in a more abstract and esoteric manner (plate 23). Compared to Hidalgo de Caviedes's murals, Dirube's sculpture is more abstract and more focused on material. Composed of plaster, metal wire, and backlit resin, Dirube's mural appears at first glance to be just an abstract pattern of geometric shapes. However, upon more careful scrutiny one can observe boats and symbols. Boats have been, and still are, a rich imagery used frequently in Cuban art, in literary as well as in visual works, and one that would not hold as much meaning to someone who does not live on an island. Whether from Spain, Africa, the American colonies, the United States, China, Jamaica, or Haiti, immigrants and visitors historically came to Cuba by boat, and the countless boats that landed on its shores made possible the rich creole culture. Boats were the only way on and off the island until quite recently, relatively speaking. They were the connection to the rest of the world, they provided Cuba's main livelihood as a colony for the first two or three centuries, and they were necessary for providing the island with all it could not produce domestically. Although probably less legible to casino visitors, Dirube's mural addresses the complexity of the simple image of the boat, the complexity of which is indicated in the rich pattern of the mural.

Boats represent not only the European discovery and colonization of the island but also the more than five hundred thousand Africans who arrived by boat to Cuba's shores as slaves, who became agents and participants in the continuation of various African faiths to carry on the fundamental concepts of their native religion.[54] The result of this movement was La Regla de Ocha-Ifá or La Regla de Lukumí. As traditionally explained, the *orishas* (deities) of the Yoruba religion are coupled with various saints of the Roman Catholic religion. This was often based on visual similarities between the saints and orishas; for example, Changó, god of fire and thunder and symbol of male potency, was coupled or merged with Santa Barbara because they were both associated with wearing red and white. An African slave who identified with Changó could publicly wear or carry images of Santa Barbara. To Catholics it appeared as if they were converted to the Catholic faith, but it was really a way for practitioners of La Regla de Lukumí to keep their faith alive and proclaim it in a coded way. The boat is an important part of the representation of the Virgen de la Caridad de Cobre, for example, the patroness of Cuba who saved three Cubans who were out at sea, one of them a slave, during a storm. The Virgen de la Caridad de Cobre is associated with Ochún, a very powerful Santería orisha who is associated with love and sensuality, women, and rivers.[55]

The symbols in the sculpture also reference different aspects of Abakuá, a secret society with African roots. An all-male fraternity, the Abakuá Society was derived from the "leopard societies" from different areas of Nigeria and Cameroon and was started in Havana in 1836. One element of the Abakuá Society is the system of symbols that hold distinct meanings. Common markings symbolically represent the trade winds, the ceiba tree, crocodiles, arrows, death, rebirth, and much more. The symbols in Dirube's mural are unintelligible to the uninitiated. The oval and cross designs he employed may represent the different branches of peoples of Africa that the Abakuá was based upon or may be simply his own creations. Even if they are his inventions, they are based upon the Abakuá vocabulary of marks such as ovals, crosses, dots, and arrows, which are used to compose intelligible symbols. To the untrained viewer this work may carry little significance, but to one with even a basic understanding of this religion, the mural comes alive with powerful references.

*La Religión del Palo*, also by Rolando López Dirube, was the most prominently displayed artwork in the Havana Riviera (figure 5.4). This large-scale dynamic sculpture hung from the center of the spiral staircase located toward the back of the lobby area, centrally located near the reception desk. Although representational, it is a highly abstracted piece. The title refers to Palo, or Las Reglas de Congo, a religion that developed in Cuba mostly among slaves who came from the Congo Basin.[56] *Palo*, which means "stick" in Spanish, references the wooden sticks used in altar preparation. Basic tenets of the faith revolve around natural or earth powers and the spirits of ancestors. Like the Abakuá Society, the Palo faith uses a system of symbols, and in their form, the society and the faith are not dissimilar. Undoubtedly, guests could not have fully grasped these pieces, but one wonders what the two works by Dirube may have meant to the countless Cuban workers who were familiar with or practitioners of these religions. The Havana Riviera contained more imagery of Cuban culture than guests could comprehend.

Figure 5.4. Upward view of the sculpture *La Religión del Palo* by Rolando López Dirube, with the grand staircase wrapping around it. Located in the lobby area of the Havana Riviera Hotel. 1986-222-340, Annette and Rudi Rada Photographs Collection, HistoryMiami Museum.

Like Eduardo Abelo, member of the vanguardia who painted *El Triunfo de la Rumba*, Dirube was a white Cuban.[57] This fact complicates our understanding of his work in the Havana Riviera. Although his work is representing the cultural diversity of Cuba, we have to wonder in what ways it is problematic for someone like Dirube to be working not only on themes associated with Afro-Cuban religions but also to such a depth as to indicate an understanding of secret symbolic systems. Although he may have had genuine intentions of honoring these faiths through his work, he was also profiting from their use, and it is quite possible that practitioners of these religions were offended by these artworks.

Entering into the hotel from this perspective allows for a useful reevaluation of the spiral staircase and sculpture, which are often regarded as simply a cheap imitation of Morris Lapidus's "stairs to nowhere" in the 1954 Fontainebleau Hotel in

Miami. First, the nickname given to Lapidus's staircase is not accurate as it actually does lead somewhere (though just to a cloakroom). Although the Fontainebleau's interior design does not follow the traditional layout of a grand staircase in a hotel leading to important areas such as a ballroom or a restaurant, the design incorporates the staircase as a stage for the spectacle of guests descending into the lobby. Second, the two are formally very different. Lapidus's staircase hugs a curved wall, which was decorated with an oversized reprint of Giovanni Battista Piranesi's 1772 etching *View of Campo Vaccino*. The Havana Riviera staircase avoids reference to styles of the past. The light treads with open backs warrant more comparison with the Caribe Hilton than with the Fontainebleau. In a time when high-rise hotels were serviced by elevators and open sprawling pedestal forms allowed for a single floor of public spaces, the staircase and sculpture combination was an ingenious design addition. In fact, in the Havana Riviera, the staircase and sculpture create one unified artwork, it is impossible to tell if the staircase complements the sculpture or vice versa. Referencing the grand staircases of the great hotels of the past, the design also reveals the antiquity of the concept of the grand staircase by rendering the staircase as nothing more than a sculpture. This was modern art best complemented by modern design.

Although perhaps not as obvious, other aspects of the lobby proclaim the cubanidad of the hotel. In general, Cuban society embraced the modern design of midcentury. The large boom in residential building meant that many middle- and upper-class Cubans were looking to match their interior design to their now modern home, and there was a general high literacy in terms of design in Havana in this period. Like architecture, interiors were a way for Cubans to proclaim their modernity and their participation in a global world of design and commerce. The Havana Riviera's use of modern furniture not only mirrored general furniture trends in Havana but also did this by using Cuban materials and Cuban-produced designs.

As one enters through the front door, the lobby walls stretched in front, alternating between panels of decorative concrete grilles and marble panels that were produced in Cuba out of Cuban materials (see figure 5.3). The use of this marble presents a striking contrast to other approaches to materials in hotel design. Whereas luxury was usually expressed through imported materials such as marble from Italy, the Havana Riviera did not take the standard path of relying on the cache of iconic foreign luxury materials, a practice particularly popular in hotel design. Instead, the Havana Riviera worked to connect notions of luxury with Cuba itself, by displaying Cuban marble in the same fashion as Italian marble would be implemented in design.

Although US furniture, and modern furniture at that, was locally available (a Knoll store and a shop that carried Herman Miller furniture were located within

Figure 5.5. Interior lobby area of the Havana Riviera Hotel, showing modern Cuban furniture, with ocean visible in the background, ca. 1957. Havana, Cuba. Photograph by Rudi Rada, 8 x 10 inches. 1986-222-325, Igor B. Polevitzky Photographs Collection, HistoryMiami Museum.

the city limits), all of the modern furniture in the main lobby was made in Cuba (figure 5.5). This is notable since postwar Cuban culture subscribed to a US notion of modernity, and Cubans had ready access to a wide array of US goods. Despite the heavy reliance on US imports, however, within the architecture and design community there was keen interest in developing design, including furniture, on the island. The Cuban design journal *Espacio* indicates that there were at least two furniture design studios in Havana in the 1950s, and *Espacio* and *Arquitectura* both fostered a dialogue between Cuban architecture and furniture design during this period. This is all the more notable when compared to Miami, another major city in the area, which did not have a modern design store until the Arango Design Store opened in 1959.[58]

Research in the interiors and the furniture reveals how pushing beyond dominant, and still prioritized, methods of research into other types of archives and ways of valuing information can help us write more nuanced histories. In this case, it is worth detailing the research as it reveals just how much the traditional archive privileges US voices over Cuban ones. Although there was an emphasis on Cuban materials, furniture, and artwork in the main public areas of the Havana Riviera, it seems striking that in documents Alvin Parvin, of the Parvin-Dohrmann Company of Los Angeles, is listed as being responsible for designing all of the furniture in the hotel.[59] Parvin, who had designed other hotels in Las Vegas, surely had established means for producing his designs for those hotels in the United States. However, it would have been a daunting task for him to make all of these new connections and business arrangements in a foreign country. The Parvin-Dohrmann Company may have been listed officially as head of interior design, but it is more probable that there was a local designer or design firm associated with the project, a ubiquitous practice in Cuba when foreign architects or designers came in to complete projects.[60]

Typical of performing research in Cuba, where there tends to be very little preserved documentation pertaining to these projects, much of the history of twentieth-century architecture in Cuba exists as oral histories that have yet to be recorded and often cannot be verified against archival documents. This is the case with the Havana Riviera. Architect Daniel Bejerano was responsible for the restoration of the hotel in the 1990s, which was the most historically accurate restoration of the hotel to date. The research necessary for the restoration made Bejerano the authority on the hotel's design and history, and he asserts that the furniture was made in Cuba. Given that he knows how to accurately mine the somewhat scholarly unorthodox avenues of information in Cuba, his account is likely the most accurate one.[61]

The furniture in the main lobby area was typical of midcentury design. Long, low-slung couches filled the area with simple lines and neat angular forms. These were complemented by equally minimal and low-slung coffee tables, decorated with organically shaped, abstract marble sculptures. Some tropical vegetation was incorporated into the space, neatly contained in rectangular planters built into the center of stone benches. While an open plan defined the main floor, the lobby lounge area was clearly demarcated through the arrangement of the cubic furniture, which clearly delimited the space.

## *The Politics of Reception*

The name of the hotel played no small part in shaping the hotel's identity and that of Havana and Cuba more broadly. Riviera, of course, refers to the chic coastal portion of France to which many aspired to travel. It was a nice complement to Havana's moniker as the "Paris of the Caribbean." The sophistication and glamor of Paris and the French Riviera were borrowed and attached to Havana and the Havana Riviera hotel. The hotel's tagline, "Havana in the Grand Manner," underscored this association, positioning the Havana Riviera as the key element in experiencing the ultimate in Caribbean vacationing (see plate 19). French references were sprinkled throughout the hotel, from the Regency style fittings that decorated parts of the hotel to the restaurant and bar names such as L'Aiglon Restaurant and L'Elegante Bar. The interest in emphasizing the French theme in the hotel is apparent in the name of L'Elegante Bar. The "e" at the end is not grammatical in French, but to US visitors it makes the word seem foreign. The Havana Riviera carefully blended French sophistication, modernist design, and Cuban culture in its architecture and design to give US guests a perfectly constructed vision of life in Havana, a life that was very different from that lived by Cubans. The combination of furniture, materials, and artworks that composed the interior design created a spatial and visual experience of cubanidad, which was defined by attention to its cultural heritage and natural resources.

Although it is true that high-rise resort hotel building did boom in Miami earlier in the decade than in Havana, hotel architecture in Havana was not a lazy copy of Miami instances. Designs tended to be more thoughtful and less kitschy in Cuba because there was a stronger sense of cultural identity and a commitment to engaging with it through art and design. Miami, on the other hand, always struggled to develop a clear identity to project to the rest of the world. Florida promoters could not entice people with an exotic culture, as south Florida was part of the United States and was understood to no longer have any deeply rooted culture.[62] What differentiated Florida the most was its climate, and images of sunshine, palms, and oranges were commonly evoked.[63] Hotels in Florida often relied upon a variety of adopted themes to offer an alternative to cultural experience. Some touched on potentially valid historic topics that were, however, grossly exaggerated, like pirate themes. Others blatantly had nothing to do with Florida, such as Polynesian themes and the French Baroque styling of the Fontainebleau. One hotel that was perhaps an attempt to situate Florida within the greater context of the Americas was Morris Lapidus's 1955 Americana hotel in Bal Harbour, Florida (unfortunately demolished in 2007). The hotel's location in a US state was recognized in the interior decoration, which explicitly referenced various part of the United States. In addition, the concept of Miami as connected with and similar to Central and South American was showcased through designs that focused on tropical vegetation or on the cultures of these regions. In this sense, the design echoed a larger tendency in the period to promote Miami as a crossroads in the Pan-American world or even as a truly Pan-American city.

Unfortunately, observations about the extensive engagement and display of Cuban culture in the Havana Riviera's design have really only been made in retrospect. During this period, the architectural world was firmly under the influence of the European avant-garde and the ideas of such critics as Henry-Russell Hitchcock and Siegfried Giedion. This group promoted a definition of modernism that would have relegated a great deal of the Havana Riviera to kitsch design. More recently, a group of scholars with more wide-ranging and less Western-centric views of design have reappraised designs such as that of the Havana Riviera.

US publications of the period acknowledged the innovative architecture of the Havana Riviera, which they tied to a growing internationalism in the city.[64] Despite US newspaper headlines such as "Cuba's Newest Hotel Brings Tropical Beauty Indoors," it was the gambling and other illicit activities offered by the Havana Riviera—"a self-contained orbit for the pleasure seeker"—that were highlighted in the articles.[65] Indeed, once construction began, the image of the hotel was marred by the image of Cuba as the playground of the United States. The tourism and the hotels that were developed under the corruption of Batista's dictatorship catapulted gambling, prostitution, drinking, and drug use to new levels in the country.[66] After the Cuban Revolution, Fidel Castro positioned the Havana Riviera and other postwar hotels, as well as the Tropicana and other places of entertainment, as symbols of the deleterious effects of US imperialism, and they were leveraged to denounce the Batista government and its relationship with the United States.

Castro argued that Batista's approach to tourism was deeply corrupt and poisonous to Cuban culture and society. These claims echoed others about the Batista regime. Castro did not blame everything on Batista; he also faulted the United States for Cuba's problems. He held the United States accountable for doing business with and supporting a dictator such as Batista in order to continue the legacy of US imperialism on the island, and he condemned the behavior of US tourists in Havana for the deleterious effect it had on Cuban society.[67] Castro associated the ills of capitalism—greed, corruption, gambling, drug and alcohol abuse, and prostitution—with the places where he felt this took place: casinos, cabarets, and hotels. These spaces were also tainted because most of them were owned or operated by US businessmen, many of whom

Figure 5.6. During the Revolution in 1959, Cubans took to the streets and looted and burned casino equipment. Photograph by Fernando Lezcano taken January 1, 1959. Courtesy of Lezcano/AP.

were mobsters, and because these spaces seemed to epitomize the imposition of US interests in Cuba. Every US business operating in Cuba meant one less business run by a Cuban. Castro's revolution aimed to take back Cuba for the Cubans.

In the second half of the 1950s, hotels, nightclubs, and casinos became symbolic to many Cubans of all that was wrong in the country, and throughout the revolutionary struggle many actions played out in these spaces as a means to reclaim them for the Cuban people (figure 5.6). After Castro's government was firmly in place in 1959, these buildings continued to carry the negative connotations that developed during the revolutionary fight and those connotations have been solidified in Cuban discourse. With his rise to power, Castro strategically reclaimed these sites of US imperialism for the Cuban people. Most famously, he set up temporary headquarters in the Havana Hilton. A fact less known is that Castro repurposed the Copa Room at the Havana Riviera, the space used for the cabaret shows, and hosted a press conference there shortly after taking power. During this press conference he underscored the popular nature of the Revolution and its commitment to having the Cuban people determine their own destiny and reject foreign interference. Moreover, the Castro regime legally reclaimed these sites through nationalization of these businesses and buildings. In the process, the Castro regime solidified an understanding of the design of these hotels as insignificant or harmful. In particular, the design of the Havana Riviera has been described as everything from thoughtless, to kitsch, to an imitation of Miami design, but most commonly it is referred to as all three—thoughtless Miami kitsch. The Havana Riviera was referred to simplistically as an example of imported Miami design, a characterization that served a larger program of vilifying all things associated with the United States. As a result, the notion of the interior design as an exploration of Cuban identity was erased from discourse.

We have much to lose by continuing to subscribe to these appraisals. The current state of tourism reveals the inherent conflict in this simplistic understanding of the Havana Riviera's design and suggests a shift in attitude toward an appreciation bordering on respect of these designs. The Cuban government has restored the Havana Riviera's interiors to closely resemble their original appearance. Relatively faithful restoration allows the Cuban state, which owns the building, to profit from tourists' desires to experience a particular representation of Havana. Capturing the original 1950s design in many ways sensationalizes for touristic consumption the history of the mob and of corruption in Havana and, in so doing, legitimizes the Revolution's fight against it. The state's control over these sites renders them ideologically safe—they are relics of a time passed, a past that the state can parade as being over and done, beaten, with no fear of it returning.

What we need to remember is that, at the time of its construction, the Havana Riviera promoted modern design as something that was not foreign, that was part of local practices, and that was, above all, desirable, given the state's and much of the general population's support in the project of coloniality/modernity. In many ways, the hotels built in the 1950s represented the strong ties of Cuba to the economy and culture of the United States and beyond, demonstrating Cuba's struggle to propose and realize its own national identity, which was not always at odds with US attributes or modernity and was also understood as internationally situated. The significance of the Havana Riviera's design lies in its existence within competing, and at times conflicting, discursive agendas. This is evidenced by the numerous agents—US and insular governments, designers and artists, owners and operators, guests and workers—who were involved in the creation and life of these midcentury hotels and who realized the power of design in projecting identity and shaping international and cross-cultural encounters and opinions.

Plate 14. Postcard of the Caribe Hilton with Fortín de San Gerónimo in the foreground on the left and historic San Juan in the background at the top. The Hotel Normandie is behind the Caribe Hilton to the right. Author's collection.

Plate 15. Brochure for the Caribe Hilton. Hospitality Industry Archives, Conrad Hilton College, University of Houston.

Plate 16. Postcard of the Aruba Caribbean Hotel, designed by Morris Lapidus, opened 1959, Noord, Aruba. Author's collection.

Plate 17. *Visit Cuba: So Near Yet So Foreign*. Postcard by Conrado Walter Massagüer. Instituto Cubano del Turismo, Havana, Cuba. Author's collection.

Plate 18. Cover of guidebook *Cuba, Ideal Vacation Land: Tourist Guide*, by Conrado Walter Massagüer, 1955–1956. 7.4 x 5.5 inches. Instituto Cubano del Turismo, Havana, Cuba. Gift of Vicki Gold Levi, XC2002.11.4.246. The Wolfsonian–Florida International University, Miami Beach, Florida.

Plate 19. Clipping of advertisement for the Havana Riviera Hotel, Cabana Club & Casino, 1955. Gift of Vicki Gold Levi, XC2002.11.4.268. The Wolfsonian–Florida International University, Miami Beach, Florida.

Plate 20. View of the Carlton Terrace Apartments, 1956, Bal Harbour, Florida. 1986-222-713, Igor B. Polevitzky Photographs Collection, HistoryMiami Museum.

Plate 21. Hipólito Hidalgo de Caviedes, mural in L'Aiglon Restaurant in the Havana Riviera, ca. 1957. Author's collection.

Plate 22. Hipólito Hidalgo de Caviedes, mural in L'Aiglon Restaurant in the Havana Riviera, ca. 1957. Author's collection.

Plate 23. Rolando López Dirube, *Abstracción*, ca. 1957. Mixed media. Photograph courtesy José Quevedo.

Plate 24. Carolina Caycedo, *The People of Puerto Rico Is Justly Indebted*, 2020. From the series Distressed Debt. Digital print on silk, 98.5 x 53 inches. Courtesy of the artist.

Plate 25. Carolina Caycedo, *Let Us Tell You about the Bonds of Puerto Rico*, 2020. From the series Distressed Debt. Digital print on silk, 98.5 x 53 inches. Courtesy of the artist.

# Conclusion

# *Development Persistent*

### Familiar Constants and New Forms

**Brightly colored and detailed with images, frames, and seals, bonds are the** focus of artist Carolina Caycedo's *Distressed Debt* series. Comprised of a number of collages, the series takes the materiality of historical municipal government and corporate bonds from the 1800s to the 1970s as matter to reveal concerns about debt and bonds in the contemporary world and their historical relationship to slavery. Indeed, the term "bond" as used in the financial world in fact comes from the word "bondage" in reference to slavery, as the first bonds were used to mortgage slaves to other individuals or companies.[1] Through the visual imagery of bonds, Caycedo draws forth a troubled history of how this earlier practice of slavery-related bonds continued to support the modernity/coloniality project through to the present. Caycedo associates this with a financial slavery and oppression for some states, such as Puerto Rico, which has fifteen times the bond debt of other states in the contiguous United States. When credit agencies downgraded numerous bond issues to junk status in 2014, Puerto Rico entered a debt crisis. With their debt bought, sold, and valued by others, so much of the financial fate of a state such as Puerto Rico lies outside its control.

Caycedo's work points to the connection between financial histories or contexts and Puerto Rican identity through formal imagery such as seals, shields, and insignias as well as more popular imagery. For example, her work includes a 1952 Puerto Rican bond for five thousand dollars to support a public works series, and an irrigation work in particular. Depicting predominantly Black folks working in a cane field, the image plays with notions of history, perhaps suggesting a timelessness of cane cultivation in Puerto Rico, as the scene could just as easily be found in the 1950s as in the 1850s (plate 24). Whether depicting past or present, these intricately designed pieces of paper represent value and real changes to the built environment of a place. Thinking through words the way Caycedo does (from bonds to the bondage of slavery, for example), one way to view these objects is to view the Puerto Rican government as selling itself into slavery for the sake of development. These complex and unequal flows of capital and power are, as Caycedo notes, couched in terms such as "trust" and "bond," which we think we understand, but which contribute to a "tyrannical" financial world that creates loopholes for those with power to avoid accountability.[2]

In one work from the series *Let Us Tell You about the Bonds of Puerto Rico*, Caycedo squarely locates the intersection of the notion of Puerto Rico as a space of leisure and tourism with financial investment (plate 25). Tourist and investor are conflated in the words from the bond campaign that Caycedo has placed in large type within the work: "If you think the charm of Puerto Rico is unique, let us tell you about the bonds of Puerto Rico." A 1970s project of the Banco Gubernamental de Fomento para Puerto Rico (Puerto Rico Government Development Bank), the campaign suggests that all of Puerto Rico is attractive and up for grabs.[3] Bonds, piña coladas, urban works, and sandy beaches all collapse into one large phenomenon of consumption. The artwork reminds viewers of tourism's role in financial markets and in the complex and diverse ways that slavery, colonialism, imperialism, tourism, modernity, and tropical paradise are woven together across time.

## *Thinking Across, Together, Against*

Recognizing Puerto Rico, the Dominican Republic, and Cuba as centers of creative hotel design is a corrective to traditional approaches that would consider innovative design as always produced in specific "central" areas and merely copied or reproduced in other marginal areas around the globe. The Grand Condado Vanderbilt, a hotel that at first glance seems to reinforce colonialist histories of empire, was integrated into larger suburban development projects, specifically the development of Condado, an area conceived for the upper-class inhabitants of San Juan. Although many may have seen the hotel as an imposition of the influence of contiguous-US business interests, the situation is more complicated than that, as history also shows how the city took on the hotel as a symbol of its modernity and good taste. Upper-class Puerto Ricans, especially those living in Condado, likely invoked the Grand Condado Vanderbilt as one example of movement toward modernity. Years later, the perceived power of the Grand Condado Vanderbilt to function as a symbol of the island—and by extension the power of a symbol to raise the economic situation of the island—shines through at the moment when the local government fought to purchase the hotel with federal government funds. Although nothing came from this campaign, the episode sets the stage for later moments in government-sponsored hotel building while also reminding us of how the project of coloniality/modernity forms the backbone of tourism development for all of the local governments covered in this study.

In recognizing that hotel design was a potent form of soft power, these government officials and hotel owners had to support designs that made a statement. As a result, the strikingly extravagant hotels that were built had an impact beyond San Juan, Ciudad Trujillo, and Havana. Images of these hotels spread throughout the world. The view of these hotel designs as being globally influential stems in part from the local governments' promotion of hotel building as a practice for identity projection as well as an opportunity for economic profit. In all of the case studies explored in this book, insular government officials recognized the value not just of investing in tourism but of supporting the hotel design of grand suburban resorts as a means to project a national identity. Of course, in each hotel the particular image of national identity was different, was not always supported by the citizens, and negotiated a fine line between conveying an image that maintained self-respect and one that met tourist expectations. In all cases, however, the projected image was defined by categories of the modern, the historic, and the tropical—to varying extents and in varying forms and combinations.

Projection of national identity was not just about empty symbols. In all these cases, tangible material development was happening on a large scale, and it was through these projects, leveraged by governments to evidence modernity through development, that development becomes associated, and often to no small extent, with national identity. In tandem with other projects tied to national identity, coloniality becomes once again forcefully reasserted. This not only insists that Western-style modernity is the only path forward but, as Maldonado-Torres articulates, also reinscribes coloniality and its understandings of race and gender that result from the "naturalization of the non-ethics of war." In articulating the *ego conquiro*, which predates René Descartes's *ego cogito*, Maldonado-Torres explains how the ego conquiro and the project of colonization stand on doubt or skepticism that allows for the questioning of the humanity of colonized peoples. Concepts of race and gender are deployed to create formulas that not only justify colonization but continue to undergird coloniality and modernity.[4]

As these case studies show, we cannot view the agents involved in these projects and their interests in absolute terms. Although the different governments were involved to varying degrees—whether sponsoring the project (Hotel Nacional, Hotel Jaragua, and Caribe Hilton), providing legislation that encouraged private business (Havana Riviera), or approving urban development plans that were attractive to hotel developers (Grand Condado Vanderbilt)—they were only one component in a complex set of relationships among multiple agents. These case studies illustrate that, in addition to the local governments, there were local business interests, US business interests, tourism boosters (both local and US-sponsored), tourists, and locals all playing a part in the conception and the life of these hotels. Each hotel reveals a unique mix of these agents and their connections to the hotel design, revealing how various and often differing interests are manifest in the building's design. For example, the Caribe Hilton's "ultra-modern" form reveals the unwillingness of the Puerto Rican government to consider Conrad Hilton's preference for a Mediterranean Revival design; in the case of the Havana Riviera, the Cuban government can only claim a role in the design insofar as legislation stipulated the construction cost minimums and allowed tall buildings. The complex relationships among different people and entities complicate traditional histories that would suggest unidirectional flows of influence, whether in terms of the politics, economics, or architecture.

In tracing the themes of the modern, the tropical, and the historic across all the case studies, continuity, rather than rupture, shines through, which we can read, I contend, as reflecting tourism's position within the modernity/coloniality project. The major shift in thinking about the modern is in how the modern should look. Connotations of hygiene embodied in the wicker furniture of the Grand Condado Vanderbilt were replaced with the easy-to-clean forms of Jens Risom's chairs in guest rooms at the Caribe Hilton. The aesthetic was different, but the goal was the same. The unornamented cubic forms and open plan of the International Style inspired modernism of the Hotel Jaragua, the Caribe Hilton, and the Havana Riviera replaced the Beaux Arts design of the Grand Condado Vanderbilt and the Hotel Nacional. Both approaches were concerned with functionality and efficiency—they just came in different "packaging." From this perspective, we can start to rethink traditional understandings of architectural modernism.

## CONCLUSION: DEVELOPMENT PERSISTENCE

The contrast between the architecture of the Grand Condado Vanderbilt and the Havana Riviera, for example, becomes less pronounced when we consider style as only one aspect of the design to be analyzed.

The notion of the tropical is embedded in all these hotels, and although it takes on different visual forms, at the core the various representations are all concerned with expressing an exoticness or otherness, largely through an emphasis on vegetation and climate. As hotels had to convey tropicality in a manner that did not overwhelm their guests, visual forms reinforced that modern man (and indeed, the image was quite intentionally gendered) had control over tropicality. For example, the Grand Condado Vanderbilt had gardens organized in neat rectilinear forms representing control, while bedside table consoles in the Caribe Hilton were meant to demonstrate how tropicality could be manipulated and fused with modern design. The containment of vegetation and more conceptual notions of the tropical alike underscored the idea that man had tamed tropicality.

All the hotels addressed notions of the tropical from a climatic standpoint through their design. The way the designs did this ranges from the Hotel Nacional's canvas overhangs and the Caribe Hilton's concrete grills, which both provided shade, to the Grand Condado Vanderbilt's open loggias and the Havana Riviera's air-conditioning, which both provided cooler air inside the public areas of the hotels. Tropical climate was also referenced in other design details. Historic styles that referenced the Mediterranean, North Africa, or the Middle East carried with them the connotations of the warmer climes associated with those places. Furniture that incorporated native materials such as the mahogany furniture in the Hotel Nacional and the ARKLU furniture that incorporated native woods and fibers also reminded guests of their temporary presence in a tropical location.

Engagement with notions of the historic was a key counterpoint to the modernity proposed by these hotels. The Grand Condado Vanderbilt and the Hotel Nacional took on the concept of the historic in a more visual and literal way in the hotel design through their historicist architecture. This, however, was not a slavish re-creation of a specific historical style; rather, it was an adoption and a fusion of various aspects of different historical styles in order to create a unique design. The reinterpretation, as opposed to copying, of historical styles visually signified modern design. The designs gave visitors a taste of the Spanish colonial past through tile work, exposed wood roof beams, or colonial style furniture, but that was not the only design factor. This sample spoonful allowed just enough of the historic; for, just like the tropical, the historic could not be overwhelming or else visitors would fear for their safety in that foreign place.

## CONCLUSION: DEVELOPMENT PERSISTENCE

Engagement with the Spanish colonial past, largely through the built environment of a colonial zone or other monuments, squarely located insular narratives of history as white while sidelining any Black, Indigenous, or Asian legacies or current presence. In the case of the Caribe Hilton, the historic was not located within the architecture or the interior design of the hotel but, rather, was positioned as a contrast or complement to the hotel through historic structures and spaces that were both geographically and discursively connected to the hotel. In terms of geography, Fortín de San Gerónimo, located right next to the hotel, offered a foil to the new modern Caribe Hilton. Promotional materials reveal to us the importance of the restoration of San Juan Viejo in the 1950s and its packaging as a tourist site. Historic San Juan Viejo was often discussed in brochures and flyers right next to the Caribe Hilton. Together, the two proposed to the potential tourist the complete package—accommodations in a modern hotel and daily sightseeing in the historic city center. The brochures may have been taking a cue from Trujillo's triangulation of the Hotel Jaragua in relation to the colonial zone in Ciudad Trujillo. In Cuba, the historic was addressed less through contrast with the modern and more by incorporating the themes of heritage and tradition into new, modern designs. In all three cities, colonial zones were interpreted primarily in terms of Spanish colonial history. Narratives revolved around the romantic conquest by Christopher Columbus and the daring feats of pirates, not the ways in which these places were established and exploited for profit from the (usually forced) labor of Black, Indigenous, and Asian people. In setting up these simplistic and straightforward histories, these narratives also legitimized the current structure of coloniality and offered assurances of unproblematic presents and futures.

The historic was not only leveraged as a past that was employed as a foil to the present. The Havana Riviera hotel positioned the notion of cubanidad as both dynamic and evolving. through Cuban avant-garde art that touched on aspects of Cuban heritage, with a particular emphasis on the packaging of the marginalized sphere of Afro-Cuban religions for guest consumption. In this case, cubanidad thrives on continuation and the constant evolution of heritage. However, its heavy reliance on Afro-Cuban culture reveals a slippage that invites us to consider racial power dynamics and the trope of non-Western groups as "timeless." Although we can problematize how different agents engaged with the historic, at the time of the hotels' construction, government leaders, hotel operators, and tourism boosters sought to project simplified, carefree, and engaging representations of the historic. Indeed, conveying appealing notions of the historic was a significant goal of hotel owners and government officials as it was a major attraction for tourists and a means to promote national identity programs. In this respect, San Juan, Ciudad Trujillo, and Havana, with their rich histories and cultures, had an advantage over other tropical destinations such as Florida, which struggled to find a way to define itself in the absence of significant marketable heritage.

## *Development Revised*

Although consistencies in hotel building continued to a certain extent and tourism marched on in one form or another, there is a moment around 1960 that also marks a turning point in tourism on the islands. In the 1960s, Puerto Rico underwent a shift consistent with other trends in the Caribbean toward developing ex-urban, beach-oriented, all-inclusive resorts while still targeting the US market. Predictably, this shift had a profound effect on hotel building on the island. In the Dominican Republic, tourism did not flourish during the later years of the Trujillo regime, and it was only with new leadership in the 1960s and a focus on ex-urban resort tourism that it became a central industry. In Cuba, there was a dramatic turn after 1959. As relations deteriorated with the United States, Fidel Castro's government focused on developing vacationing in Cuba primarily for Cuban citizens.[5]

The example of the Dorado Beach Resort in Puerto Rico illustrates one major trend in tourism development in the Hispanic Caribbean—the shift to an inward-looking format that was removed from local engagement. Since the 1940s, Laurence and Nelson Rockefeller had been interested in tourism, especially decentralized tourism, as a means to improve relations between Latin American countries and the United States and to promote private contiguous-US business in Latin America. Laurence Rockefeller formed a company called RockResorts with the intent to build decentralized, nature-centered resorts starting first in the Caribbean. After converting an old sugar plantation in St. John into the Caneel Bay Resort (1956), Rockefeller turned toward Puerto Rico in a move that also reaffirmed the family's commitment to assisting with the economic development of Puerto Rico.[6] In 1953, Teodoro Moscoso introduced Laurence Rockefeller to the estate of Alfred T. Livingston, which had already been chosen by golf course architect Robert Trent Jones Sr. as the site of a golf course, and Rockefeller bought the 225 acres of beachfront property. The new Dorado Beach Resort opened in December 1958, partially funded by loans from the Puerto Rican government. No matter whether government funding was involved, an increase in foreign companies entering in the resort business defined this shift throughout the Hispanic Caribbean.[7]

## CONCLUSION: DEVELOPMENT PERSISTENCE

As historian Evan Ward asserts, these first two RockResorts were pioneering in the field of low-density resort design, an approach that would become the dominant trend.[8] Focusing on nature as the central theme of a relaxing vacation, Rockefeller strove to blend the modern cottages, beach houses, and auxiliary buildings, as well as the renovated extant plantation building, with the natural setting. There was a stress on horizontal rather than vertical development and an attempt to remove from view all references to modern civilization, such as telephone wires. Guests still enjoyed all the amenities of modern living, however, including air-conditioning in all rooms. Designed by the New York architectural firm Goldstone and Dearborn, the new buildings were predominantly two stories high and were expressed in a tropical modern style in the footsteps of earlier work by Toro y Ferrer. The architecture emphasized balconies, in order to take advantage of breezes, as well as brise-soleils to provide ventilation and shade. The extant buildings of the Livingston estate were from the 1930s, and Rockefeller kept their Spanish Colonial style. From its opening, the Dorado Beach Resort was a success, and Rockefeller immediately began thinking of an expansion. Toro y Ferrer designed additional buildings for the complex in keeping with the low-slung horizontal profile of the resort; one hundred more rooms were added between 1959 and 1962, and another seventy-two were added between 1964 and 1966.

It is worth lingering for a moment on the fact that this resort is located on the grounds of a former plantation, and the renovated plantation structures serve as the main core of the public spaces of the hotel. Here the plantation becomes commodified and incorporated into the vacation experience and the colonial/imperial past and present becomes romanticized. However, it is not too long a leap to move from the enslavement and forced labor of the past—and the racism that is born out of the justification of these social relations—to the service industry that operates in this space as it takes on its resort form. This is not specific to RockResorts, Puerto Rico, or even the Hispanic Caribbean (Jamaica Kincaid eloquently describes this phenomenon in her local Antigua), and it extends beyond to other Caribbean locales.

Rockefeller still had much bigger ideas, and he partnered with Eastern Airlines in 1967 to create the high-rise Cerromar Beach Hotel as a new addition to the Dorado Beach Resort. Designed in a modernist idiom that by then was the norm for hotel design, the new addition to the complex was an eight-story hotel with 503 rooms and suites designed specifically with conferences in mind. Opened in 1972, the Cerromar Beach Hotel was poles apart from the intimate beach houses and cottages of the Dorado Beach Resort, and the large number of rooms it offered were ill timed with the general oversupply of rooms in San Juan combined with the slump in tourism that occurred in Puerto Rico after 1969. The practice of high-rise building was not unique, however, and others of this type popped up elsewhere in San Juan, Havana, and Santo Domingo.

## *The Modern Becomes Historic and Other Tales of Preservation*

No longer considered new, all the hotels under study here have taken on changed roles, and many have been utilized to create new historical narratives. These hotels have been neglected, abandoned, destroyed, or rehabilitated in varying ways, reflecting how those subsequently in power understood the hotels and their contexts and how that understanding related, or not, to more contemporary values and concerns. At the beginning of 2014, one of the most notable of the modernist hotels constructed in the 1950s, the Hotel Capri, reopened its doors in Havana. Built in late 1957, the tall, slim hotel occupies a portion of a city block located close to the Hotel Nacional at the corner of Calles 21 and N. Funded by Miami hoteliers and mobsters, the Hotel Capri was conceived as a way to take advantage of Batista's Ley de Hoteles 2074, which was also utilized at the Havana Riviera. Cuban architect José Canaves Ugalde designed the nineteen-floor hotel with a rooftop pool as a design solution to address the limited footprint of the hotel. The idea of "swimming in the sky" was an attractive modern addition to the modern styling of a hotel devoted primarily to promoting gambling in its casino.

The notorious gangsters who ran the hotel and casino left when Castro came to power, and the hotel subsequently became property of the state. The Hotel Capri became run-down and shabby over time, like other hotels of the 1950s, as these structures and international tourism were simply not a priority of the Castro regime. In 1997, militant anti-Castro exiles detonated a bomb in the lobby, inflicting even more damage to the aging hotel. The hotel finally closed its doors in the early 2000s and then, during the same decade, underwent renovation and restoration efforts.

The new Hotel Capri that has reopened is a model example of the current government's approach to hotel design and tourism. Like the majority of hotels on the island, the Hotel Capri is a joint business venture between the state and a foreign operating company (in this case the Spanish hotel chain NH Hoteles SA), in which the Cuban government retains a majority share of the business.[9] In a totalitarian state, the government ultimately retains control over everything, and with this in mind we can look at what the design of the hotel suggests about current attitudes concerning national identity.

The Cuban government has finally embraced the economic opportunities of taking what was once modern—the hotels of the 1950s—and packaging them as historic entities for tourists with a hunger for nostalgia. In an ironic move, the Cuban government now financially profits from packaging and selling a part of Cuban history that they had struggled to quash with the Revolution in 1959. This move is possible, and comfortable, for the Cuban government because there is no fear of a return to the Havana of the 1950s, which, after more than fifty years of communism/socialism, is not felt to be a huge threat to the regime's maintenance of power. Indeed, the ability to package and sell this history, something that can only be done after enough time has elapsed, most likely makes the current government feel even more secure, as it creates even more distance between the pre-communist past and the socialist present.

In renovating the hotel, designers have restored and preserved a number of original pieces such as the lobby chandeliers and the lobby desk, in order to maintain the 1950s feel. This decade is historicized in the old Havana cityscape photos that decorate the guest rooms and is rendered glamorous as a means for the government to profit. However, concern has also been to produce a modern hotel. New amenities such as Wi-Fi have been incorporated into the hotel. In a country with antiquated public telecommunications technology, an element such as Wi-Fi is no small detail. Likewise, the rooftop pool, restored and reopened, provides guests with the reminder that they are in a tropical setting.

The Hotel Capri demonstrates how what was once the modern or contemporary has now been fixed into a consumable past. The midcentury past is contrasted with modern amenities that meet the expectations of today's tourists such as high-speed Internet and Wi-Fi, spas, and fitness centers. The mid-century historicism of these hotels is complemented by continued efforts to restore and preserve colonial centers, which have become even more important with the growing interest in cultural and heritage tourism. In the present context, guests find that these hotels meet their present-day expectations while simultaneously guests can also experience the historic. The hotels represent a layered concept of history to twenty-first-century guests who stay in these twentieth-century hotels and who visit historic zones that represent an earlier colonial moment. Preserved to a great extent in their original forms, modernist hotels such as the Hotel Capri continue to convey notions of the tropical through their emphasis on tropical vegetation and vistas and their architectural features that highlight climate, such as concrete screens and blurred distinctions between interior and exterior.

## CONCLUSION: DEVELOPMENT PERSISTENCE

The attack on the Hotel Capri in 1997 earns its place in a larger phenomenon of terrorist attacks that take place at hotels. Between 2002 and 2011, eighteen major terrorist attacks against hotels occurred worldwide with the opportunity for mass casualty cited as the motivating factor.[10] Notably, many hotels that have suffered attacks are part of recognizable chains associated with the United States, such as Marriott, Intercontinental, Hilton, and Days Inn, and many of these hotels cater to westerners. One cannot help but wonder if—or even assume that—US global imperialism in its many forms played into the decision to select these hotels as targets. US imperialism and the machadato's relationship with the United States certainly played into the decision to attack the Hotel Nacional in the Revolution of 1933.

That hotels are targets for terrorist attacks reveals how politically charged these structures are. Although, in some cases, they are seen by locals as an imposition of a foreign influence, many hotels reflect local influence, which shapes attitudes and opinions of guests and locals as well. Even given mixed opinions on the value of tourism, it is still seen as a form of development, which is also contested. Thanks to histories such as those of the Hispanic Caribbean, people are increasingly questioning tourism and development more broadly. To that end, design has played a potent role in tourism, and a critical engagement with the role that tourism design plays in shaping foreign relations, global economics, identity politics, and cultural exchange is important for understanding the past, present, and possible future. It is within the seemingly trivial details such as wicker furniture, neo-Plateresque ornamentation, indoor ponds, and artwork by local artists that attitudes and opinions about a place and culture are shaped. The seemingly carefree vacations of tropical ambiance and colonial charm in the Caribbean are so much more than they appear at first glance, and Hispanic Caribbean hotel design has shaped attitudes and practices in ways that continue to resonate today.

# Notes

**Introduction: Development Begun**

1. Joiri Minaya, *I can wear tropical print now series*, https://www.joiriminaya.com/I-can-wear-tropical-print-now.

2. Kincaid, *Small Place*, 55.

3. Quijano, "Coloniality of Power."

4. Niell, "Architecture, Domestic Space, and the Imperial Gaze," 105.

5. The terms of the conclusion of the war were that Cuba would gain its independence, although the United States was heavily involved in the nation's government. By the end of 1898, the United States claimed Puerto Rico, Guam, the Philippines, and Hawai'i as its possessions.

6. Sheller, *Consuming the Caribbean*, 60. See also Strachan, *Paradise and Plantation*, 9, where he cites Taylor, *To Hell with Paradise*, 53.

7. "Porto Rico: The Island of Enchantment" (The Condado-Vanderbilt Hotel, n.d), n.p., box 454, Archives of the Office of the Governor, Archivo General de Puerto Rico, San Juan, Puerto Rico. Charles Berwind and his family owned the New York & Porto Rico Steamship Company, and he helped fund the Grand Condado Vanderbilt Hotel.

8. Strachan, *Paradise and Plantation*, 7

9. See Rivera Cusicanqui, *Ch'ixinakax utxiwa*, ch. 3.

10. For a useful discussion of the cultural side of tourism as an extractive practice, see Herva, Varnajot, and Pashkevich, "Bad Santa."

11. It was rare for tourism boosters or guidebooks from the 1910s to 1960s to mention Indigenous built spaces.

12. Quijano, "Coloniality and Modernity/Rationality," 170.

13. In this case, the use of the term "American" is meant to refer specifically to the United States.

14. Arnold, "Illusory Riches."

15. Stepan, *Picturing Tropical Nature*.

16. Manthorne, *Tropical Renaissance*.

17. Thompson, *Eye for the Tropics*, 5. Thompson also notes the paradox that, although "tropicalization was a forward-looking project for elites, a revisioning of the modern future of these societies, it was based on a reconstruction of these islands as living in the past" (15).

18. Thompson, *Eye for the Tropics*, 98.

19. Cocks, *Tropical Whites*.

20. Thompson, *Eye for the Tropics*, 15 (also ch. 4 for a longer study of local racial politics).

21. Sidney Mintz, "Goodbye Columbus: Second Thoughts in the Caribbean Region at Mid-Millenium," Walter Rodney Memorial Lecture delivered at the Centre for Caribbean Studies, University of Warwick, England, in May 1993, later published as a pamphlet. David Scott used it as an epigraph in Scott, "Modernity that Predated the Modern," 191.

## 1. The Grand Condado Vanderbilt

1. After taking control of the island, the US government started using the spelling "Porto Rico," a more anglicized version of the Spanish name. *Picturesque Cuba, Porto Rico, Hawaii, and the Philippines.*

2. On the public nature of hotels, see Sandoval-Strausz, *Hotel*, 36–39.

3. *Washington Post*, 1898. The US title of the war, the "Spanish-American War," does not clearly represent the Cubans, Puerto Ricans, and Filipinos who fought for their countries. It also does not accurately reflect the actual history of warring; Cubans had been engaged in armed struggle for their liberation from Spain at different periods ever since 1868, for example.

4. On tourism and hotels in San Juan in the twentieth century, see Torres Santiago, "La invención de los umbrales del Edén."

5. US imperialism is figured as having a strong influence because of this chapter's focus on a hotel developed by a New York businessman and the early period of tourism to the island by predominantly contiguous-US citizens. However, just as Ayala and Bernabe point out, this is not to suggest that US imperialism was either static or monolithic, nor that it was responsible for all significant historical shifts in Puerto Rico. Ayala and Bernabe, *Puerto Rico in the American Century*, 10.

6. The two booklets are "Porto Rico: 'The Switzerland of the Tropics'" and "Porto Rico: The Island of Enchantment" (Condado-Vanderbilt Hotel, n.d), n.p., located in box 454, Archives of the Office of the Governor, Archivo General de Puerto Rico, San Juan, Puerto Rico (hereafter cited as Archivo General de Puerto Rico).

7. "Island of Enchantment," n.p., Archivo General de Puerto Rico.

8. "Switzerland of the Tropics," Archivo General de Puerto Rico. Theodore Roosevelt, *Letters to His Children*, ed. Joseph Bucklin Bishop (New York: C. Scribner's Sons, 1919), 189; Theodore Roosevelt, "December 11, 1906: Message Regarding the State of Puerto Rico" (speech, December 11, 1906, Washington, DC), Miller Center, University of Virginia, https://millercenter.org/the-presidency/presidential-speeches/december-11-1906-message-regarding-state-puerto-rico.

9. The quote refers not only to the fact that US involvement was brief and the United States lost few troops but that Hay was sworn in as secretary of state only two months before the war ended.

10. Coaling stations were seemingly neutral ways to dedicate space and personnel to the US military. On the strategic use of coaling stations in the Dominican Republic, see Roorda, *Dictator Next Door*, 11.

11. Ayala and Bernabe, *Puerto Rico in the American Century*, 26–27. These authors also offer a balanced overview of the economics, politics, and culture of Puerto Rico with useful pre-1898 background.

12. Ayala and Bernabe, *Puerto Rico in the American Century*, 58.

13. Grandin, *Empire's Workshop*, 3, 17, 23.

14. However, by the time the hotel was constructed and opened, the Jones Act extended US citizenship to Puerto Ricans, and in the same year Puerto Ricans voted on a referendum on the prohibition of alcohol in Puerto Rico, which passed.

15. Berwind New York & Porto Rico Steamship Company sold to Charles Morse's Consolidated Steamship Lines. "Morse Here To-Day," *New York Tribune*, February 16, 1908, 1. On Flagler and Plant in Florida, see Braden, *Architecture of Leisure*.

16. Ayala, *American Sugar Kingdom*, 270n140.

17. Jean-Marie Ruiz, "Scientific Rhetoric and the American Empire: Two Versions," in Delmas, Vandamme, and Andréolle, *Science and Empire*, 118.

18. Many in the United States were hesitant to integrate these places fully into the United States as they viewed their populations as non-white, less primitive, and thus potentially harmful to the civilized status of US citizens. On this topic see Jacobson, *Barbarian Virtues*, 225–34.

19. On Florida, see Braden, *Architecture of Leisure*.

20. Sheller, *Consuming the Caribbean*, 60.

21. Henry L. Hartzell, San Juan, to Governor Blanton Winship, San Juan, May 22, 1934, box 286, Archives of the Office of the Governor, Archivo General de Puerto Rico. This was part of Hartzell's effort to convince the governor that the insular government had to take action regarding the ownership and operation of the hotel.

22. According to Nina Gray and Pamela Herrick, none of Frederick Vanderbilt's papers exist to aid in research. See Gray and Herrick, "Decoration in the Gilded Age."

23. The brothers acquired a tiny telephone company in 1914. By 1917, they were installing telephones throughout Puerto Rico and Cuba, and in 1920, their company was formally known as the International Telephone and Telegraph Corporation.

24. Mary Frances Gallart, "Ahora seremos felices: modelos de urbanizaciones en San Juan" ['Ahora seremos felices': Models of Private Housing Developments in San Juan], in Vivoni Farage, *San Juan siempre nuevo*, 37.

25. "Grand Condado Vanderbilt," San Juan (State Historic Preservation Office, US Department of the Interior, 2009), 50.

26. Gallart, "Ahora seremos felices," in Vivoni Farage, *San Juan siempre nuevo*, 39.

27. Latin American suburban development was based on theories and practices from Europe and the United States, reformulated to account for local cultural, social, and political contexts. On urban and suburban development in Latin American cities, see Almandoz, *Planning Latin America's Capital Cities*; Alonso and Casciato, *Metropolis in Latin America*.

28. Sepúlveda Rivera, *Puerto Rico urbano*, 392. Condado residences such as these were centered along Avenida Ashford.

29. The Behn brothers came to Puerto Rico via the Virgin Islands, though their parents were originally from Europe.

30. Charles Wetmore and Whitney Warren founded their firm in 1898. Warren had studied at the École des Beaux Arts in Paris, and his approach to architecture in his practice in the United States reflected the program's emphasis on studying classical architecture and incorporating historical styles in design. After Warren designed a country house for Charles Wetmore and during the construction the two became friends, Wetmore decided to abandon his job as an attorney, commence architectural training, and form an architectural firm with Warren. On the firm, see Pennoyer and Walker, *Architecture of Warren & Wetmore*.

31. Reference files for this project are located in Warren & Wetmore Architectural Photographs and Records, 1889–1938, Drawings and Archives Collection, Avery Architectural and Fine Arts Library, Columbia University, New York, New York.

32. A bohío is a type of house or dwelling found throughout parts of the Caribbean. It can vary in form and material. In Puerto Rico they were typically constructed from parts of palm and other types of trees.

33. Plateresque was a style of architecture that developed in the late Gothic and early Renaissance period in Spain and its territories. Plateresque architecture is characterized by the eclectic mix of a variety of decorative components and is visually recognizable by decorative façades covered in a profusion of ornamentation.

34. The coat of arms is now inscribed with a CV, but at the time of construction this lettering did not exist.

35. An undated drawing for an unspecified hotel project in Havana contains details of the surrounding area that suggest it was their proposal for the Sevilla-Biltmore project. Folder 7, box 19, Warren & Wetmore Architectural Photographs and Records, 1889–1938, Drawings and Archives Collection, Avery Architectural and Fine Arts Library, Columbia University, New York, New York. On the history of the extension for the Sevilla-Biltmore, see Erica Morawski, "Havana's Early Modern Hotels: Accommodating Colonialism, Independence and Imperialism," in Hartman, *Imperial Islands*, 189–207.

36. It seems as though Warren & Wetmore's design for the Sevilla-Biltmore proposed the demolition of the existing hotel structure and other extant structures on the block in order to build a massive fourteen-story hotel with a roof garden. Their proposal to demolish so much extant architecture may have been why the owner decided to hire another firm of architects who composed a design that incorporated the existing hotel.

37. The proposal for the presidential palace can be found in folder 8, box 19, and the photo of the Hotel Inglaterra in folder 3, box 29, of Warren & Wetmore Architectural Photographs and Records, 1889–1938, Drawings and Archives Collection, Avery Architectural and Fine Arts Library, Columbia University, New York, New York. For a more extensive analysis of the Hotel Inglaterra, see Morawski, "Havana's Early Modern Hotels," in Hartman, *Imperial Islands*.

38. Warren & Wetmore scholars Peter Pennoyer and Anne Walker describe the Bermuda Golf Club as an "undercooked Mediterranean design." Pennoyer and Walker, *Architecture of Warren & Wetmore*, 212.

39. Skwiot, *Purposes of Paradise*, 103. Skwiot traces the history of attempts by Castle & Cooke and Matson Navigation Lines, as well as other interested parties, to support the "production of narratives of Waikiki as a place reserved for royalty, once Hawaiian, now Anglo-Saxon, [which] proceeded in tandem with the construction of the Royal Hawaiian Hotel" (96).

40. Skwiot, *Purposes of Paradise*, 103–4.

41. Rexford Newcomb, *Mediterranean Domestic Architecture in the United States* (Cleveland: J. H. Hansen, 1928), iv.

42. There were no doors or openings to allow access to this balcony, there were only windows located above it, so it was clearly meant to be decorative.

43. This staircase was part of a tradition of grand staircases in hotel design. Staircases were more than just a means for transporting guests between floors; their grandness and often opulent design was meant to project the status of the hotel. Likewise, guests who paraded these stairs, a social act of being seen and watching others, took on this status.

44. Adamson, *American Wicker*, 120.

45. "Island of Enchantment," Archivo General de Puerto Rico. A floor typically contained thirty-three bedrooms (for a total of one hundred in the hotel), and many could open to other bedrooms so as to create suites.

46. Strain, *Public Places, Private Journeys*, 2. The idea of the tourist gaze was first thoroughly examined in Urry, *Tourist Gaze*. Strain, in *Public Places, Private Journeys*, extends the idea of the tourist gaze to a much more inclusive group of participants.

47. Insular Government Bureau of Information, *Porto Rico: The Riviera of the West* (San Juan: Porto Rico Publishing Company, 1912), 79, box 454, Archives of the Office of the Governor, Archivo General de Puerto Rico.

48. Niell, "Architecture, Domestic Space, and the Imperial Gaze," 105. This essay introduced me to the important scholarship by Faye Caronan.

49. Caronan, "Colonial Consumption and Colonial Hierarchies," 36, 39.

50. There could be additional bound booklets, but these two brochures offer sufficient material to analyze, and it is probably safe to assume that additional booklets would employ the same strategies and rhetoric.

51. *Riviera of the West*, 79, Archivo General de Puerto Rico.

52. On the topic of islands and science during the modern period in the broad sense, see Gillis, *Islands of the Mind* (esp. ch. 6). On science as knowledge and a form of control and its Enlightenment roots, see Aronowitz, *Science as Power*, 7. See also Catherine Delmas, Vandamme, and Andréolle, *Science and Empire*.

53. "Switzerland of the Tropics," 9, Archivo General de Puerto Rico.

54. Monmonier, *How to Lie with Maps*, 90; Simon Ryan, "Inscribing Emptiness: Cartography, Exploration, and the Construction of Australia," in Tiffin and Lawson, *De-Scribing Empire*, 116.

55. "Switzerland of the Tropics," Archivo General de Puerto Rico.

56. In fact, many publications made an effort to depict the Spanish roots of Puerto Rico in order to claim that the inhabitants of Puerto Rico were of a higher nature than, say, people from Africa and in order to suggest there was a greater chance, then, of improving the island and its people. Caronan, "Colonial Consumption and Colonial Hierarchies," 39. As this practice of racial mapping relates to how depictions of built structures participated in discourses of race, see Niell, "Architecture, Domestic Space, and the Imperial Gaze," 108–10.

57. Seiler, *Republic of Drivers*, 7 (quote), 9.

58. "Switzerland of the Tropics," Archivo General de Puerto Rico.

59. *Picturesque Cuba, Porto Rico, Hawaii, and the Philippines*, 32; Niell, "Architecture, Domestic Space, and the Imperial Gaze," 109.

60. William Dinwiddie, *Puerto Rico: Its Conditions and Possibilities* (New York: Harper & Brothers Publishers, 1899), iii, 185.

61. Paving roads was just one of many projects that commenced after 1898. It is difficult to characterize these projects as either Puerto Rican or US-driven as the two were so enmeshed. A certain number of directives regarding improvement programs came from the US government in Washington, DC, but others were developed through the local government, which did have Puerto Rican representatives. Likewise, some of the funding for these projects came directly from the US government, but in other cases taxes levied on the island covered the costs.

62. Henry L. Hartzell, San Juan, to Governor Blanton Winship, San Juan, May 22, 1934, box 286, Archives of the Office of the Governor, Archivo General de Puerto Rico. The governor of Puerto Rico was appointed by the United States until 1948, when Puerto Ricans were allowed to vote for governor.

63. This period is marked by the Ponce Massacre of March 21, 1937. Initially meant as a peaceful civilian march in protest of the US government's imprisonment of Pedro Albizu Campos, leader of the Puerto Rican Nationalist Party, it turned deadly when police killed nineteen Puerto Ricans and injured more than two hundred others. Earlier, in October of 1935, the Río Piedras Massacre took place on the campus of the Universidad de Puerto Rico in the San Juan suburb of Río Piedras. Four Nationalist Party supporters and one police officer were killed when local police officers opened fire on supporters of the Puerto Rican Nationalist Party.

64. The Gran Condado Vanderbilt attracted the type of tourist that Hartzell clearly favored—the social elite, who responded favorably to the hotel's high level of service and accommodations under Berwind's management. Hartzell attributed to Prohibition the influx to Puerto Rico of the upper class over lower socioeconomic classes. Although contiguous-US citizens were inclined to travel outside the United States to "wet" islands in the Caribbean, Hartzell seemed unaware that the non-elite often traveled to other islands than Puerto Rico not because these islands offered drinking but because they had tourism programs and prices specifically geared to middle- and working-class US vacationers. Puerto Rico developed a reputation as catering to the social elite. In Hartzell's opinion, upon undertaking a program of tourism development the local government should remain focused on targeting a higher class of tourist as Puerto Rico could never compete with the "less desirable attractions of Havana." Hartzell to Governor Winship, May 22, 1934, box 286, Archivo General de Puerto Rico.

65. From his letter, it is clear that Hartzell saw the Grand Condado Vanderbilt as a business opportunity and as a symbol of the US control in Puerto Rico that should be kept up. He was from the United States, and the tone and wording of his writing clearly indicate his belief that US politicians should be ruling Puerto Rico, as well as an obvious subscription to the idea that contiguous-US citizens were superior to Puerto Ricans. Hartzell to Governor Winship, May 22, 1934, box 286, Archivo General de Puerto Rico.

66. Hartzell certainly was not alone in his thinking that the island and its businesses were best managed by contiguous-US citizens; since 1898 and up until that point in 1934 Puerto Rico had a local government (composed primarily of contiguous-US citizens) that was appointed by the US president and was always headed by a governor from the United States.

67. This is based on a document in the government archives that was most likely written in the summer of 1934, box 286, Archives of the Office of the Governor, Archivo General de Puerto Rico. No other papers from this period document Winship's intention to obtain the hotel and the federal funds he needed to facilitate the acquisition. Whether Hartzell's letter was the first time anyone proposed that the Puerto Rican government purchase the hotel remains unclear.

68. Governor Blanton Winship, San Juan, to Bureau of Insular Affairs, Washington, DC, July 1934, box 286, Archives of the Office of the Governor, Archivo General de Puerto Rico. To further convince the bureau of the positive possibilities of the hotel, Winship mentioned that Colonel Byoir, head of Doherty Hotel interests in Miami and Palm Beach, was intrigued by tourist development in Puerto Rico. He suggested that Byoir might be a potential operator for the Grand Condado Vanderbilt hotel. Winship's reference to a US company's interest in operating the hotel was undoubtedly meant to instill faith in a US government decision to invest funds in the hotel.

69. In the end, the Hotel Normandie cost an estimated two million dollars, a not insignificant amount for that time. Torres Santiago, "La Invención de los umbrales del Edén," 138.

70. Braden, *Architecture of Leisure*, 280.

## 2. The Hotel Nacional de Cuba

1. The Spanish term *machadato* can refer to either President Machado's regime or the period of his presidency, and I use it in both senses in this chapter. Joseph R. Hartman has written extensively on the machadato's efforts at nation building and constructing national identity through built and visual works. I am deeply indebted to his work for providing a current and thorough reading of the machadato's work through cultural terms. See the bibliography for a list of his relevant scholarly studies.

2. *Album fotográfico . . . por el General Gerardo Machado y Morales*.

3. Hartman, "Silent Witnesses," 294.

4. Hartman, "Race, Gender, Giants," 181.

5. A work on foreign soil built after the firm's peak years, the Hotel Nacional de Cuba is an architectural commission that falls outside the norm of the architectural firm's standard history. Most scholarly works focus on the firm's earlier period. For example, Roth's *Architecture of McKim, Mead & White, 1870–1920* does not cover the firm's works after 1920. By the time the Hotel Nacional project came up, all of the founding partners were either retired or deceased.

6. The Revolution of 1933 has often been downplayed in Cuban history. Antoni Kapcia, "Siege of the Hotel Nacional, Cuba, 1933."

7. My positioning of national histories within transnational or international frameworks is influenced by such works as Fallan and Lees-Maffei, *Designing Worlds*; Jilly Traganou, "From Nation-Bound Histories to Global Narratives of Architecture," in Adamson, Riello, and Teasley, *Global Design History*, 166–73; and Traganou and Mitrašinović, *Travel, Space, Architecture*.

8. The monument was designed by Moisés de Huerta and Félix Cabarrocas in 1925 and was built the same year. It was subsequently rebuilt in 1926 after a devastating hurricane hit Havana.

9. La Guerra Necessaria (1895–1898) was the last of three wars—preceded by La Guerra de los Diez Años (Ten Years' War, 1868–1878) and la Guerra Chiquita (1879–1880)—that Cubans fighting for independence launched against Spain. The United States entered into the conflict for its last three months, at which point it was also called the Spanish-American War by those in the United States. Negative

sentiment about US involvement in Cuba continued well beyond the period under study here In 1961 a mob of Cubans removed the eagle and the busts of President William McKinley, Leonard Wood, and Theodore Roosevelt, which they considered symbols of imperialism.

10. Many of these studies offer excellent documentation of the built environment of Havana, though stylistic groupings are the major organizing force. They include works by Rodríguez, especially *La Habana: arquitectura del siglo XX*; Sambricio and Segre, *Arquitectura en la ciudad de la Habana*; and other volumes in which the focus is solely on, for example, the eclecticism of Vedado mansions, Art Deco in Havana, or Cuban modernist architecture. This is not to suggest that the scholarship is static, however. There are scholars who question the boundaries of stylistic groupings or who look at Cuban architecture from a different perspective. For the former, see Rodríguez, "Theory and Practice of Modern Regionalism in Cuba"; for the latter, see Hyde, *Constitutional Modernism*, and Hartman, *Dictator's Dreamscape*. The most compelling recent work is by Joseph R. Hartman. Because his work is not narrow architectural history, it invites more expanded methods for understanding the built environment.

11. The hotel is not known for some of the creole architectural elements most associated with Cuban architecture such as *guarda vecinos* and *vitrales*, most predominantly found in residential design, but its tiles and furniture certainly spoke to a Cuban architectural language. Édouard Glissant played a formative role in theorizing creole culture. Considered a groundbreaking work, his 1981 *Le Discours antillais* positively framed the Caribbean as a place of flux, transformation, and exchange, all of which defined *antillanité*, or Caribbeanness. I find Jay D. Edwards's work useful in setting up a theory of creolization that is applicable to architectural studies. See Edwards, "Creolization Theory and the Odyssey of the Atlantic Linear Cottage."

12. This is consistent with the fact that the first version of the Plan Proyecto de La Habana was produced in the same year, 1925, and there probably was already informal conversation about including a national hotel as part of this urban plan. The majority of McKim, Mead & White's archival materials related to the Hotel Nacional de Cuba are located at the McKim, Mead & White Architectural Records Collection, Department of Prints, Photographs and Architectural Collections, New-York Historical Society Museum & Library (hereafter cited as McKim, Mead & White Collection, New-York Historical Society).

13. Damián J. Fernández, "Cuba and *lo Cubano*, or the Story of Desire and Disenchantment," in Fernández and Cámara Betancourt, *Cuba, the Elusive Nation*, 94.

14. On land speculation and development relative to the tourist industry, see Schwartz, *Pleasure Island*.

15. Hartman, *Dictator's Dreamscape*, 10; Venegas Fornias, *La urbanización de las murallas*.

16. The urban works of President Machado included highways and bridges, monumental individual architectural works such as the Hotel Nacional de Cuba and the Capitolio, and large master plans that were never fully realized. Of all the machadato's priorities, only one of its projects was worker housing.

17. Faced with increasing opposition, Machado assembled a constitutional convention in 1928, which resulted in abolishing the vice presidency and giving Machado the power to take a second six-year term in office (to run from 1929 to 1935) without reelection. Thomas, *Cuba*, 587; Pérez, *Cuba*, 196.

18. *Album fotográfico . . . por el General Gerardo Machado y Morales*.

19. El Plano de la Ciudad Universitaria (University City Plan) was designed by Jean-Claude Nicolas Forestier, and the commemorative album contains his second plan for the campus, which was completed in 1929. Many university buildings already existed, and there was an overall scheme to amplify and cohere the extant campus. Forestier's second plan followed the model of Columbia University, though the major parts of his plan were not built until the late 1930s. Lejeune, "City as Landscape." Images of the Hotel Nacional de Cuba in the album included a photograph of the building under construction and a drawing of the design.

20. "Decree No. 1867 of October 30, 1928, Call for Bids for the Lease of the Lands of Santa Clara Battery for the Erection of a Magnificent National Hotel," box 273, McKim, Mead & White Collection, New-York Historical Society.

21. Presidential Decree no. 1867, October 30, 1928, n.p., box 273, McKim, Mead & White Collection, New-York Historical Society. The Monument to the Victims of the USS *Maine* was meant to mark an entry into the neighborhood of Vedado in El Plan de Embellecimiento y Ampliación de la Habana, or as it was also known in Spanish, El Proyecto del Plano Regulador de La Habana y sus Alrededores (I use Hartman's translation for English, the Havana City Project). Forestier originally designed this square with small gardens, streetlamps, and benches. Geometric gardens around the monument provided a visual connection to the gardens on the grounds of the Hotel Nacional de Cuba on the promontory above. On Forestier's design for this plaza, see Hartman, "Silent Witnesses," 303–4.

22. All monetary figures for the hotel's construction were discussed in US dollars. Monetary figures are cited here in their original 1928–1930 quantities (one dollar at that time would be worth between eighteen and nineteen dollars in 2025). With the construction of the Hotel Nacional already underway, Hartman suggests that, in the proposal, the Maine Plaza was seen as a site that would be of tourist interest.

23. "Decree No. 1867 of October 30, 1928, Call for Bids for the Lease of the Lands of Santa Clara Battery for the Erection of a Magnificent National Hotel," box 273, McKim, Mead & White Collection, New-York Historical Society.

24. These documents can be found in box 273, McKim, Mead & White Collection, New-York Historical Society.

25. This would be the equivalent of around $7.6 million in 2025 dollars, according to numerous inflation calculators.

26. Letter to the National Hotel of Cuba Corporation from McKim, Mead & White, February 19, 1930, box 273, Mead & White Collection, McKim, Mead & White Collection, New-York Historical Society.

27. Contracts can be found in box 273, McKim, Mead & White Collection, New-York Historical Society.

28. Invoices can be found in in box 273, McKim, Mead & White Collection, New-York Historical Society.

29. Fernández, "Cuba and *lo Cubano*," 83, 94.

30. On Céspedes, see Schwartz, *Pleasure Island*.

31. Báez and de la Hoz, *Hotel Nacional de Cuba*, 14–15.

32. For histories of the Havana City Project, see Lejeune, "City as Landscape"; Hyde, *Constitutional Modernism*; Rodriguez, *La Habana*; Hartman, *Dictator's Dreamscape*; Hartman, "Silent Witnesses."

33. Quoted in Lejeune, "City as Landscape," 164. At this point Forestier was an accomplished landscape architect and a self-taught city planner who had already developed plans for Lisbon, Paris, and Buenos Aires.

34. Forestier was by no means the first to develop a master plan for Havana. Other plans had been proposed including those by Raúl Otero (1905), Camilo García de Castro (1916), Walfrido de Fuentes (1916), and Pedro Martínez Inclán (1922). Many of these Cuban designers ended up working on the plan attributed to Forestier. On these plans, see Segre, Coyula, and Scarpaci, *Havana*, 54. *La Habana Actual* did have a major focal area where the Plaza Cívica was later located. However, in Martínez Inclán's plan this area is defined in terms of traffic as a vehicular circulatory hub rather than a monumental civic space. Despite this difference, Forestier's plan for Vedado is strikingly similar to Martínez Inclan's. See Hyde, *Constitutional Modernism*, 115.

35. The Havana City Plan imagined a large artery connecting the Plaza Cívica and the Hotel Nacional and the Maine Plaza, but this was never realized. The Plaza Cívica was later renamed Plaza de la Revolución after the Revolution in 1959.

36. I agree with Eduardo Luis Rodríguez's claim that the importance of Forestier in Havana has been greatly exaggerated in the last years due to international recognition of his career as an urban planner. Rodríguez, *La Habana*, 41. The comparison that Hyde presents in *Constitutional Modernism* of the similarity of Forestier's plan to extant plans developed by Cuban planners and architects supports Rodríguez's evaluation and suggests that more scholarly attention should be paid to these Cuban figures. However, Hartman, in "Silent Witnesses," offers a compelling framework for viewing the unbuilt parts of Forestier's plans and how those unbuilt parts represent a continuation of the modernity/coloniality project.

37. Hartman, "Silent Witnesses," 294.

38. Although Machado had his own plans to develop tourism, other actors of all levels were already heavily invested in the tourist industry after the commencement of the Eighteenth Amendment, or Prohibition, in the United States in 1920. In this period, Havana was constructed as the natural destination to escape Prohibition. See Schwartz, *Pleasure Island* for a historical analysis; and T. Philip Terry, *Terry's Guide to Cuba* (Boston: Houghton Mifflin, 1926) for a Prohibition-era view of the US attraction to vacationing in Cuba.

39. Merrill, *Negotiating Paradise*, 107.

40. Airline service did not start until 1928, and only the wealthy could afford it for some time afterward.

41. Merrill, *Negotiating Paradise*, 107. Merrill's figures are derived from *Terry's Guide to Cuba* (1926).

42. Brown and Dawson, "Cuba, Refuge of the Frivolous and Thirsty," *New York Times*, August 31, 1919, 69. Shortly after Prohibition started in the United States, bars and drinking establishments became greater in number and focus in Cuba. Many US bar owners packed up and moved down to Cuba, where they reopened their business and catered to US tourists. Pérez, *On Becoming Cuban*, 168.

43. All figures on tourist numbers in Cuba and the Caribbean are from Villalba Garrido, *Cuba y el turismo*, 21.

44. On the history of Vedado, see Pavez Ojeda, *El Vedado, 1850–1940*, 55–65. The design of Vedado was different from the typical urban layout, especially when it came to residences, in which landscaping was traditionally focused to the rear of the house around the patio, while street façades usually reached right to the sidewalk, sometimes covering the sidewalk with a portico. Urban regulations of Vedado called for houses to be set back from the street, allowing for the development of green spaces between houses and sidewalks and also between sidewalks and streets. Vedado was not populated rapidly; in 1870 there were still only twenty houses in the neighborhood, and it was not until the 1910s that a significant amount of building occurred when it became the favored neighborhood for the wealthy. Vedado remained predominantly residential, defined by detached villas often in revival styles, akin to the eclectic villa designs of the United States of the nineteenth and early twentieth centuries.

45. De las Cuevas Toraya, *500 años de construcciones en Cuba*, 107–8, 157–66, 173–74.

46. Up until the early twentieth century, Marianao was a rather rural area on the outskirts of the city, dotted with the stately summer residences of Cuban officials and sugar growers. During the US occupation from 1906 to 1909, US military headquarters were located in Camp Columbia in Marianao, and utilities such as water and electricity were extended to this area. The addition of modern infrastructure, combined with the rolling green hills and beautiful vistas, positioned Marianao as an attractive site for future development.

47. Although George A. Fuller was listed on the contract, it seems this contractor did not have much involvement in building the Hotel Nacional. Likewise, the United States Realty Company had nothing to do with ownership of the land or the building, as the Cuban government ultimately owned it. The two may have been involved merely as investors. The United States Realty Company was a parent company of George A. Fuller, among other companies, whose focus was on construction, development, and real estate holdings. Some documents in the McKim, Mead & White Collection at the New-York Historical

Society suggest that George A. Fuller and the United States Realty Corporation tried to back out of the contract, but the Cuban government would not allow the removal of their names. The exact details of these relationships are difficult to tease out of the documents.

48. Pérez, *Cuba in the American Imagination*.

49. Pérez, *Cuba in the American Imagination*. Changing ideas over time included annexing Cuba as a state and administering Cuba as a colony.

50. For an overview of US interest in not allowing complete Cuban independence, the US intervention and immediate steps to limit sovereignty in Cuba in 1898, see Pérez, *Cuba*, 135–44.

51. In 1926, for example, roughly two-thirds of the sugar crop was produced by US-owned mills, and five US banks and three British banks controlled more than 75 percent of banking interests. Pérez recounts that, in 1925, estimates of US capital interests in Cuba had risen to between $1.1 billion and $2.0 billion, which could be found distributed through every sector of the Cuban economy. Pérez, *Cuba under the Platt Amendment*, 258. Cuban leaders who wanted to thrive in this environment had to cater to US interests as the United States was a dominant force in commerce, had an increasing influence in the real estate market, and was a looming authority ready to intervene if political matters ran contrary to US interests.

52. The Spanish-American War was dubbed such by the United States. In Cuba, the period of 1895–1898 is referred to as the Necessary War, which was the third of three defined liberation wars, beginning with the Ten Years' War (1868–1878) and the Little War (1879–1880).

53. On US architects in Cuba, see José A. Gelabert-Navia, "American Architects in Cuba," *Journal of Decorative and Propaganda Arts* 22 (1996), 132–49.

54. The company's roots were in New York, where they developed as a structural engineering and construction firm; they gained a reputation for their work on skyscrapers and other buildings that involved modern building techniques.

55. They may have also offered kickbacks or enticing incentives to obtain contracts. As Schwartz has thoroughly documented in *Pleasure Island*, the land speculation and building market in Cuba during this period was defined by a culture of kickbacks and favors. Schwartz suggests that there was perhaps no building project that was not touched by this type of corruption. Purdy & Henderson's established reputation in the United States and in Cuba is surely what made them the obvious choice for the Hotel Nacional.

56. Cited in Lejeune, "City as Landscape," 159.

57. The firm later produced designs that were not Beaux Arts, but this was long after all the founders had died and after the Hotel Nacional was built. The earliest drawings for the hotel date to 1925, five years after the last of the founding partners had retired.

58. Charles H. Reilly, *McKim, Mead & White* (London: E. Benn, 1924).

59. National City Bank expanded rapidly under the chairmanship of Charles E. Mitchell, bringing the bank to more than twenty-three countries outside the United States. On National City Bank's involvement in the tourism industry and the bank business in Cuba, see Villalba Garrido, *Cuba y el turismo*, 40–41.

60. Pérez, *Cuba under the Platt Amendment*, 165.

61. In general, US hotels and hotel operating companies were globally recognized for leading the field in hospitality. On this topic, see Sandoval-Strausz, *Hotel*. In the case of the Hotel Almendares, for example, hotel owners specifically sought out a US citizen to manage the hotel, probably because they felt a US manager was better equipped to run a hotel in a manner that met US expectations and US visitors would be more drawn to a hotel with a US manager.

62. Some hotels were US ventures, such as the Sevilla-Biltmore, which was owned and operated under the Biltmore chain. On the other hand, many Cuban-owned hotels opted for US management, such as the

Hotel Almendares, which hired a US manager and actively advertised his US origins as indicative of the quality of the hotel. The majority of tourists traveling to Cuba in the 1920s were US citizens.

63. The project was budgeted for a cost of $46,250,000, more than double the amount required by the presidential decree.

64. The terms stipulated that the lease would last for thirty years, at which point there would be an option to renew for thirty more years. After that, the hotel would fall into the hands of the state.

65. The lease payment was required when the bid was submitted.

66. McKim, Mead & White to Purdy & Henderson, September 9, 1929, box 273, PR 42, McKim, Mead & White Collection, New-York Historical Society.

67. All invoices and costs had to be reported to McKim, Mead & White. Purdy & Henderson corresponded the most with the architects' office in New York about construction concerns. The correspondence suggests that the architects saw themselves working as much against Purdy & Henderson as with them. They may have sensed that the contractor felt more inclined to work in favor of the Cuban government than the hotel project syndicate. Purdy & Henderson had to account for any difference in cost from what was agreed upon in the preapproved budget. An extensive amount of correspondence in the archives chronicles the details of this reporting. Whenever Purdy & Henderson needed or wanted to stray from what was planned, they had to generate a form letter into which they entered all the details of the changes. While the interiors were being finished, there was a great number of changes to plan, mostly in favor of cutting costs. Small changes—such as cutting crown molding from the guest rooms, substituting cheaper tiles in some places, and opting for brass chromium plated fixtures instead of the proposed white metal fixtures—saved thousands of dollars in decorating costs.

68. "Decree No. 1867 of October 30, 1928, Call for Bids for the Lease of the Lands of Santa Clara Battery for the Erection of a Magnificent National Hotel," n.p., box 273, McKim, Mead & White Collection, New-York Historical Society.

69. Schwartz, *Pleasure Island*; Peréz, *Cuba under the Platt Amendment*.

70. Although Machado was deposed and the Platt Amendment abrogated in 1933, there was still much turmoil in the country in the later 1930s. It was only once a climate of perceived economic and political stability was achieved under President Fulgencio Batista (during his first term as president from 1940 to 1944) that constituents from different political groups gathered to draft a new constitution.

71. Kapcia, "Siege of the Hotel Nacional," 286. Tension had been brewing within the ranks of the military since the liberal rebellion in 1917, after which President Mario García Menocal placed a significant number of conservatives in position in the military so as to counter liberal power. The conflict between liberals and conservatives was grounded largely in different attitudes concerning national sovereignty and the role the United States should or should not play in the governing of the island after Spanish colonialism ended in 1898.

72. Machado was not the first president to be met with civil dissension. In 1917, President Mario García Menocal (1913–1921) faced the "February Revolution" organized by liberals. President Alfredo Zayas (1921–1925) faced numerous revolts and protests launched by a growing number of organizations that were formed with the intention of improving Cuban civil society and government and increasing national sovereignty.

73. Kapcia, "Siege of the Hotel Nacional," 286. Historical narratives vary in their portrayal of the military's agency in making these decisions. Other accounts present the chain of events as being largely imposed and manipulated by the US government, through the ambassador Sumner Welles, who was appointed by President Franklin Roosevelt specifically for the purpose of dealing with revolution in Cuba.

74. Pérez, *Cuba under the Platt Amendment*, 318.

75. Kapcia, "Siege of the Hotel Nacional," 288. Intervention was justified through the 1901 Platt Amendment.

76. The leftist radical group Pro Ley y Justicia was established in August 1933. The Ejercito del Caribe was formed by the DEU (Directorio Estudiantil Universitario), a student group founded in 1927. ABC Radical was an offshoot of the ABC group, which was originally a secret society agitating against Machado that received its name in 1931. ABC Radical split off from ABC because of disagreements over whether they should participate in mediation coordinated by the United States.

77. As a result of their refusal to participate in mediation, these groups missed their opportunity to position themselves as US allies and gain a greater voice through political representation during Céspedes's presidency and subsequent provisional government (referred to as the Pentarchia). Robbed of representation in politics, these groups were committed to protest and revolt, often through violence, as a means to convey their message. Likewise, these groups were more committed to a complete revolution against the government, rather than reform, which was often promised but never delivered.

78. Although the activist groups were content that the ex-officers were being transported to jail to await trial for their actions under the machadato, firing resumed briefly while some remaining officers were still awaiting transportation at the hotel.

79. "Cuban Hotel Battlefield Sets Sightseeing Hours," *New York Times*, 8 October 1933.

80. I would characterize what we see at the Hotel Nacional not just as symptomatic of the general shift toward privatization as a management strategy to capture more revenue but also as particular to the fact that this was a hotel for international visitors. US visitors mingling with locals in a Cleveland hotel would not have been the same as US tourists mingling with Cuban locals in a Havana hotel.

81. Hilton wanted to privatize public spaces as a means to earn more revenue, for example. What were once spaces open to anyone became clearly defined as bars, restaurants, and lounges that required consumption and the expenditure of money.

82. Peréz, *Cuba under the Platt Amendment*, 279–84.

83. The idea of a constant struggle to realize the goals of the nineteenth-century independence movement has defined the contours of the understanding of the Cuban nation since 1898 and continues to this day. Many historians touch on this in works that deal with other topics while Louis A. Pérez Jr. has made this the focus of study. In *The Structure of Cuban History*, he masterfully outlines the framework within which this rhetoric is sustained and perpetuated.

84. The idea of what actually constitutes sovereignty may have been quite different during the two periods. A number of Cubans fighting for independence in the nineteenth century believed that members of the elite Creole class were more qualified to run an independent Cuba than a popularly elected government.

85. The prime location allowed one to monitor movement for miles around, and the cliff running along the ocean side of the site made for a difficult armed approach. Indeed, throughout history the site has been utilized with consideration of its defensive properties.

86. "When the Smoke of Battle at National Hotel Cleared Away," *Newark Evening News*, October 5, 1933.

87. Will Taylor to Lawrence G. White, October 28, 1933, box 273, McKim, Mead & White Collection, New-York Historical Society.

88. Santa Clara was originally set up as a military outpost by Charles III after the English conquest of 1762.

89. Thomas, *Cuba*, 581.

90. The Capitolio took much longer to build than expected, resulting in exorbitant cost overruns. Over the years, the design went through a number of changes, all by Cuban architects, and Purdy & Henderson were responsible for construction during the final phase. On the Capitolio, see Hartman, *Dictator's Dreamscape*, ch. 1.

91. Cost was a major point of criticism, but the design's resemblance to US and French predecessors was also criticized. Lejeune, "City as Landscape," 179.

92. Author's translation of a quote cited in de las Cuevas, *500 años de construcciones en Cuba*, 259. Machado ran on a platform that challenged the US involvement in Cuba, but upon taking office his government continued to support foreign investors, which prompted critics to question the headway he made on workers' rights, an issue at the fore in those days.

93. Roig was against imperialism and foreign intervention and influence, either US or Spanish. He was progressive in the area of social liberties and rights and promoted Cuban culture as an important basis for the nation. Castellanos claims that Roig was never officially affiliated with any particular party. See Gerardo Castellanos, *Emilio Roig de Leuchsenring* (Havana: Molina y Compañia, 1938). However, in other instances, Roig is listed as a member of the Junta Cubana de Renovación Nacional (Cuban Committee for National Renewal), which published a manifesto upon its founding that called for national reform. See Hyde, *Constitutional Modernism*, 9.

94. Pérez, *Cuba*, 183; Whitney, *State and Revolution in Cuba*, 55–80.

## 3. The Hotel Jaragua

1. Baez, "Constructing the Nation," 93.
2. Rancier, "Santo Domingo," 54.
3. On the connection between el Ciclo de San Zenón and nation building, see Anderson, *Disaster Writing*, ch. 1.
4. Anderson, *Disaster Writing*, 29.
5. See Roorda, *Dictator Next Door*, 11.
6. Attitudes about involvement in the Caribbean were anything but unanimous; Roosevelt did face significant anti-imperialist opponents in Congress. To intervene in Dominican finances, Roosevelt used executive power to conclude a "modus vivendi" with the Dominican Republic. Roorda, *Dictator Next Door*, 14.
7. Roorda, *Dictator Next Door*, 15.
8. Roorda, *Dictator Next Door*, 17.
9. Rancier, "Santo Domingo," 53.
10. Pérez Montás, "Los paradigmas de la nacionalidad," 158.
11. Some of the residences he designed were situated in the Condado area of San Juan, not far from the Grand Condado Vanderbilt Hotel. On Nechodoma in the Dominican Republic, see Pérez Montás, "Los paradigmas de la nacionalidad," 210.
12. Pérez Montás, "Los paradigmas de la nacionalidad," 212, 221.
13. Pérez Montás, "Los paradigmas de la nacionalidad," 200.
14. Blackmore, "Hubristic Hydraulics," 117. See also Anderson, *Disaster Writing*, 33; Blackmore, "Hubristic Hydraulics," 118.
15. Roorda, *Dictator Next Door*, 21–22.
16. Roorda, *Dictator Next Door*, 22.
17. Anderson, *Disaster Writing*, 31.
18. Lara, "Smarting Wound," 469.
19. Lara, "Smarting Wound," 470. Here Lara is also drawing on the work of Ginetta E. B. Calendario, *Black behind the Ears: Dominican Racial Identity from Museums to Beauty Shops* (Durham: Duke University Press, 2007).
20. Turits, "World Destroyed," 592.
21. Jolly, *Creating Pátzcuaro, Creating Mexico*.

22. Turits, *Foundations of Despotism*, 81.
23. Turits, *Foundations of Despotism*, 83.
24. Blackmore, "Hubristic Hydraulics," 120. See also Blackmore, "Hubristic Hydraulics"; Blackmore, "Counterflows."
25. Turits, *Foundations of Despotism*, 216.
26. Turits, "World Destroyed," 596.
27. Turits, "World Destroyed," 593.
28. Turits, "World Destroyed," 604.
29. Turits recounts early episodes in Trujillo's rule that indicate his advisors and other intellectuals were more anti-Haitian than he was. Turits, "World Destroyed," 609–12.
30. Turits, "A World Destroyed," 625, 629.
31. Blackmore, "Hubristic Hydraulics," 118.
32. Martínez and Messina, *Jaragua no cae*, 49.
33. Blackmore, "Hubristic Hydraulics," 119.
34. On the Columbus Lighthouse project, see chapter 3 of Robert Alexander González, *Designing Pan-America*.
35. National Bureau of Tourism, *Guia de Ciudad Trujillo República Dominicana: la ciudad más antigua de América* (Ciudad Trujillo: Ucar, Garcia u Compañia, 1940).
36. *Guia de Ciudad Trujillo*, 6.
37. *Guia de Ciudad Trujillo*, 12.
38. Martínez and Messina, *Jaragua no cae*, 59.
39. Martínez and Messina, *Jaragua no cae*, 59. Pedro Agudo, manager of the Grand Condado Hotel, wrote Trujillo about getting out of the private sector, no doubt trying the escape the troubled times the Grand Condado was experiencing while also looking to the perceived success of new state hotel projects in Cuba and Venezuela.
40. Martínez and Messina, *Jaragua no cae*, 79.
41. The Export-Import Bank of Washington was created under Executive Order 6581 in 1934.
42. Martínez and Messina, *Jaragua no cae*, 81.
43. Martínez and Messina, *Jaragua no cae*, 185. At this point in time the peso was equal to one US dollar, making this close to twenty-five million dollars in 2025.
44. Another beachside hotel of this type was the Hotel Guarocuya in Barahona.
45. "Hotel Montaña," *Archivos de Arquitectura Antillana* 54 (March 2015): 90.
46. Martínez and Messina, *Jaragua no cae*, 187.
47. Martínez and Messina, *Jaragua no cae*, 187.

## 4. The Caribe Hilton

1. "Spectacular Luxury in the Caribbean: The Caribe Hilton Hotel at San Juan, Puerto Rico," *Architectural Forum* 92 (March 1950): 97.
2. Clipping of Mel Heimer's, "My New York," from an unidentified publication, folder 1, box 6, Hospitality Industry Archives, Conrad Hilton College, University of Houston.
3. Primary sources refer to this style with a number of different names: tropical modern, tropical modernism, architecture for the tropics (in publications so entrenched in modernism they just assume the modern aspect of it).
4. Liane Lefaivre and Alexander Tzonis, "The Suppression and Rethinking of Regionalism and Tropicalism after 1945," in Tzonis, Lefaivre, and Stagno, *Tropical Architecture*, 14.
5. According to architectural historian Jerry Torres Santiago, the architectural discourse of Puerto

Rican modernism was propelled and defined by the quest to articulate the tropical environment through architectural forms. Torres Santiago, "La invención de los umbrales del Edén," 152.

6. This was nothing new; this was manifest in the early twentieth century in Puerto Rico (see chapter 1). I am indebted to Paul Niell for providing such a compelling application of both Quijano's and Mignolo's work to Puerto Rico. See Niell, "Architecture, Domestic Space, and the Imperial Gaze."

7. Rodríguez, "To Be for (an)*other*," 179.

8. Maldonado, *Teodoro Moscoso*, 25–30. Fomento was officially created on May 11, 1942, with Bill 188, signed by Rexford Guy Tugwell, the last appointed governor of Puerto Rico from the contiguous states. Formally titled the Administración de Fomento Económico (Economic Development Administration), Fomento, and its implementation of Operación Manos a la Obra, had its roots in the New Deal–esque initiative of Governor Tugwell, who oversaw the establishment of a number of state-owned factories. When Luis Muñoz Marín was popularly elected in 1948, he reorganized government agencies, which effectively made PRIDCO a public corporation, which acted primarily as Fomento's real estate arm. Many of the goals of Operación Manos a la Obra complemented the aims of the President Truman's Point Four Program of technical assistance for "developing countries" that the United States was implementing in Puerto Rico at the same time.

9. On Operación Manos a la Obra, see Ayala and Bernabe, *Puerto Rico in the American Century*; Maldonado, *Teodoro Moscoso*.

10. On Moscoso, see Maldonado, *Teodoro Moscoso*.

11. For details of the conditions, see Ayala and Bernabe, *Puerto Rico in the American Century*, 189. Ayala and Bernabe summarize the conditions well: "The Industrial Incentives Act of 1947 granted private firms exemption from insular income, property, and other taxes and the payment of fees for licenses until 1957. Since US corporations operating in Puerto Rico paid no federal income taxes, this offered them an almost tax-free environment. Moreover, federal minimum wage laws were not automatically applicable to the island." Ayala and Bernabe, *Puerto Rico in the American Century*, 189. Minimum wages were much lower in Puerto Rico than in the United States, a common characteristic found in colonial relations.

12. For a history of the relationship between Operación Manos a la Obra and government planned tourism, see Merrill, *Negotiating Paradise*.

13. Puerto Rican government officials studied data on other Caribbean and tropical destinations such as Jamaica, Hawai'i, and Mexico so as to determine the best type of image to cultivate and how and what kind of tourism initiatives to implement in order to appeal to tourists.

14. For example, see Paul J. C. Friedlander, "Island for Tourists," *New York Times*, December 8, 1949, 17.

15. The plan aimed to attract 16 percent of the Caribbean tourist market, which would bring in an estimated annual revenue of fifteen million dollars. Lee E. Cooper, "Puerto Rico Opens a $6,000,000 Hotel," *New York Times*, December 10, 1949, 29.

16. For example, see "Porto Rico: 'The Switzerland of the Tropics'" and "Porto Rico: The Island of Enchantment" (Condado-Vanderbilt Hotel, n.d), box 454, Archivo General de Puerto Rico, the brochures and promotional literature analyzed in chapter 1.

17. Krista Thompson analyzes the palm tree as a visual signifier of the tropics, in *An Eye for the Tropics*, 100–102.

18. In discussing the growth of international tourism by US citizens in the postwar years, Dennis Merrill reports that "by the early 1960s Americans alone spent $3 billion per year traveling overseas." Merrill, "Negotiating Cold War Paradise," 180. See also Merrill, *Negotiating Paradise*; Ward, *Packaged Vacations*.

19. On the increasing affordability of vacations for contiguous-US citizens and the incorporation of vacation time into the work sphere, see Aron, *Working at Play*.

20. Aron, *Working at Play*, 10.

21. Diana Rice, "Field of Travel," *New York Times*, September 5, 1948, 11.

22. On reduced airfares, the Point Four Program, and Puerto Rican emigration to the United States, see Grosfoguel, *Colonial Subjects*, 109.

23. Merrill, "Negotiating Cold War Paradise," 181.

24. The role of the contiguous United States as regards the actions of both government and businesses and the Puerto Rican government's adoption of what critics consider a "US mentality" in the 1940s and 1950s constitute a contested topic. While some scholars saw modernization programs as creating jobs and higher standards of living, others saw the commitment to industrialization as a rejection of the agricultural sector, which forced many rural residents to abandon their livelihoods and relocate to cities or emigrate to the contiguous states for job opportunities. Nevertheless, there was an air of paternalism in contiguous-US literature, which in some cases presented the United States as Puerto Rico's savior, suggesting that the contiguous United States first had to invest in the island, and more than just financially, before Puerto Rico would be able to "lift itself up by its bootstraps."

25. For example, see "1950 Hotel Accommodations at the Crossroads of the Nation," *Hotel Monthly* 58, no. 683 (February 1950): 27–40.

26. While the United States' interest in Pan-Americanism dates back to the nineteenth century, President Franklin Roosevelt rekindled attention through his Good Neighbor Policy and his attention to the Americas during World War II and this continued under subsequent Cold War administrations.

27. Maldonado, *Teodoro Moscoso*, 123.

28. Oscar E. Bowline, "Bustling Caribbean," *New York Times*, December 5, 1948, 18.

29. For an entertaining overview of the history of Hilton's hotel empire, see Hilton, *Be My Guest*. Hilton took over operations of an extant hotel in Chihuahua, Mexico, which was subsequently dubbed the Palacio Hilton. He later pulled out of the hotel, and although his experience in Mexico did not end well, it did not seem to hinder his engagement in the Caribe Hilton arrangement.

30. Ward, *Packaged Vacations*, 26. On Hilton's ideological reasons for wanting to get into international hotels, see Wharton, *Building the Cold War*, 8–11.

31. The original proposition stipulated that the operating company was to be responsible for interior decoration, but Hilton convinced Fomento officials that they should pay for it. In the end, Hilton only had to invest $195,000 in the hotel project.

32. Maldonado, *Teodoro Moscoso*, 124.

33. Torregrosa retired from the firm in 1952, and the firm continued under the name Toro y Ferrer and then later Toro-Ferrer.

34. Torres Santiago, "La invención de los umbrales del Edén," 147. For this attitude in the fine arts, see the following chapters in *Puerto Rico: Arte e identidad*: Silvia Álvarez Curbelo, "El proyecto de modernización," 109–39; Marimar Benítez, "La década de los cincuenta: Afirmación y reacción," 141–47; José Antonio Torres Martino, "Las artes gráficas de Puerto Rico," 149–77.

35. This rhetoric was presented in publications produced in Puerto Rico that discussed topics such as the program of modernization, modern architecture in Puerto Rico, and tourism. The association between contiguous-US education and modernization in Puerto Rico was largely incorporated into contiguous-US publications as well, where developments were presented as the result of help from the contiguous United States and the adoption of a contiguous-US attitude toward modernization, industrialization, labor, and progress, as well as architecture. The assumption that Osvaldo Toro and Miguel Ferrer were somehow better suited than other architects to design for tropical climates completely disregards the fact that they had just spent years in New York where their education, given the location, probably did not focus much on building in tropical climates.

36. Roberto Segre traces the rejection of colonial and ornamented architecture for a rationalist design approach in the Caribbean in "Antillean Architecture of the First Modernity: 1930–1945," in

Brillembourg, *Latin American Architecture*, 116–35. One of the best-known examples of this is President Getúlio Vargas's embrace of modern architecture as the new form for Brazil under his leadership. He invested in avant-garde architects to design works that he wanted to symbolize the Brazilian state, typically buildings such as social housing that identified the government's commitment to its people. Perhaps the most iconic of these is the building for the Ministério da Educação e Saúde (Ministry of Education and Health, 1936–1942, Rio de Janeiro), in which Lúcio Costa led a team of Brazilian architects in designing the building and even convinced the government to agree to have Le Corbusier consult on the project.

37. The use of architectural modernism to represent the modern state has been thoroughly documented by architectural historians. For a general discussion, see Fernando Kusnetzoff, "Architecture, History, and Society in Latin American," trans. Andrew Gordon, in Segre and Kusnetzoff, *Latin America in Its Architecture*, 12. For more recent engagement with the topic, see Bergdoll, Comas, Liernur, and del Real, *Latin America in Construction*; Carranza and Lara, *Modern Architecture in Latin America*.

38. For an overview of a more critical reception of Operación Manos a la Obra, especially in the arts, see *Puerto Rico: Arte y identidad*; Ayala and Bernabe, *Puerto Rico in the American Century*, 211–18.

39. The small farms component of the reform never took off. Ayala and Bernabe, *Puerto Rico in the American Century*, 185.

40. Merrill, *Negotiating Paradise*, 187.

41. Maldonado, *Teodoro Moscoso*, 124, 125–26.

42. Maldonado, *Teodoro Moscoso*, 124.

43. The entire issue of the *Caribe News* from December 9, 1949, for example, was devoted to articles and advertisements about the Caribe Hilton and its inauguration.

44. "Spectacular Luxury in the Caribbean: The Caribe Hilton Hotel at San Juan, Puerto Rico," *Architectural Forum* 92 (March 1950): 97.

45. Kropp, *California Vieja*, 4.

46. Brazil was not the only country to think about modernization's relationship with the use of the historic in national identity. On Mexico, see Berger and Wood, eds., *Holiday in Mexico*; Oles, *South of the Border*.

47. SPHAN was created in 1936.

48. Castriota, "Living in a World Heritage Site," 12.

49. Segawa, *Architecture of Brazil, 1900–1990*, 106.

50. Maldonado, *Teodoro Moscoso*, 131.

51. For a brief history of the restoration of San Juan Viejo, see Maldonado, *Teodoro Moscoso*, 131–32; Merrill, *Negotiating Paradise*, 202.

52. Shortly after the Caribe Hilton was built, the company acquired the Pan American Guest House and demolished it so as to make way for an extension that was completed in 1955.

53. Many brochures such as these can be found in box 454, Archivo General de Puerto Rico.

54. Aline B. Louchheim, "Bold New Design for San Juan Hotel," *New York Times*, October 23, 1949, 3.

55. These photographs can be found in a variety of publications and are often the same publicity photographs reprinted in brochures and the popular press.

56. On the history and significance of the landscaping of colonial land, see Casid, *Sowing Empire*.

57. In particular, in *Tropical Renaissance*, Katherine Manthorne traces the association of the tropical environment with notions of primordial, primitive, and uncivilized, as well as the connection of the tropical environment with depictions of the Garden of Eden. See also Stepan, *Picturing Tropical Nature*; Thompson, *Eye for the Tropics*.

58. Whether the climate was in fact ideal is another point. The incorporation of air-conditioning in

all the guest rooms suggests that visitors might have found it too hot, for example, and anecdotes report that some open areas had to be enclosed because the "soft ocean breezes" were actually overly strong winds; rainstorms complicated matters as well.

59. "The Caribe Hilton: An Object Lesson," *Interiors + Industrial Design* (April 1950): 77.

60. At first Risom designed for others such as Knoll, but by 1946 he had established his own firm that designed, manufactured, and distributed furniture to contract and residential clients in the United States and abroad.

61. For example, see Obniski, "Selling Folk Art and Modern Design."

62. Newspapers throughout the United States published articles citing the shipment of furniture from the contiguous states to San Juan for the furnishing of the Caribe Hilton, hailing it as the largest peacetime air shipment to date. See, for example, "Caribe Hilton—World's First Hotel to Be 'Moved by Air!'" *Hotel Bulletin* (February 1950): 43.

63. Klumb and Arneson were both former Taliesin Fellows. The name of the firm was derived from the combination of the first letters of their last names.

64. On Klumb's career in Puerto Rico, see Vivoni Farage, *Klumb*.

65. Obfuscating the distinction between indoor and outdoor was central to Klumb's architectural practice. For example, he designed his residence walls to fold open to such an extent that the living room was little more than a space with a roof. He also used the same pieces of ARKLU furniture that were in the Caribe Hilton in the outdoor areas around his own home.

66. Advertisement located in the Henry Klumb archives at Archivo de Arquitectura y Construcción, University of Puerto Rico, Rio Piedras, San Juan, Puerto Rico. Although the archive is extensive concerning Klumb's architecture, the amount of materials related to ARKLU and his furniture design are quite small.

67. There are other claims for the invention of the piña colada. For example, Barrachina, a restaurant in San Juan Viejo, has a plaque mounted outside their establishment that claims the piña colada was invented there in 1963.

68. Stewart, *On Longing*, 134 (for an extended discussion of the souvenir, see ch. 5).

69. Newspaper clippings, box 6, Hospitality Industry Archives, Conrad Hilton College, University of Houston.

70. Merrill, *Negotiating Paradise*, 197. Also see Maldonado, *Teodoro Moscoso*, 128.

71. Paul J. C. Friedlander, "Island for Tourists," *New York Times*, December 8, 1949, X17.

72. The old airport was located south, and slightly east, of San Juan Viejo.

73. Government regulations curbed new hotel building in Condado in the 1950s, and as a result, many of the subsequent San Juan hotels were built in Isla Grande, while the Dorado Beach Hotel and Golf Club was located outside the city to the west. The 1950s and 1960s also witnessed the construction of modernist hotels in other parts of the island, such as the Ponce Intercontinental Hotel in Ponce and the El Conquistador in Fajardo. Fernández, in *Architecture in Puerto Rico*, lists extant hotels, as well as a slew of other projects either being proposed or already under construction.

74. Merrill, *Negotiating Paradise*, 201.

75. Merrill, *Negotiating Paradise*, 185.

76. Hilton, *Be My Guest*, 232–33.

77. Wharton examines Hilton International hotels in her book *Building the Cold War*. She does not study the Caribe Hilton in depth, but she does note that the basic plan of the Caribe Hilton was adopted in other Hilton hotels. I would contend that this is not just a characteristic of Hilton hotel architecture but the path that hotel design takes in general in this period. However, as Evan Ward also points out, this architecture can conversely be seen from the point of view of the locals (what could be considered a Latin

American viewpoint), a perspective that considers earlier modernist architecture in Latin America as precedents for these hotels.

78. The design of the Trinidad Hilton utilized an inverted pedestal base and tower configuration on account of the topography of the land on which it was built. Toro y Ferrer were hired as consulting architects for this project.

79. Ward, *Packaged Vacations*, 35. In the case of the Caribe Hilton, the inability of Puerto Rico to manufacture the furniture needed for the hotel meant that most of it was shipped in from Marshall Field & Company in Chicago, in what was described in the press as the largest peacetime air shipment in history. See "New Ultra-Modern Hotel at San Juan a Milestone in Campaign for Tourist Trade," *New York Herald Tribune*, December 5, 1949, 6. In other Hiltons, such as the Continental Hilton, there was a sufficient local furniture industry to supply the majority of the furniture.

80. For detailed accounts of how this plays out in cities such as Berlin, Rome, Istanbul, and Cairo, see Wharton, *Building the Cold War*, 189.

81. For wonderfully detailed accounts of the role of the Havana Hilton in the Cuban Revolution, see Merrill, *Negotiating Paradise*; Ward, *Packaged Vacations*.

## 5. The Havana Riviera

1. Batista staged a coup d'état in 1952, suspended the Cuban Constitution shortly thereafter, and led as dictatorial president until he was overthrown in 1959 by rebel forces led by Fidel Castro.

2. *Malecón* means "seawall" in Spanish.

3. For more on the concept of cosmopolitan cubanidad, see Morawski, "Tropicana Cabaret."

4. Lionnet, "Cosmopolitan or Creole Lives?," 27.

5. Fernández, *Cosmopolitanism in Mexican Visual Culture*, 7–21.

6. Despite what actually happened, there were discussions of demolishing parts of Habana Vieja in the name of urban development. Perhaps the best-known instance is the ideas and proposals of Town Planning Associates (TPA, a firm that produced urban design and city planning in various South American cities), who were commissioned by the government through the Junta Nacional de Planificación (National Planning Board). Relevant to the topic of tourism development, TPA proposed a man-made island to jut out from the city, to be filled with hotels and to function as a space predominantly for tourists. On the TPA in Havana, see Hyde, *Constitutional Modernism*.

7. Scarpaci, Segre, and Coyula, *Havana*, 73–74.

8. Scarpaci, Segre, and Coyula, *Havana*, 121.

9. Merrill, *Negotiating Paradise*, 124.

10. This is not to say that there were not plenty of US travelers who would visit Havana and stay in some of the older hotels in the historic city center. Certainly, there were tourists who would have preferred this experience, but the most modern hotels with the most amenities were the new hotels outside the historic center.

11. Scarpaci, Segre, and Coyula, *Havana*, 122.

12. In 1837, Cuba was the first Spanish-speaking country and sixth country in the world to have a railroad; it developed telephone service in 1881; and it continuously led Latin America in incorporating running water, sewage systems, electricity, and transportation infrastructure into the urban environment. Scarpaci, Segre, and Coyula, *Havana*, 36. Louis A. Pérez Jr. links these developments to the extreme intervention of US military and business interests after the end of the War for Cuban Independence in 1898. Pérez, *On Becoming Cuban*, 97–164.

13. This way of thinking is still present in Cuba and the popular phrase, "Cuba is Havana and the rest is just beaches," which has existed for some time, evokes this attitude.

14. Merrill, *Negotiating Paradise*, 105, 111–13.

15. Merrill, *Negotiating Paradise*, 111–12. One major exception to the focus on Havana was the popularity of Varadero, a peninsula with white sandy beaches located about ninety miles from Havana. Varadero developed as an oasis for foreigners and Cuba's upper classes to enjoy sun, sand, and surf on mostly privatized beaches.

16. Although there was growth in the tourist sector in Cuba, the island's share of the Caribbean market decreased from 43 percent in 1949 to 31.4 percent in 1954. It is a stark comparison when one considers that Puerto Rico doubled its number of tourists, Haiti quintupled its number of visitors, and Cuba increased tourist arrivals only by 30 percent. On statistics, see Merrill, *Negotiating Paradise*, 112; Schwartz, *Pleasure Island*, 148.

17. Skwiot, *Purposes of Paradise*, 155.

18. Merrill, *Negotiating Paradise*, 122. See also Pérez, *On Becoming Cuban*, 434–35. This airport is now known as José Martí International Airport.

19. Cubans still talk today about how they, their mothers, aunts, and grandmothers would fly to Miami for the day or the weekend to shop and go to the beauty parlor. Despite the bad relations between the US government and the Cuban government since 1959, memories and stories of the relationships Cubans had with the United States continue to be kept alive in oral histories. Most people I have talked to either speak fondly of this relationship, if they were a part of it, or speak positively of it when recounting what their relatives told them.

20. Merrill, *Negotiating Paradise*, 122.

21. Pérez, *On Becoming Cuban*, 347.

22. Fernandez, *Cruising the Caribbean*, 270; Pérez, *On Becoming Cuban*, 327. Likewise, the United States supported the Cuban economy by receiving 92 percent of Cuba's exports.

23. Scarpaci, Segre, and Coyula, *Havana*, 74.

24. In general, this prosperity was at the expense of workers' rights and those who lived in rural areas.

25. Schwartz, *Pleasure Island*, 152.

26. Schwartz, *Pleasure Island*, 153.

27. Merrill, *Negotiating Paradise*, 113. This sheds some light on the economic difficulties encountered by the Castro regime. When the revolutionary government nationalized private entities, it lost its outside sources for loan repayment to the state bank and lending institutions. Now the state hotel had to repay the state bank.

28. They are often referred to as the Kefauver hearings for the chair, Senator Estes Kefauver of Tennessee, who led the probe into organized crime's connections to drugs, gambling, and political corruption.

29. Schwartz, *Pleasure Island*, 144.

30. As Schwartz recounts, Lansky missed out on some significant business opportunities in Las Vegas because he was serving a short prison term in Saratoga, New York. By the time he was out, Cuba seemed a more lucrative opportunity than Las Vegas. Schwartz, *Pleasure Island*, 149.

31. Schwartz, *Pleasure Island*, 145.

32. Although there is no doubt that Lansky was running the project, he was not listed on the papers as an investor. In fact, the closest he was connected to the hotel was through his nominal position as Head of Kitchens. The hotel's papers listed a Toronto hotelier company run by brothers Ben and Harry Smith as the operating company, but in reality, Lansky had complete control over all operations.

33. Schwartz, *Pleasure Island*, 157.

34. In addition, areas outside of the historic center may have offered better water, sewage, electricity, and other services, as these things in Habana Vieja were always problematic. Residents were constantly dealing with antiquated systems that could not adequately support the number of inhabitants in this part of the city.

35. The disagreement between Johnson and investors is stated in Rodríguez, *Havana Guide*, 140. It does not seem to be published anywhere, but the anecdote about the proposal for dice on the ceiling and Johnson's response is the accepted history among Cuban architectural historians.

36. Moruzzi, *Havana before Castro*, 184.

37. We can see this in its using architecture to make tropical climate more agreeable, as in the Caribe Hilton, and in its use of colors that meshed with the ocean and the surrounding buildings. Also, the hotel continued an approach already established in Havana, with the construction of the Malecón, to connect urban infrastructure to the sea.

38. Born in Russia in 1911, Igor Polevitzky had lived in Pennsylvania with his family since the age of eleven. He studied architecture at the University of Pennsylvania, where the department had an excellent reputation due to the presence of Paul Philippe Cret, whose work was associated with modern classicism and whose writings addressed such issues as functional planning and modern styling. Although the school was still officially teaching a Beaux Arts approach to architecture, Cret and other like-minded instructors ensured that the modern movement had a firm presence as well. Shulman, "Igor Polevitzky's Architectural Vision," 335–36.

39. Allan T. Shulman, "Polevitzky's Birdcage Houses," in Shulman, *Miami Modern Metropolis*, 385.

40. Shulman, "Igor Polevitzky's Architectural Vision," 359. This was made possible by innovations in building materials that allowed Polevitzky to design with light aluminum frames and screen infill.

41. Shulman, "Polevitzky's Birdcage Houses," in Shulman, *Miami Modern Metropolis*, 389.

42. Allan T. Shulman, "The Fontainebleau Hotel: Modernity, Decadence and the Iconography of Leisure," in Shulman, *Miami Modern Metropolis*, 313.

43. Shulman, "Igor Polevitzky's Architectural Vision," 336.

44. Later interpretations of modernism focused on it as a tool to master man's environment, in this case most notably by the incorporation of air-conditioning.

45. Rocco Ceo and Allan T. Shulman, "Privileged Views and Underwater Antics: Swimming Pools, Diving Towers and Cabana Colonies," in Shulman, *Miami Modern Metropolis*, 340, 343.

46. According to Shulman and Lejeune, by the late 1950s apartment high-rises had replaced resort hotels as the main paradigm of beachfront development in Miami. Allan T. Shulman and Jean-François Lejeune, "Postwar Towns: Bal Harbour Village and Bar Harbor Islands," in Shulman, *Miami Modern Metropolis*, 194.

47. I use the term "modern" loosely as it was never discussed in such terms at the time. Recently, Victor Deupi and Jean-François Lejeune have discussed the Havana Riviera in terms of Synthesis of the Arts in their broader study of Cuban Modernism. Both terms work to capture how all public areas were considered zones for integrating the latest in Cuban art and design. See Deupi and Lejeune, *Cuban Modernism*.

48. While the term *Santería*, which means "way of the saints" was used for a long time, many now reject this term because of its emphasis on the Catholic and syncretic elements and at the expense of the African legacy in the practice.

49. Frédéric Miahle, *Viaje pintoresco al redador de la isla de Cuba* (Havana: L. Marquier, 1848).

50. *Vanguardia* is Spanish for "avant-garde." The year 1927 is considered the year that Cuban modern art was born, thanks to *Exposición de arte nuevo*, organized by *Revista de Avance*, a journal that promoted avant-garde Cuban art. This exhibition was the first devoted exclusively to modern art and featured at least twenty-one Cuban artists.

51. On the vanguardia's use of Afro-Cuban culture, for example, see Hartman, *Dictator's Dreamscape*, 156–57.

52. The term *mulata* was a racial and gender designation for a woman of mixed European and African ancestry and was understood as a type in a range of gendered racial categories. The mulata represented

the conflicts and tensions in Cuban history and identity. On the mulata in Cuban culture, see Fraunhar, *Mulata Nation*.

53. The Carlton Terrace Apartments were designed before the Havana Riviera, but photographs of the lobby interior in the HistoryMiami Museum archives show Florencio Gelabert's sculpture *Ritmo Cubano* in the space. It is not clear when these photographs were taken, and thus not clear if there was one sculpture moved from Florida to Cuba, or if multiple copies were cast. Regardless, it affirms the strong connections between Havana and Miami design at the time. Photographs of Carlton Terrace Apartments, folder 11, box 1, series 1, Igor B. Polevitzky Photographs Collection, HistoryMiami Museum, Miami.

54. Chasteen, *Born in Blood and Fire*, 17.

55. Traditional explanations in scholarship of these African-based religions tend to be Western-centric and highlight the connections with Catholicism. Different framings, which can be found increasingly in scholarship, question the emphasis on the association with saints among other Western-centric characterizations of the practice.

56. It is also commonly referred to as Palo Monte.

57. In all photographs of Dirube, he presents as a person who would have been understood as white. I have reviewed the Rolando López Dirube archives in the Cuban Heritage Collection at the University of Miami, and there are no references to him understanding himself or being understood by others as mixed-race or Black. In fact, a complete absence of reference to race often suggests whiteness.

58. Anthony J. Abbate, "Arango Design: Progressive Style and Latin Influence," in Shulman, *Miami Modern Metropolis*. Jorge and Judith Arango felt there was a lack of contemporary design and an overabundance of kitsch design in Miami. To remedy this they opened their design store, which was the first in Miami to offer pieces by designers such as Arne Jacobsen, Alvar Aalto, and Charles and Ray Eames.

59. This is cited in Moruzzi, *Havana before Castro*, 186.

60. James McQuaid was in charge of the interior design at the Havana Hilton, for example. However, scholar Fredo Rivera reports that the common narrative in Cuba is that the interior designer worked with a well-known Cuban art collector and dealer, Ramón Osuna, and with the architect Gabriela Menéndez on everything from the art to the furnishing. What we can confirm is that much of the Havana Hilton's furniture—such as the rattan furniture in the Hurricane Bar and the metal furniture in the Sugar Bar Terrace—was locally produced.

61. Interviews with Daniel Bejerano, February 2011. Moruzzi's overview of furniture claims that all furniture was designed by Alvin Parvin, of the Parvin-Dohrmann Company of Los Angeles, which is probably based on what he found listed in official documents. See Moruzzi, *Havana before Castro*, 186.

62. Indigenous groups native to Florida (which were many) were largely no longer present in Florida by the end of the eighteenth century. After this, a few Indigenous groups have moved and settled in Florida; notable among these are the Seminole and the Miccosukee.

63. Even the palm was not as culturally and historically potent a symbol in Florida as it was in Cuba.

64. "Havana Riviera to Open Dec. 10," *Boston Globe*, December 1, 1957, B22.

65. "Cuba's Newest Hotel Brings Tropical Beauty Indoors," *Boston Globe*, December 8, 1957, B36.

66. On the devolution of tourism in the 1950s, see Schwartz, *Pleasure Island*. The initial development of mass tourism in Cuba was in the 1920s, when US travelers flocked to Cuba to escape Prohibition. This period firmly established Cuba as a place of boozing, where one could escape the strictures of life in the United States.

67. Merrill, *Negotiating Paradise*, 142–44, 154–55, 169–70.

**Conclusion: Development Persistent**

1. Carolina Caycedo, "Portfolio," from www.carolinacaycedo.com, 47.

2. Katy Donoghue, "Carolina Caycedo Centers Social and Environmental Justice Conversation around Care, *Whitewall*, August 17, 2021, https://whitewall.art/art/carolina-caycedo-centers-social-and-environmental-justice-conversation-around-care.

3. The Banco Gubernamental de Fomento para Puerto Rico was created under Rexford Guy Tugwell's administration in 1942. It was one of a number of government entities brought into being through legislation as part of an integrated initiative for development on the island. One of the other entities created through this legislation was PRIDCO, which was responsible for the development of the Caribe Hilton.

4. Maldonado-Torres, "On the Coloniality of Being," 249. I have tried to make the connection between modernity/coloniality and race particularly clear in chapter 3, though it is certainly at play in all of the case studies covered in this book.

5. While there was a strong Russian presence in the 1960s, Castro focused official government tourism programs on tourism for Cuban citizens.

6. Ward, *Packaged Vacations*, 16.

7. In Cuba, this did not occur until the late 1970s as the first twenty years after the Revolution were dedicated to domestic vacationing. The Dominican Republic and Cuba had more Spanish companies than US companies coming in to set up resorts.

8. Ward, *Packaged Vacations*, 16.

9. This arrangement is the most typical type of business arrangement, which has predominated in Cuba since the 1990s when the government started looking to other parts of the world for foreign hotel chains to operate state-owned hotels. This filled a deficiency on the part of the Cuban government to run a hotel efficiently and according to contemporary practices that meet the desires of today's tourists.

10. "Threat Assessment: Major Terror Attacks against Hotels, 2002–2011" (New York: New York State Intelligence Center, 2012), 2–3.

# Bibliography

Adalet, Begüm. *Hotels and Highways: The Construction of Modernization Theory in Cold War Turkey.* Stanford University Press, 2018.

Adamson, Glenn, Giorgio Riello, and Sarah Teasley. *Global Design History.* Routledge, 2011.

Adamson, Jeremy. *American Wicker: Woven Furniture from 1850 to 1930.* National Museum of American Art, 1993.

Adolphus, Anabelle Reynoso. "La dictadura de Rafael Leonidas Trujillo y la arquitectura moderna en república dominicana: El Hotel Jaragua, Santo Domingo, 1939–1985." Masters thesis, Pontificia Universidad Catolica de Chile Escuela de Arquitectura, Santiago, Chile, 2008.

Akcan, Esra. *Architecture in Translation: Germany, Turkey, and the Modern House.* Duke University Press, 2012.

*Album fotográfico de los actos celebrados con motivo de la toma de posesión de la presidencia de la república por el General Gerardo Machado y Morales.* Secretaria de Obras Públicas, 1929.

Almandoz, Arturo, ed. *Planning Latin America's Capital Cities, 1850–1950.* Routledge, 2002.

Alonso, Alejandro G., Pedro Contreras, and Martino Fagiuoli. *Havana Deco.* W. W. Norton, 2007.

Alonso, Idurre, and Maristella Casciato, eds. *The Metropolis in Latin America, 1830–1930: Cityscapes, Photographs, Debates.* Getty Research Institute, 2021.

Alsayyad, Nezar, ed. *Consuming Tradition, Manufacturing Heritage: Global Norms and Urban Forms in the Age of Tourism.* Routledge, 2001.

Alsayyad, Nezar, ed. *Hybrid Urbanism: On the Identity Discourse and the Built Environment.* Praeger, 2001.

Álvarez Curbelo, Silvia, and Carmen I. Raffucci, eds. *Frente a La Torre: ensayos del centenario de la Universidad de Puerto Rico, 1903–2003.* Editorial de la Universidad de Puerto Rico, 2005.

Andermann, Jens. *The Optic of the State: Visuality and Power in Argentina and Brazil.* University of Pittsburgh Press, 2007.

Anderson, Benedict. *Imagined Communities: Reflections on the Origin and Spread of Nationalism.* Rev. ed. Verso, 2006.

Anderson, Mark D. *Disaster Writing: The Cultural Politics of Catastrophe in Latin America.* University of Virginia Press, 2011.

Aparicio, Frances R., and Susana Chávez-Silverman, eds. *Tropicalizations: Transcultural Representations of Latinidad.* University Press of New England, 1997.

Appadurai, Arjun. *Modernity at Large: Cultural Dimensions of Globalization.* University of Minnesota Press, 1996.

Arnold, David. "'Illusory Riches': Representations of the Tropical World, 1840–1950." *Singapore Journal of Tropical Geography* 21, no. 1 (2000): 6–18.

Aron, Cindy S. *Working at Play: A History of Vacations in the United States.* Oxford University Press, 1999.

Aronowitz, Stanley. *Science as Power: Discourse and Ideology in Modern Society.* University of Minnesota Press, 1988.

Aste, Richard, ed. *Behind Closed Doors: Art in the Spanish American Home, 1492–1898*. Monacelli Press and Brooklyn Museum, 2013.

Avermaete, Tom, and Anne Massey, eds. *Hotel Lobbies and Lounges: The Architecture of Professional Hospitality*. Routledge, 2013.

Ayala, César J. *American Sugar Kingdom: The Plantation Economy of the Spanish Caribbean, 1898–1934*. University of North Carolina Press, 1999.

Ayala, César J., and Rafael Bernabe. *Puerto Rico in the American Century: A History since 1898*. University of North Carolina Press, 2007.

Bacchilega, Christina. *Legendary Hawai'i and the Politics of Place: Tradition, Translation, and Tourism*. University of Pennsylvania Press, 2007.

Baez, Jennifer. "Constructing the Nation at the 1955 Ciudad Trujillo World's Fair." *Athanor* 32 (2014): 93–101.

Báez, Luis, and Pedro de la Hoz. *Hotel Nacional de Cuba: revelaciones de una leyenda*. Editorial Capitán San Luis, 2011.

Barnes, Natasha. *Cultural Conundrums: Gender, Race, Nation, and the Making of Caribbean Cultural Politics*. University of Michigan Press, 2006.

Baver, Sherrie L. *The Political Economy of Colonialism: The State and Industrialization in Puerto Rico*. Praeger, 1993.

Bederman, Gail. *Manliness and Civilization: A Cultural History of Gender and Race in the United States, 1880–1917*. University of Chicago Press, 1995.

Benítez-Rojo, Antonio. *The Repeating Island: The Caribbean and the Postmodern Perspective*. 2nd ed., translated by James E. Maraniss. Duke University Press, 1997.

Bergdoll, Barry, Carlos Eduardo Comas, Jorge Francisco Liernur, and Patricio del Real. *Latin America in Construction: Architecture 1955–1980*. Museum of Modern Art, 2015.

Berger, Dina, and Andrew Grant Wood, eds., *Holiday in Mexico: Critical Reflections on Tourism and Tourist Encounters*. Duke University Press, 2010.

Berger, Molly W., ed. "The American Hotel." *Journal of Decorative and Propaganda Arts* 25 (2005): special issue.

Berger, Molly W. *Hotel Dreams: Luxury, Technology, and Urban Ambition in America, 1829–1929*. Johns Hopkins University Press, 2011.

Berman, Marshall. *All That Is Solid Melts into Air: The Experience of Modernity*. 1982. Repr. Penguin Books, 1988.

Bhabha, Homi K. *The Location of Culture*. Routledge, 1994.

Birkenmaier, Anke, and Esther Whitfield, eds. *Havana beyond the Ruins: Cultural Mappings after 1989*. Duke University Press, 2011.

Black, Megan. *The Global Interior: Mineral Frontiers and American Power*. Harvard University Press, 2018.

Blackmore, Lisa. "Counterflows: Hydraulic Order and Residual Ecologies in the Dominican Landscape." *Iberoamericana* 19, no. 72 (November 2019): 57–80.

Blackmore, Lisa. "Hubristic Hydraulics: Water, Dictatorship, and Modernity in the Dominican Republic." *Latin American and Latinx Visual Culture* 2, no. 1 (January 2020): 115–25.

Blackmore, Lisa. *Spectacular Modernity: Dictatorship, Space and Visuality in Venezuela, 1948–1958*. University of Pittsburgh Press, 2017.

Bondil, Nathalie, ed. *Cuba: Art and History from 1868 to Today*. Prestel, 2008.

Braden, Susan R. *The Architecture of Leisure: The Florida Resort Hotels of Henry Flagler and Henry Plant*. University Press of Florida, 2002.

Briggs, Laura. *Reproducing Empire: Race, Sex, Science, and U.S. Imperialism in Puerto Rico*. University of California Press, 2002.

Brillembourg, Carlos, ed. *Latin American Architecture, 1929–1960: Contemporary Reflections*. Monacelli Press, 2004.

Burnard, Trevor, and John Garrigus. *The Plantation Machine: Atlantic Capitalism in French Saint-Domingue and British Jamaica*. University of Pennsylvania Press, 2016.

Bush, Gregory W. "'Playground of the USA': Miami and the Promotion of Spectacle." *Pacific Historical Review* 68, no. 2 (May 1999): 153–72.

Cabán, Pedro A. *Constructing a Colonial People: Puerto Rico and the United States, 1898–1932*. Westview Press, 1999.

Cabezas, Amalia L. *Economies of Desire: Sex and Tourism in Cuba and the Dominican Republic*. Temple University Press, 2009.

Canizaro, Vincent B., ed. *Architectural Regionalism: Collected Writings on Place, Identity, Modernity, and Tradition*. Princeton Architectural Press, 2007.

Carley, Rachel. *Cuba: 400 Years of Architectural Heritage*. Whitney Library of Design, 1997.

Caronan, Faye C. "Colonial Consumption and Colonial Hierarchies in Representations of Philippine and Puerto Rican Tourism." *Philippine Studies* 53, no. 1 (2005): 32–58.

Carranza, Luis E., and Fernand Luiz Lara. *Modern Architecture in Latin America: Art, Technology, and Utopia*. University of Texas Press, 2014.

Casid, Jill H. *Sowing Empire: Landscape and Colonization*. University of Minnesota Press, 2004.

Castañeda, Luis M. *Spectacular Mexico: Design, Propaganda, and the 1968 Olympics*. University of Minnesota Press, 2014.

Castillo, Greg. *Cold War on the Home Front: The Soft Power of Midcentury Design*. University of Minnesota Press, 2010.

Castriota, Leonardo. "Living in a World Heritage Site: Preservation Policies and Local History in Ouro Preto, Brazil." *TDSR X* 2 (Spring 1999): 7–19.

Ceo, Rocco, and Allan T. Shulman. "Privileged Views and Underwater Antics: Swimming Pools, Diving Towers and Cabana Colonies." In *Miami Modern Metropolis: Paradise and Paradox in Midcentury Architecture and Planning*, edited by Allan T. Shulman, 338–45. Bass Museum of Art, 2009.

Chastain, Andra B., and Timothy W. Lorek, eds. *Itineraries of Expertise: Science Technology and the Environment in Latin America's Long Cold War*. University of Pittsburgh Press, 2020.

Chasteen, John Charles. *Born in Blood and Fire: A Concise History of Latin America*. 2nd ed. W. W. Norton, 2006.

Chomsky, Aviva, Barry Carr, and Pamela Maria Smorkaloff, eds. *The Cuba Reader: History, Culture, Politics*. Duke University Press, 2003.

Cocks, Catherine. *Doing the Town: The Rise of Urban Tourism in the United States, 1850–1915*. University of California Press, 2001.

Cocks, Catherine. *Tropical Whites: The Rise of the Tourist South in the Americas*. University of Pennsylvania Press, 2013.

Cody, Jeffrey W. *Exporting American Architecture, 1870–2000*. Routledge, 2003.

Cooper, Frederick, and Ann Laura Stoler, eds. *Tensions of Empire: Colonial Cultures in a Bourgeois World*. University of California Press, 1997.

Covert, Lisa Pinley. *San Miguel de Allende: Mexicans, Foreigners, and the Making of a World Heritage Site*. University of Nebraska Press, 2017.

Crain, Edward E. *Historic Architecture in the Caribbean Islands*. University Press of Florida, 1994.

Cuevas Toraya, Juan de las. *500 años de construccion en Cuba*. D. V. Chavín, Servicios Gráficos y Editoriales, 2001.

Cuevas Toraya, Juan de las. *Cuba: para guardar la memoria*. Junta de Andalucía, Consejería de Obras Públicas y Transportes, Dirección General de Arquitectura y Vivienda, 2006.

Cullen, Deborah, and Elvis Fuentes. *Caribbean: Art at the Crossroads of the World*. El Museo del Barrio and Yale University Press, 2012.

Dávila, Arlene M. *Sponsored Identities: Cultural Politics in Puerto Rico*. Temple University Press, 1997.

Delbourgo, James, and Nicholas Dew, eds. *Science and Empire in the Atlantic World*. Routledge, 2008.

Delmas, Catherine, Christine Vandamme, and Donna Spalding Andréolle, eds. *Science and Empire in the Nineteenth Century: A Journey of Imperial Conquest and Scientific Progress*. Cambridge Scholars, 2010.

Denby, Elaine. *Grand Hotels, Reality and Illusion: An Architectural and Social History*. Reaktion Books, 1998.

Derby, Lauren. *The Dictator's Seduction: Politics and the Popular Imagination in the Era of Trujillo*. Duke University Press, 2009.

Derby, Lauren, and Marion Werner. "The Devil Wears Dockers: Devil Pacts, Trade Zones, and Rural-Urban Ties in the Dominican Republic." *New West Indian Guide/Nieuwe West-Indische Gids* 87, no. 3–4 (2013): 294–321.

Deupi, Victor, and Jean-François Lejeune. *Cuban Modernism: Mid-century Architecture, 1940–1970*. Birkhauser, 2021.

Duany, Jorge, ed. *Picturing Cuba: Art, Culture, and Identity of the Island and in the Diaspora*. University Press of Florida, 2019.

Duany, Jorge. *The Puerto Rican Nation in the Move: Identities on the Island and in the United States*. University of North Carolina Press, 2002.

Dubois, Laurent, and Richard Lee Turits. *Freedom Roots: Histories from the Caribbean*. University of North Carolina Press, 2019.

Dunlop, Beth, ed. "Florida." *Journal of Decorative and Propaganda Arts* 23 (1998): special issue.

Duval, David Timothy, ed. *Tourism in the Caribbean: Trends, Development, Prospects*. Routledge, 2004.

Edwards, Jay D. "Creolization Theory and the Odyssey of the Atlantic Linear Cottage." *Etnofoor* 23, no. 1 (2011): 53–85.

Elliott, J. H. *Empires of the Atlantic World: Britain and Spain in America, 1492–1830*. Yale University Press, 2006.

Endy, Christopher. *Cold War Holidays: American Tourism in France*. University of North Carolina Press, 2004.

English, T. J. *Havana Nocturne: How the Mob Owned Cuba . . . and Then Lost It to the Revolution*. HarperCollins, 2007.

Escobar, Arturo. *Designs for the Pluriverse. Radical Interdependence, Autonomy, and the Making of Worlds*. Duke University Press, 2017.

Escobar, Arturo. *Encountering Development: The Making and Unmaking of the Third World*. Rev. ed. Princeton University Press, 2011.

Esperdy, Gabrielle. "'I Am a Modernist': Morris Lapidus and His Critics." *Journal of the Society of Architectural Historians* 66, no. 4 (December 2007): 494–517.

Fallan, Kjetil, and Grace Lees-Maffei, eds. *Designing Worlds: National Design Histories in an Age of Globalization*. Berghahn, 2016.

Fernández, Damián J. "Cuba and *lo Cubano*, or the Story of Desire and Disenchantment." In *Cuba, the Elusive Nation: Interpretations of National Identity*, edited by Damián J. Fernández and Madeline Cámara Betancourt, 79–99. University of Florida Press, 2000.

Fernández, Damián J., and Madeline Cámara Betancourt, eds. *Cuba, the Elusive Nation: Interpretations of National Identity*. University Press of Florida, 2000.

Fernández, José Antonio. *Architecture in Puerto Rico*. Architectural Book Publishing, 1965.

Fernández, María. *Cosmopolitanism in Mexican Visual Culture*. University of Texas Press, 2014.

Fernandez, Ronald. *Cruising the Caribbean: U.S. Influence and Intervention in the Twentieth Century*. Common Courage Press, 1994.

Fernandez, Ronald. *The Disenchanted Island: Puerto Rico and the United States in the Twentieth Century*. 2nd ed. Praeger, 1996.

Field, Thomas C., Jr., Stella Krepp, and Vanni Pettinà, eds. *Latin America and the Global Cold War*. University of North Carolina Press, 2020.

Fishkin, Shelley Fisher. "Crossroads of Culture: The Transnational Turn in American Studies—Presidential Address to the American Studies Association, November 12, 2004." *American Quarterly* 57, no. 1 (March 2005): 17–57.

Flores, Tatiana. "'Latinidad Is Cancelled': Confronting an Anti-Black Construct." *Latin American and Latinx Visual Culture* 3, no. 3 (July 2021): 58–79.

Fox, Claire F. *Making Art Panamerican: Cultural Policy and the Cold War*. University of Minnesota Press, 2013.

Fraser, Valerie. *Building the New World: Studies in the Modern Architecture of Latin America, 1930–1960*. Verso, 2000.

Fraunhar, Alison. *Mulata Nation: Visualizing Race and Gender in Cuba*. University Press of Mississippi, 2018.

Friedman, Alice T. *American Glamour and the Evolution of Modern Architecture*. Yale University Press, 2010.

Fry, Maxwell, and Jane Drew. *Tropical Architecture in the Dry and Humid Zones*. 2nd ed. Robert E. Krieger, 1982.

Fuente, Alejandro de la. *A Nation for All: Race, Inequality, and Politics in Twentieth-Century Cuba*. University of North Carolina Press, 2001.

Funes Monzote, Reinaldo. *From Rainforest to Cane Field in Cuba: An Environmental History since 1492*. Translated by Alex Martin. University of North Carolina Press, 2008.

Galeano, Eduardo. *Open Veins of Latin America: Five Centuries of the Pillage of a Continent*. Translated by Cedric Belfrage. Monthly Review Press, 1997.

Gaonkar, Dilip Parameshwar, ed. *Alternative Modernities*. Duke University Press, 2001.

García Canclini, Néstor. *Consumers and Citizens: Globalization and Multicultural Conflicts*. Translated by George Yúdice. University of Minnesota Press, 2001.

García Canclini, Néstor. *Hybrid Cultures: Strategies for Entering and Leaving Modernity*. Translated by Christopher L. Chiappari and Silvia L. López. University of Minnesota Press, 1995.

Garlock, Maria E. Moreyra, and David P. Billington. *Félix Candela: Engineer, Builder, Structural Artist*. Yale University Press and Princeton University Art Museum, 2008.

Gasson, Richard H. *The Birth of American Tourism: New York, the Hudson Valley, and American Culture, 1790–1830*. University of Massachusetts Press, 2008.

Gelernter, Mark. *A History of American Architecture: Buildings in Their Cultural and Technological Context*. University Press of New England, 2001.

Gibson, Carrie. *Empire's Crossroads: A History of the Caribbean from Columbus to Present Day*. Atlantic Monthly Press, 2014.

Gillem, Mark L. *America Town: Building the Outposts of Empire*. University of Minnesota Press, 2007.

Gillis, John R. *Islands of the Mind: How the Human Imagination Created the Atlantic World*. Palgrave Macmillan, 2004.

Gilroy, Paul. *The Black Atlantic: Modernity and Double Consciousness*. Harvard University Press, 1995.

Gimeno-Martínez, Javier. *Design and National Identity*. Bloomsbury, 2016.

Glissant, Édouard. *Caribbean Discourse: Selected Essays*. Translated by J. Michael Dash. Rev. ed. University of Virginia Press, 1999.

Go, Julian. *American Empire and the Politics of Meaning: Elite Political Cultures in the Philippines and Puerto Rico during U.S. Colonialism*. Duke University Press, 2008.

Go, Julian. "Chains of Empire, Projects of State: Political Education and U.S. Colonial Rule in Puerto Rico and the Philippines." *Comparative Studies in Society and History* 42, no. 2 (April 2000): 333–62.

Goldhage, Sarah Williams, and Réjean Legault, eds. *Anxious Modernisms: Experimentation in Postwar Architectural Culture*. MIT Press and Canadian Centre for Architecture, 2000.

González, Robert Alexander. *Designing Pan-America: U.S. Architectural Visions for the Western Hemisphere*. University of Texas Press, 2011.

Grandin, Greg. *Empire's Workshop: Latin America, the United States, and the Rise of the New Imperialism*. Metropolitan Books, 2006.

Gray, Nina, and Pamela Herrick. "Decoration in the Gilded Age: The Frederick W. Vanderbilt Mansion, Hyde Park, New York." *Studies in the Decorative Arts* 10, no. 1 (Fall–Winter 2002–2003): 98–141.

Griffith, Cathryn. *Havana Revisited: An Architectural Heritage*. W. W. Norton, 2010.

Grosfoguel, Ramón. *Colonial Subjects: Puerto Ricans in a Global Perspective*. University of California Press, 2003.

Harrison, David, ed. *Tourism and the Less Developed World: Issues and Case Studies*. CABI, 2001.

Hartman, Joseph R. *Dictator's Dreamscape: How Architecture and Vision Built Machado's Cuba and Invented Modern Havana*. University of Pittsburgh Press, 2019.

Hartman, Joseph R. "Hurricanes in Havana: El Ciclón de '26 as Cultural Agent in Machado's Cuba." *Cuban Studies* 52 (2023): 71–100.

Hartman, Joseph R., ed. *Imperial Islands: Art Architecture and Visual Experience in the US Insular Empire after 1898*. University of Hawai'i Press, 2022.

Hartman, Joseph R. "Race, Gender, Giants: Consensus and Dissensus in Cuban Cultural Politics." *Cultural Politics* 14, no. 2 (2018): 174–97.

Hartman, Joseph R. "Silent Witnesses: Modernity, Colonialism, and Jean-Claude Nicolas Forestier's Unfinished Plans for Havana." *Journal of the Society of Architectural Historians* 78, no. 3 (September 2019): 292–311.

Hartman, Saidiya. *Lose Your Mother: A Journey along the Atlantic Slave Route*. Farrar, Straus and Giroux, 2007.

Haslip-Viera, Gabriel, ed. *Taíno Revival: Critical Perspectives on Puerto Rican Identity and Cultural Politics*. Wiener, 2001.

Healy, David. *Drive to Hegemony: The United States in the Caribbean, 1898–1917*. University of Wisconsin Press, 1988.

Hernández, Felipe, Mark Millington, and Iain Borden, eds. *Transculturation: Cities, Spaces and Architectures in Latin America*. Critical Studies, edited by Myriam Diocaretz, vol. 27. Rodopi, 2005.

Hertz, John B. "Authenticity, Colonialism, and the Struggle with Modernity." *Journal of Architectural Education* 55, no. 4 (May 2002): 220–27.

Herva, Vesa-Pekka, Alex Varnajot, and Albina Pashkevich. "Bad Santa: Cultural Heritage, Mystification of the Arctic and Tourism as an Extractive Industry." *Polar Journal* 10, no. 2 (2020): 375–96.

Higman, B. W. *A Concise History of the Caribbean*. Cambridge University Press, 2011.

Hilton, Conrad. *Be My Guest*. Prentice Hall, 1957.

Hoganson, Kristin L. *Consumer's Imperium: The Global Production of American Domesticity, 1865–1920*. University of North Carolina Press, 2007.

Hoganson, Kristin L. *Fighting for American Manhood: How Gender Politics Provoked the Spanish-American and Philippine-American Wars.* Yale University Press, 1998.

hooks, bell. *Black Looks: Race and Representation.* South End Press, 1992.

Howard, David. "Development, Racism, and Discrimination in the Dominican Republic." *Development in Practice* 17, no. 6 (November 2017): 725–38.

Hyde, Timothy. *Constitutional Modernism: Architecture and Civil Society in Cuba, 1933–1959.* University of Minnesota Press, 2012.

Immerwahr, Daniel. *How to Hide an Empire: A History of the Greater United States.* Farrar, Straus and Giroux, 2019.

Jacobson, Matthew Frye. *Barbarian Virtues: The United States Encounters Foreign Peoples at Home and Abroad, 1876–1917.* Hill and Wang, 2001.

Jakle, John A. *The Tourist: Travel in Twentieth-Century America.* University of Nebraska Press, 1985.

Jay, Martin, and Sumathi Ramaswamy, eds. *Empires of Vision: A Reader.* Duke University Press, 2014.

Jolly, Jennifer. *Creating Pátzcuaro, Creating Mexico: Art, Tourism, and Nation Building under Lázaro Cárdenas.* University of Texas Press, 2018.

Joseph, Gilbert M., Catherine C. Legrand, and Ricardo D. Salvatore, eds. *Close Encounters of Empire: Writing the Cultural History of U.S.–Latin American Relations.* Duke University Press, 1998

Judd, Dennis R., and Susan S. Fainstein, eds. *The Tourist City.* Yale University Press, 1999.

Kapcia, Antoni. *Havana: The Making of Cuban Culture.* Berg, 2005.

Kapcia, Antoni. "The Siege of the Hotel Nacional, Cuba, 1933: A Reassessment." *Journal of Latin American Studies* 34, no. 2 (May 2002): 283–309.

Kaplan, Amy. *The Anarchy of Empire in the Making of U.S. Culture.* Harvard University Press, 2002.

Kaplan, Amy, and Donald E. Pease, eds. *Cultures of United States Imperialism.* Duke University Press, 1993.

Kincaid, Jamaica. *A Small Place.* Farrar, Straus and Giroux, 1988.

King, Anthony D, ed. *Re-presenting the City: Ethnicity, Capital and Culture in the 21st-Century Metropolis.* New York University Press, 1996.

King, Anthony D., ed. *Spaces of Global Cultures: Architecture, Urbanism, Identity.* Routledge, 2004.

Klein, Naomi. *The Shock Doctrine: The Rise of Disaster Capitalism.* Picador, 2007.

Knight, Franklin W., and Colin A. Palmer, eds. *The Modern Caribbean.* University of North Carolina Press, 1989.

Kropp, Phoebe S. *California Vieja: Culture and Memory in a Modern American Place.* University of California Press, 2006.

Lamonaca, Marianne, and Jonathan Mogul, eds. *Grand Hotels of the Jazz Age: The Architecture of Schultze & Weaver.* Princeton Architectural Press, 2005.

Langley, Lester D. *The Banana Wars: An Inner History of American Empire, 1900–1934.* University Press of Kentucky, 1983.

Langley, Lester D. *The United States and the Caribbean in the Twentieth Century.* 4th ed. University of Georgia Press, 1989.

Lara, Ana-Maurine. "A Smarting Wound: Afro-Dominicanidad and the Fight against Ultranationalism in the Dominican Republic." *Feminist Studies* 43, no. 2 (2017): 468–84.

Lasansky, D. Medina, and Brian McLaren. *Architecture and Tourism: Perception, Performance and Place.* Berg, 2004.

Lejeune, Jean-François. "The City as Landscape: Jean Claude Nicolas Forestier and the Great Urban Works of Havana, 1925–1930." Translated by John Beusterein and Narciso G. Menocal. *Journal of Decorative and Propaganda Arts* 22 (1996): 150–85.

Lejeune, Jean-François, ed. *Cruelty and Utopia: Cities and Landscapes of Latin America*. Princeton Architectural Press, 2005.

Lejeune, Jean-François, and Allan T. Shulman. *The Making of Miami Beach, 1933–1942: The Architecture of Lawrence Murray Dixon*. Bass Museum of Art, 2000.

León, Ana María. *Modernity for the Masses: Antonio Bonet's Dreams for Buenos Aires*. University of Texas Press, 2021.

Levi, Vicki Gold, and Steven Heller. *Cuba Style: Graphics from the Golden Age of Design*. Princeton Architectural Press, 2002.

Limerick, Jeffrey, Richard Oliver, and Nancy Ferguson. *America's Grand Resort Hotels*. Pantheon Books, 1979.

Lionnet, Françoise. "Cosmopolitan or Creole Lives? Globalized Oceans and Insular Identities." *Profession* (December 2011): 23–43.

Llanes, Llilian. *Havana Then and Now*. Thunder Bay Press, 2004.

Lobo Montalvo, Maria Luisa. *La Habana: arquitectura y historia de una ciudad romántica*. Montacelli Press, 2009.

Loeffler, Jane C. *The Architecture of Diplomacy: Building America's Embassies*. Princeton Architectural Press, 1998.

Löfgren, Orvar. *On Holiday: A History of Vacationing*. University of California Press, 1999.

Loomis, John A. *Revolution of Forms: Cuba's Forgotten Art Schools*. Princeton Architectural Press, 1999.

López-Durán, Fabiola. *Eugenics in the Garden: Transatlantic Architecture and the Crafting of Modernity*. University of Texas Press, 2018.

Lowinger, Rosa, and Ofelia Fox. *Tropicana Nights: The Life and Times of the Legendary Cuban Nightclub*. Harcourt, 2005.

Lu, Duanfang, ed. *Third World Modernism: Architecture, Development, and Identity*. Routledge, 2011.

MacCannell, Dean. *The Tourist: A New Theory of the Leisure Class*. University of California Press, 1999.

Malavet, Pedro A. *America's Colony: The Political and Cultural Conflict between the United States and Puerto Rico*. New York University Press, 2004.

Maldonado, A. W. *Teodoro Moscoso and Puerto Rico's Operation Bootstrap*. University Press of Florida, 1997.

Maldonado-Torres, Nelson. "On the Coloniality of Being: Contributions to the Development of a Concept." *Cultural Studies* 21, no. 2–3 (March–May 2007): 240–70.

Manthorne, Katherine Emma. *Tropical Renaissance: North American Artists Exploring Latin America, 1839–1879*. Smithsonian Institution Press, 1989.

Marks, Robert B. *The Origins of the Modern World: A Global and Environmental Narrative from the Fifteenth to the Twenty-First Century*. 3rd ed. Rowman and Littlefield, 2015.

Martín Zequeira, María Elena, and Eduardo Luis Rodríguez Fernández. *La Habana: guía de arquitectura [Havana, Cuba: An Architectural Guide]*. Bilingual ed. Junta de Andalucía, Consejería de Obras Públicas y Transportes, Dirección General de Arquitectura y Vivienda, 1998.

Martínez Suárez, Alex, and Rab Messina. *Jaragua no cae [Jaragua Won't Crumble]*. Bilingual ed. Centro Cultural Eduardo León Jimenes, 2021.

Marvel, Thomas S. *Antonin Nechodoma, Architect, 1877–1928: The Prairie School in the Caribbean*. University Press of Florida, 1994.

McClintock, Anne. *Imperial Leather: Race, Gender, and Sexuality in the Colonial Contest*. Routledge, 1995.

McCoy, Alfred W., and Francisco A. Scarano, eds. *Colonial Crucible: Empire in the Making of the Modern American State*. University of Wisconsin Press, 2009.

McEwen, Abigail. *Revolutionary Horizons: Art and Polemics in 1950s Cuba*. Yale University Press, 2016.

McLaren, Brian L. *Architecture and Tourism in Italian Colonial Libya: An Ambivalent Modernism*. University of Washington Press, 2006.

Medina, Eden, Ivan da Costa Marques, and Christina Holmes, eds. *Beyond Imported Magic: Essays on Science, Technology, and Society in Latin America.* MIT Press, 2014.

Menocal, Narciso G., ed. "Cuba." *Journal of Decorative and Propaganda Arts* 22 (1996): special issue.

Merrill, Dennis. "Negotiating Cold War Paradise: U.S. Tourism, Economic Planning, and Cultural Modernity in Twentieth-Century Puerto Rico." *Diplomatic History* 25, no. 2 (Spring 2001): 179–214.

Merrill, Dennis. *Negotiating Paradise: U.S. Tourism and Empire in Twentieth-Century Latin America.* University of North Carolina Press, 2009.

Mignolo, Walter. *The Darker Side of Western Modernity: Global Futures, Decolonial Options.* Duke University Press, 2011.

Mignolo, Walter. *Local Histories/Global Designs: Coloniality, Subaltern Knowledges, and Border Thinking.* Princeton University Press, 2000.

Mintz, Sydney W. "Enduring Substances, Trying Theories: The Caribbean Region as Oikoumenè." *Journal of the Royal Anthropological Institute* 2, no. 2 (June 1996): 289–311.

Mintz, Sydney W. "Plantations and the Rise of a World Food Economy: Some Preliminary Ideas." *Review (Fernand Braudel Center)* 34, no. 1/2 (2011): 3–14.

Mintz, Sydney W. *Sweetness and Power: The Place of Sugar in Modern History.* Penguin Books, 1985.

Monmonier, Mark. *How to Lie with Maps.* University of Chicago Press, 1991.

Moraña, Mabel, Enrique Dussel, and Carlos A. Jáuregui, eds. *Coloniality at Large: Latin America and the Postcolonial Debate.* Duke Univeristy Press, 2008.

Morawski, Erica. "The Tropicana Cabaret: Designing Cosmopolitan Cubanidad." *Journal of Design History,* Special Issue on Latin American Design 32, no. 1 (February 2019): 52–68.

Moré, Gustavo Luis, ed. "Caribbean Modernist Architecture." *Archivos de Arquitectura Antillana* 34 (2009): special edition.

Moré, Gustavo Luis, ed. *Historias para la construcción de la arquitectura dominicana, 1492–2008* Grupo León Jimenes, 2008.

Moruzzi, Peter. *Havana before Castro: When Cuba Was a Tropical Playground.* Gibbs Smith, 2008.

Murray, N. Michelle, and Akiko Tsuchiya, eds. *Unsettling Colonialism: Gender and Race in the Nineteenth-Century Global Hispanic World.* State University of New York Press, 2019.

Musicant, Ivan. *The Banana Wars: A History of United States Military Intervention in Latin America from the Spanish-American War to the Invasion of Panama.* MacMillan, 1990.

Nelson, Louis P. *Architecture and Empire in Jamaica.* Yale University Press, 2016.

Niell, Paul B. "Architecture, Domestic Space, and the Imperial Gaze in the Puerto Rico Chapters of *Our Islands and Their People* (1899)." In *Imperial Islands: Art, Architecture, and Visual Experience in the U.S. Insular Empire after 1898,* edited by Joseph R. Hartman, 103–21. University of Hawai'i Press, 2022.

Niell, Paul. *Urban Space as Heritage in Late Colonial Cuba: Classicism and Dissonance on the Plaza de Armas of Havana, 1754–1828.* University of Texas Press, 2015.

Obniski, Monica. "Selling Folk Art and Modern Design: Alexander Girard and Herman Miller's Textiles and Objects Shop (1961–67)." *Journal of Design History* 28, no 3 (September 2015): 254–74.

Ochoa Aloma, Alina. *Desafío de una utopía: una estrategia integral para la gestión de salvaguarda de la Habana Vieja = Challenge of a Utopia: A Comprehensive Strategy to Manage the Safeguarding of the Old Havana.* Gobierno de Navarra, 1999.

Ockman, Joan, ed. *Architecture School: Three Centuries of Educating Architects in North America.* MIT Press, 2012.

Ockman, Joan, and Salomon Frausto, eds. *Architourism: Authentic, Escapist, Exotic, Spectacular.* Prestel, 2005.

Offner, Amy C. *Sorting Out the Mixed Economy: The Rise and Fall of Welfare and Developmental States in the Americas.* Princeton University Press, 2019.

Oles, James, ed. *South of the Border: Mexico in the American Imagination, 1914–1947*. Smithsonian Institution Press, 1993.

O'Rourke, Kathryn E. *Modern Architecture in Mexico City: History, Representation, and the Shaping of a Capital*. University of Pittsburgh Press, 2016.

Palmié, Stephan, and Francisco A. Scarano, eds. *The Caribbean: A History of the Region and Its Peoples*. University of Chicago Press, 2011.

Paterson, Thomas G. *Contesting Castro: The United States and the Triumph of the Cuban Revolution*. Oxford University Press, 1994.

Patricios, Nicholas N. *Building Marvelous Miami*. University Press of Florida, 1994.

Pattullo, Polly. *Last Resorts: The Cost of Tourism in the Caribbean*. Cassell, 1996.

Pavez Ojeda, Jorge. *El Vedado, 1850–1940: de monte a reparto: territorio e identidades de un barrio habanero*. Editorial Linotipia Bolívar, 2003.

Pennoyer, Peter, and Anne Walker. *The Architecture of Warren & Wetmore*. W. W. Norton, 2006.

Pérez, Louis A., Jr. *Cuba: Between Reform and Revolution*. 4th ed. Oxford University Press, 2011.

Pérez, Louis A., Jr. *Cuba in the American Imagination: Metaphor and the Imperial Ethos*. University of North Carolina Press, 2008.

Pérez, Louis A., Jr. *Cuba under the Platt Amendment, 1902–1934*. University of Pittsburgh Press, 1986.

Pérez, Louis A., Jr. *On Becoming Cuban: Identity, Nationality, and Culture*. University of North Carolina Press, 1999.

Pérez, Louis A., Jr. *The Structure of Cuban History: Meanings and Purpose of the Past*. University of North Carolina Press, 2013.

Pérez Montás, Eugenio. "Los paradigmas de la nacionalidad: arquitectura y desarollo económico republicanos, 1844–1930." In *Historias para la construcción de la arquitectura dominicana, 1492–2008*, edited by Gustavo Luis Moré, 149–212. Grupo León Jimenes, 2008.

Perkins, Whitney T. *Constraint of Empire: The United States and Caribbean Interventions*. Greenwood Press, 1981.

*Picturesque Cuba, Porto Rico, Hawaii, and the Philippines: A Photographic Panorama of Our New Possessions*. Mast, Crowell & Kirkpatrick, 1899.

Pratt, Mary Louise. *Imperial Eyes: Travel Writing and Transculturation*. Routledge, 1992.

Prestamo, Felipe J., ed. *Cuba: Arquitectura y Urbanismo*. Ediciones Universal, 1995.

*Puerto Rico: arte e identidad* [Puerto Rico: Art and Identity]. Bilingual ed. 2nd ed. La Editorial de la Universidad de Puerto Rico, 2004.

Quijano, Aníbal. "Coloniality and Modernity/Rationality." *Cultural Studies* 21, nos. 2–3 (2007): 168–78.

Quijano, Aníbal. "Coloniality of Power, Eurocentrism, and Latin America." *Nepantla: Views from South* 1, no. 3 (2000): 533–80.

Rabe, Stephen G. "The Caribbean Triangle: Betancourt, Castro, and Trujillo and U.S. Foreign Policy, 1958–1963." *Diplomatic History* 20 no. 1 (Winter 1996): 55–78.

Rancier, Omar. "Santo Domingo, Modernity and Dictatorship." *Docomomo* 33 (September 2005): 53–56.

Real, Patricio del. *Constructing Latin America: Architecture, Politics, and Race at the Museum of Modern Art*. Yale University Press, 2022.

Renda, Mary A. *Taking Haiti: Military Occupation and the Culture of U.S. Imperialism, 1915–1940*. University of North Carolina Press, 2001.

Rigau, Jorge. "No Longer Islands: Dissemination of Architectural Ideas in the Hispanic Caribbean, 1890–1930." *Journal of Decorative and Propaganda Arts* 20 (1994): 236–51.

Rigau, Jorge. *Puerto Rico, 1900: Turn-of-the-Century Architecture in the Hispanic Caribbean*. Rizzoli, 1992.

Rigau, Jorge. *Puerto Rico Then and Now*. Thunder Bay Books, 2009.
Rivera Cusicanqui, Silvia. *Ch'ixinakax utxiwa: On Practices and Discourses of Decolonization*. Translated by Molly Geidel. Polity Press, 2020.
Roberts, Justin. *Slavery and the Enlightenment in the British Atlantic, 1750–1807*. Cambridge University Press, 2013.
Robin, Ron. *Enclaves of America: The Rhetoric of American Political Architecture Abroad, 1900–1965*. Princeton University Press, 1992.
Rodríguez, Eduardo Luis. *La Habana: arquitectura del siglo XX*. Blume, 1998.
Rodríguez, Eduardo Luis. *The Havana Guide: Modern Architecture, 1925–1965*. Princeton Architectural Press, 2000.
Rodríguez, Eduardo Luis. "Theory and Practice of Modern Regionalism in Cuba." *Docomomo* 33 (September 2005): 10–19.
Rodríguez, Luz Marie. "To Be for (an) *Other*: The Caribe Hilton or Ambivalence as Presence in a United States Colony." In *Territories of Identity: Architecture in the Age of Evolving Globalization*, edited by Soumyen Bandyopadhyay and Guillermo Garma Montiel, 169–79. Routledge, 2013.
Roorda, Eric Paul. *The Dictator Next Door: The Good Neighbor Policy and the Trujillo Regime in the Dominican Republic, 1930–1945*. Duke University Press, 1998.
Rosenberg, Emily S. *Financial Missionaries to the World: The Politics and Culture of Dollar Diplomacy, 1900–1930*. Duke University Press, 2004.
Rosenberg, Emily S. *Spreading the American Dream: American Economic and Cultural Expansion, 1890–1945*. Hill and Wang, 1982.
Roth, Leland M. *The Architecture of McKim, Mead & White, 1870–1920: A Building List*. Garland Publishing, 1978.
Roth, Leland M. *McKim, Mead & White: Architects*. Harper and Row, 1983.
Rothman, Hal. *Neon Metropolis: How Las Vegas Started the Twenty-First Century*. Routledge, 2002.
Ryan, Simon. "Inscribing Emptiness: Cartography, Exploration, and the Construction of Australia," In *De-Scribing Empire: Post-colonialism and Textuality*, edited by Chris Tiffin and Alan Lawson, 115–30. Routledge, 1994.
Rydell, Robert W. *All the World's a Fair: Visions of Empire at American International Expositions, 1876–1916*. University of Chicago Press, 1984.
Said, Edward. *Culture and Imperialism*. Vintage Books, 1994.
Sambricio, Carlos, and Roberto Segre. *Arquitectura en la ciudad de la Habana: primera modernidad*. Electa España, 2004.
Sandoval-Strausz, A. K. "Spaces of Commerce: A Historiographic Introduction to Certain Architectures of Capitalism." *Winterthur Portfolio* 44, no. 2/3 (Summer–Autumn 2010): 143–58.
Sandoval-Strausz, A. K. *Hotel: An American History*. Yale University Press, 2007.
Santiago-Valles, Kelvin A. *"Subject People" and Colonial Discourses: Economic Transformation and Social Disorder in Puerto Rico, 1898–1947*. State University of New York Press, 1994.
Scarano, Francisco A., and Margarita Zamora. *Cuba: contrapuntos de cultura, historia y sociedad* [*Cuba: Counterpoints on Culture, History, and Society*]. Ediciones Callejón, 2007.
Scarpaci, Joseph L., and Armando H. Portela. *Cuban Landscapes: Heritage, Memory, and Place*. Guilford Press, 2009.
Scarpaci, Joseph L., Roberto Segre, and Mario Coyula. *Havana: Two Faces of the Antillean Metropolis*. John Wiley and Sons, 1997.
Schwartz, Rosalie, *Pleasure Island: Tourism and Temptation in Cuba*. University of Nebraska Press, 1997.
Scott, Blake C. *Unpacked: A History of Caribbean Tourism*. Cornell University Press, 2022.

Scott, David. "Modernity that Predated the Modern: Sidney Mintz's Caribbean." *History Workshop Journal* 58 (Autumn 2004): 191–210.

Sears, John F. *Sacred Places: American Tourist Attractions in the Nineteenth Century.* Oxford University Press, 1989.

Segawa, Hugo. *Architecture of Brazil, 1900–1990.* Springer, 2013.

Segre, Roberto, and Fernando Kusnetzoff, eds. *Latin America in Its Architecture.* Translated by Edith Grosmann. Holmes and Meier, 1981.

Seiler, Cotten. *Republic of Drivers: A Cultural History of Automobility in America.* University of Chicago Press, 2008.

Sepúlveda Rivera, Anibal. *Puerto Rico urbano, atlas histórico de la ciudad puertorriqueña.* Centro de Investigaciones Carimar, 2004.

Shaffer, Marguerite S. *See America First: Tourism and National Identity, 1880–1940.* Smithsonian Books, 2001.

Sheller, Mimi. *Consuming the Caribbean: From Arawaks to Zombies.* Routledge, 2003.

Sheller, Mimi, and John Urry, eds. *Tourism Mobilities: Places to Play, Places in Play.* Routledge, 2004.

Shulman, Allan T. "Igor Polevitzky's Architectural Vision for a Modern Miami." *Journal of Decorative and Propaganda Arts* 23 (1998): 334–59.

Shulman, Allan T., ed. *Miami Modern Metropolis: Paradise and Paradox in Midcentury Architecture and Planning.* Bass Museum of Art, 2009.

Skwiot, Christine. *The Purposes of Paradise: U.S. Tourism and Empire in Cuba and Hawai'i.* University of Pennsylvania Press, 2012.

Smith, Valene L., ed. *Hosts and Guests: The Anthropology of Tourism.* University of Pennsylvania Press, 1989.

Stepan, Nancy Leys. *Picturing Tropical Nature.* Reaktion, 2001.

Stewart, Susan. *On Longing: Narratives of the Miniature, the Gigantic, the Souvenir, the Collection.* Duke University Press, 1993.

Stoler, Ann Laura. *Carnal Knowledge and Imperial Power: Race and the Intimate in Colonial Rule.* University of California Press, 2002.

Stoler, Ann Laura, ed. *Haunted by Empire: Geographies of Intimacy in North American History.* Duke University Press, 2006.

Stout, Nancy, and Jorge Rigau. *Havana/La Habana.* Rizzoli, 1994.

Strachan, Ian Gregory. *Paradise and Plantation: Tourism and Culture in the Anglophone Caribbean.* University of Virginia Press, 2002.

Strain, Ellen. *Public Places, Private Journeys: Ethnography, Entertainment, and the Tourist Gaze.* Rutgers University Press, 2003.

Taylor, Frank Fonda. *To Hell with Paradise: A History of the Jamaican Tourism Industry.* University of Pittsburgh Press, 1993.

Thomas, Hugh. *Cuba: or the Pursuit of Freedom.* Updated ed. Da Capo Press, 1998.

Thompson, Krista A. *An Eye for the Tropics: Tourism, Photography, and Framing the Caribbean Picturesque.* Duke University Press, 2006.

Tiffin, Chris, and Alan Lawson, eds. *De-scribing Empire: Post-colonialism and Textuality.* Routledge, 1994.

Tomich, Dale W., Rafael de Bivar Marquese, Reinaldo Funes Monzote, and Carlos Venegas Fornias. *Reconstructing the Landscapes of Slavery: A Visual History of the Plantation in the Nineteenth Century.* University of North Carolina Press, 2021.

Tomlinson, John. *Globalization and Culture.* University of Chicago Press, 1999.

Torres Santiago, Jerry. "La invención de los umbrales del Edén: imágenes, arquitectura y contexto en el desarollo hotelero de San Juan [The Invention of the Gates of Paradise]." In *San Juan siempre nuevo: arquitectura y modernización en el siglo XX [Ever New San Juan: Architecture and Modernization in the Twentieth Century]*, edited by Enrique Vivoni Farage, 118–67. Bilingual ed. Archivo de Arquitectura y Construcción de la Universidad de Puerto Rico, 2000.

Traganou, Jilly, and Miodrag Mitrašinović, eds. *Travel, Space, Architecture*. Ashgate, 2009.

Trouillot, Michel-Rolph. *Silencing the Past: Power and the Production of History*. Beacon Press, 1995.

Tucker, Richard P. *Insatiable Appetite: The United States and the Ecological Degradation of the Tropical World*. Concise rev. ed. Rowman and Littlefield, 2007.

Turits, Richard Lee. *Foundations of Despotism: Peasants, the Trujillo Regime, and Modernity in Dominican History*. Stanford University Press, 2003.

Turits, Richard Lee. "A World Destroyed, a Nation Imposed: The 1937 Haitian Massacre in the Dominican Republic." *Hispanic American Historical Review* 82, no. 3 (August 2002): 589–635.

Tzonis, Alexander, Liane Lefaivre, and Bruno Stagno, eds. *Tropical Architecture: Critical Regionalism in the Age of Globalization*. Wiley-Academy, 2001.

Urry, John. *The Tourist Gaze: Leisure and Travel in Contemporary Societies*. Sage Publications, 1990.

Vale, Lawrence J. *Architecture, Power, and National Identity*. Yale University Press, 1992.

Van Vleck, Jenifer. *Empire of the Air: Aviation and the American Ascendancy*. Harvard University Press, 2013.

Venegas Fornias, Carlos. *La urbanizacion de las murallas: dependencia y modernidad*. Editorial Letras Cubanas, 1990.

Villalba Garrido, Evaristo. *Cuba y el turismo*. Editorial de Ciencias Sociales, 1993.

Vivoni Farage, Enrique, ed. *Hispanofilia: arquitectura y vida en Puerto Rico, 1900–1950 [Hispanophilia: Architecture and Life in Puerto Rico, 1900–1950]*. Bilingual ed. La Editorial de la Universidad de Puerto Rico, 1998.

Vivoni Farage, Enrique, ed. *Klumb: una arquitectura de impronta social [Klumb: An Architecture of Social Concern]*. Bilingual ed. La Editorial de la Universidad de Puerto Rico, 2006.

Vivoni Farage, Enrique, ed. *San Juan siempre nuevo: arquitectura y modernización en el siglo XX [Ever New San Juan: Architecture and Modernization in the Twentieth Century]*. Bilingual ed. Archivo de Arquitectura y Construcción de la Universidad de Puerto Rico, 2000.

Ward, Evan R. *Packaged Vacations: Tourism Development in the Spanish Caribbean*. University Press of Florida, 2008.

Watts, David. *The West Indies: Patterns of Development, Culture and Environmental Change since 1492*. Cambridge University Press, 1987.

Weisskamp, Herbert. *Hotels: An International Survey*. Frederick A. Praeger, 1968.

Wey Gómez, Nicolás. *The Tropics of Empire: Why Columbus Sailed South to the Indies*. MIT Press, 2008.

Wharton, Annabel Jane. *Building the Cold War: Hilton International Hotels and Modern Architecture*. University of Chicago Press, 2001.

Whitney, Robert. *State and Revolution in Cuba: Mass Mobilization and Political Change, 1920–1940*. University of North Carolina Press, 2001.

Williams, Eric. *From Columbus to Castro: The History of the Caribbean*. 1970. Random House, 1984.

Wood, Andrew Grant, ed. *The Business of Leisure: Tourism History in Latin America and the Caribbean*. University of Nebraska Press, 2021.

Wright, Gwendolyn. "Building Global Modernisms." *Grey Room* 7 (Spring 2002): 124–34.

Wright, Gwendolyn. *The Politics of Design in French Colonial Urbanism*. University of Chicago Press, 1991.

Zanetti, Oscar, and Alejandro García. *Sugar and Railroads: A Cuban History, 1837–1959*. Translated by Franklin W. Knight and Marry Todd. University of North Carolina Press, 1998.

# *Index*

*Note*: Page numbers in *italics* indicate figures.

Abakuá Society, 188
ABC Radical, 84, 234n76
Abela, Eduardo, 185–86.
*Abstracción* sculpture (Dirube), 187–88, 208
Agudo, Pedro, 236n39
Albizu Campos, Pedro, 227n63
*Album pintoresco alrededor de la isla de Cuba* (Miahle), 184
Almendares Hotel, Havana, 36, 76–77, 232n61, 233n62
Americana Hotel in Bal Harbour, 164
Americanization, 49, 50
Anderson, Mark, 106
anti-blackness, 111, 114
anti-Haitianism, 113–14, 131
Arango Design Store, 192
Arango, Jorge, 244n58
Arango, Judith, 244n58
*Architectural Forum*, 131, 133, 145–46, 165
ARKLU furniture in Caribe Hilton, 156–57, *157*, 215, 240n65
Arneson, Stephen, 156, 240n63
Arnold, David, 12
*Arquitectura* journal, 192
Art Deco, 54, 64, 141, 178
Aruba Caribbean Hotel, 164–65, *201*
automobile trips in tourism, 49–50
Avenida Ashford, 31–33
Avery Architectural and Fine Arts Library, 34
Ayala, César J., 224n5, 237n11

Bacardí, Edificio, 64
Baez, Jennifer, 104

Báez López-Penha, José Ramón, 120
Balaguer, Joaquín, 130
Banco de Desarollo Económico y Social (Bandes), 176
Banco de Fomento Agrícola e Industrial de Cuba (Banfaic), 176
Banco Gubernamental de Fomento para Puerto Rico, 245n3
Banco Nacional de Cuba, 176
Batista, Fulgencio, 21, 168, 170, 219, 241n1; Castro's criticism on tourism approach, 194–95; tourism development in Cuba, 172–73, 176–77; tunnel projects, 175–76
Beaux Arts approach, 33, 34, 54, 55, 104, 143, 148
Behn, Hernan, 31–32, 225n29
Behn, Sosthenes, 31–32, 225n29
Bejerano, Daniel, 192, 244n61
*Be My Guest* memoir (Hilton), 162
Benítez Rexach, Félix, 54
Benítez Rojo, Antonio, 7
Bens Arrarte, José María, *89*
Bermúdez, Cundo, 186
Berwind, John E., 29–30, 224n5, 237n11; urban development project of Condado, 31–33
Biltmore hotels, 65
Blackmore, Lisa, 109, 112
*blancos*, 110–11
*bohío*, 34, 225n32
bonds, 211–12
Borinquen Park Company, 31
Brathwaite, Edward Kamau, 7
Brownson, Leonard E., 78
*Building the Cold War* (Wharton), 240n77

261

Cabarrocas, Félix, 228n8
Cabral, William Reid, 129
Capitolio, 88–89, 90, 229n16, 234n90
Capri Hotel, 164, 178, 181, 219–21
Cárdenas, Lázaro, 111
Caribe Hilton in San Juan, 20, 132, , 136, 142, 148–51, 161–62, 171, 214; amenities for guests, 133–35; *Architectural Forum*'s review, 133, 145–46, 165; ARKLU furniture, 156–57, *157*, 215, 240n65; brochure for, *200*; courtyard at, *153*, 153–54; criticism of Puerto Ricans, 144–45, 146; design of balconies, *134*; financial terms, 163–64; with Fortín San Gerónimo, *199*; "Garden of Eden," 152; guest rooms, 154–55, *155*; historic concept, 216; lobby with pool, 154, *154*; main pool of, *152*, 152–53; as national identity, 146–47, 163; *New York Times* review, 151; opening ceremony celebration, 158–59; popularity of, 160–61; tropicality of, 147, 151–53, 158, 215, 243n37; unfixed meanings, 165; Wharton's study, 240n77. *See also* Operación Manos a la Obra project
Carlton Terrace Apartments in Bal Harbour, 182, 205, 244n53
Caro, José Antonio, 129
Caronan, Faye C., 44
cartography, 47
Castellanos, Gerardo, 235n93
Castriota, Leonardo, 148
Castro, Fidel, 194, 217, 241n1; criticism on capitalism, 194–95; negative connotations on Havana Riviera, 195–97
Caycedo, Carolina, 211; *Distressed Debt* series, 211–12; *Let Us Tell You about the Bonds of Puerto Rico* series, 212
Cayuco, Rancho, 116
Ceo, Rocco, 181
Céspedes, Carlos Miguel de, 66; urban planning projects in Havana, 72–73
Ciclón de '26 (Hurricane of 1926), 67
Ciclón de San Zenón (1930), 20, 104, 117–18; impact in Santo Domingo, 106, 109
Citibank, 79, 232n59
Ciudad Universitaria, 68
coaling stations, 27, 107, 224n10
Coamo Springs Hotel, 47, 51–53, 99

Cocks, Catherine, 13
colonial/colonialism, 5, 149; Rivera Cusicanqui's views, 7–8; Spanish, 9, 11, 16, 34, 42, 89, 139, 165, 214; and tourism development, 3–4, 8–9
coloniality. *See* modernity/coloniality project
Comité de Diseño de Obras Públicas, 156
Condado Convention Center, 53–54
Condado Residential Park, 32
*Constitutional Modernism* (Hyde), 2231n36
Continental Hilton in Mexico City, 162
cosmopolitan/cosmopolitanism, 54, 68, 72, 169, 241nn4–5
cosmopolitan *cubanidad*, 21, 169, 183, 241n3
Crane China Company, 146
creole, 65, 187, 229n11
creolization, 65, 169, 229n11
Cret, Paul Philippe, 243n38
Cuba, 4, 21, 234n83, 241n12; 1933 Revolution in Cuba, 19–20, 58, 59, 83–85, 87–88, 228n6; gaming in Cuba, 177; innovative hotel designs in, 212; relationships with United States, 77–78, 172–75, 232n51, 242n16; state-owned hotels, 245n9; tourism development in, 74–75, 242n16, 244n66. *See also* Machado y Morales, Gerardo
*Cuba, Ideal Vacation Land: Tourist Guide* guidebook, *203*
Curtis, Charles, 110

*Danza* (Dance) (Gelabert), *166*, *168*, 183, 184–86
de Castro, Pedro Adolfo, 109
Derby, Lauren, 112
Deupi, Victor, 243n47
Dinwiddie, William, 50
Dirube, Rolando López, 187, 189, 244n57; *Abstracción* sculpture, 187–88, 208; *La Religión del Palo* sculpture, 188, *189*
*Distressed Debt* series (Caycedo), 211–12
Dominican Republic, 4, 9, 20–21, 104–5, 118, 130–31, 212, 217; Inter-American Peace Force occupation of, 130–31; racial politics of labor and, 125–27, *125–26*; Trujillo's authoritarianism, 109–11; US occupation, 107–8. *See also* Trujillo Molina, Rafael Leónidas
Dorado Beach Resort in Puerto Rico, 217–18

Dos Hermanos Bar, 75
*Downes v. Bidwell* case, 27, 139
Dunand, Jean, 54
Dupas, Jean, 54

Edwards, Jay D., 229n11
El Panama Hotel in Panama City, 164
*El Triunfo de la Rumba* (Abela), 185
*El zapateado*, 184
Embajador Hotel, 104, 129–30
Emergency Relief Administration, 53
Escuela de Arquitectura (Puerto Rico), 143
*Espacio* journal, 191–92

Fernández, María, 169
Ferrer, Miguel, 143, 238n35
Financiera Nacional de Cuba, 176
Flagler, Henry, 29
Flamingo Hotel, 178
Florida: themes of hotels in, 193–94; tourism development, 29, 30
Fomento (Puerto Rico), 137, 138, 141, 142–43, 237n8
Fontainebleau Hotel in Miami, 164, 189–90, 193
Foraker Act (1900), 27
Forestier, Jean-Claude Nicolas, 72, 73, 229n19, 230n21, 2230n34
Fortín de San Gerónimo, 150, *199*, 216
France, Roy, 104, 129
Free World's Fair of Peace and Confraternity (1955), 103, 104, 129, 130

Gelabert, Florencio, *166*, 183; *Danza* in Havana Riviera Hotel, *166*, *168*, 183, 184–86; *Ritmo Cubano* in Havana Riviera Hotel, 183–84, *184*, 186, 244n53
General Electric, 146
George A. Fuller Company, 77, 145, 146, 231–32n47
Gerard Jansen y Compañia, 82
Glissant, Édouard, 229n11
González Martínez, Manuel, 53
González Sánchez, Guillermo, 20, 103, 115; collaboration with Cabral, 129; Hotel Hamaca's design by, 127, *128*; Hotel Jaragua design by, 104; Hotel Montaña's design by, 127–28; Hotel Nueva Suiza' design by, 127; Hotel Paz's design by, 159; Parque Ramfis design by, 114–15, *115*; role in Trujillo regime, 115–17
Grand Condado Vanderbilt in San Juan, 18–19, 23, 28–29, 32, 33, 117, 141, 159, 212–15, 236n39; argument about imperialistic tourism, 24–25; attracting social elite, 227n64; colonnaded gallery on ocean side, *39*, 39–40; cover for promotional brochure, *94*; imperialistic tourism promotion, 43–46; main floor and guest-room floor design, 40, *41*, 42–43; north façade of, 25; oceanfront façade, 39–40; "Porto Rico: The Island of Enchantment" booklet, 26, 44, *96*, 99, 223n7; postcards, 22, 42, *95*; promotion of automobile touring, 48–52; relationship with Porto Rico Steamship Company, 30–31; remodeling and updating, 159–60; structural design, 38, 39–40; tourism development, 52–55; Warren & Wetmore's Mediterranean Revival design, 33–35, 38, 95. *See also* "Puerto Rico: 'The Switzerland of the Tropics'" booklet
Grandin, Greg, 28
Grau San Martín, Ramón, 170, 175
Gray, Nina, 225n22
Guantanamo Bay, Cuba, 57
*Guia de Ciudad Trujillo República Dominicana*, 118–19

Haiti/Haitians: Massacre (1937), 18, 113–14, 116–17; transborder relations with Dominicans, 112–13
Hamaca Hotel, Boca Chica, 127, *128*
Hansard, Hallet Neville, 119
Hartman, Joseph R., 58, 67, 73, 228n1, 229n10, 230n21, 231n36
Hartzell, Henry L., 52, 53, 225n21, 227–28nn64–65
Havana Automobile Company, 80
Havana City Project, 230n21, 2230n35
Havana Coal Company, 30
Havana, Cuba, 15, 58, 73, 229n10; 1933 and 1959 revolutions, 18; as center of hotels, 75–77; coat of arms of, 70, 225n34; design of tourism spaces, 170; geographic limits, 57; post–World War II hotel building in, 175–77; post–World

War II tourism in, 171–75; Tropicana Special in, 167–68; urban development under Grau San Martín, 170–71. *See also* Malecón, Havana
Havana Hilton, 162, 163, 164, 171, 178, 181
Havana Riviera Hotel, 21, 164, *166*, 178, 182–93, *191*, 216; advertisement for, *204*; Castro's criticism on, 194–97; design approaches, 168–71; as example of hotel boom, 170–71; Johnson's design proposal, 178–79; Polevitzky's architectural design, 179–82; tropicality, 215; view from Malecón, *180*
Hay, John, 27
Henríquez y Carvajal, Francisco, 108
Herrick, Pamela, 225n22
Heureaux, Ulises, 107
Hidalgo de Caviedes, Hipólito, 160, 186–87, *206–7*
Hilton, Conrad, 142–44, 171, 234n81; at Caribe Hilton's opening ceremony, 158–59; preference for Mediterranean Revival style, 143, 212; system of developing international hotels, 162–63
Hilton Hotels International, 142, 162–63, 171
Hotel Jaragua in Santo Domingo, 18, 20, 105, 119–21, *100*, *120*, *121*, 121–22, 136; entertainment sections, 124–25; outdoor galleries and balconies, *123*, 123–24; racial politics of labor and, *125*–26, 125–27; rooftop view, *124*, *124*; Spanish Courtyard, at, *122*, 123; swimming pool, *100*; as symbol of Trujillo's modernity, 104, 114, 117–19, 131; US imperialism and, 130–31
Hotel Nacional de Cuba in Havana, 19–20, 55, 57, 62, 66–67, 69, 75, 90–91, 117, 215, 228n5, 229n16, 231n47; aerial view of, *76*; architectural studies, 64–65; billboard for inauguration of, *66*; construction, negotiation of, 81–83; creole type designs, 65; design of, 75–76; exterior after October 1933 bombardment, 84, *85*; exterior decoration, 71–72; interior after October 1933 bombardment, 84, *86*; main entrance, *60*, *60*; Monument to Victims of USS *Maine*, 62–63, *63*, 230n21; role of National Cuba Hotel Corporation, 59, 65, 70, 77–82; view of lobby, *60*, *61*; visual and textual references, 61–62; witnessing 1933 Revolution, 58, 59, 83–88

Huerta, Moisés de, 228n8
Hurricane San Zenón. *See* Ciclón de San Zenón (1930)

*I can wear tropical print now series* (Minaya), 3, *93*
*indios*, 110–11
Inglaterra Hotel, 23
Instituto de Cultura Puertorriqueña (ICP), 149
Instituto del Turismo Cubano (ITC), 173, 174
Insular Cases, 28. *See also* Downes v. Bidwell case
*Interiors*, 131
International Telephone and Telegraph Corporation, 225n23

Jaragua Hotel. *See* Hotel Jaragua
Johnson, Philip, 178–79
Jolly, Jennifer, 111
Jones Act (1917), 27, 28, 224n14
Jones, Robert Trent, Sr., 217

Keally, Francis, 116
Kefauver, Estes, 242n28
Kincaid, Jamaica, 6, 218
Klumb, Henry, 156, 240n63, 240n65
Kropp, Phoebe, 147

La Concha Hotel, 161; view from Ashford Avenue side, *160*
La Guerra de los Diez Años, 228n9
*La Habana actual*, 73
Lalique, René, 54
Lansky, Meyer, 171, 177–79, 242n30, 242n32
Lapidus, Morris, 164; Americana Hotel, 164, 193; Aruba Caribbean Hotel, 164–65, *201*; Fontainebleu Hotel, 164, 189–90, 193; "stairs to nowhere," 189–90
La Rampa, 170
*La Religión del Palo* sculpture (Dirube), 188, *189*
Lawson, Alan, 47
Lejeune, Jean-François, 243nn46–47
*Let Us Tell You about the Bonds of Puerto Rico* series (Caycedo), 212
Ley de Hoteles 2074 (Hotel Law 2074), 176, 219
Lionnet, Françoise, 169
Livingston, Alfred T., 25
Llompart, José, 32

# INDEX

Locher, Robert E., 82
*Los Musicos* (Bermúdez), 186

*machadato*, 228n1
Machado y Morales, Gerardo, 19, 57, 67, 68, 77–80, 90–91, 228n1, 229n16; 1933 revolt against machadato, 58, 83–84; constitutional convention (1928), 229n17; corruption and social inequality, 67; defining national identity, 66–67; demonstration of popularity, 67–69; focus on urban/modern state development, 58, 65–66, 67; Presidential Decree No. 1867, 65, 69, 228n21; tourism development in Havana, 73–74, 231n38
Maine Monument. *See* Monument to the Victims of the *USS Maine*
Maldonado-Torres, Nelson, 213–14
Malecón, Havana, 170, 178, *180*, 181
Malecón, Santo Domingo, 116, 119, 120, 122
Manthorne, Katherine, 13, 239n57
Maribona, Armando, 173, 231n46
Marrero, Ramón, 158
Martínez Inclán, Pedro, 73
Martínez, María, 119
Massagüer, Conrado Walter, 173–74; *Cuba, Ideal Vacation Land* guidebook, 203; *Visit Cuba: So Near Yet So Foreign* postcard, 202
McAllister, Wayne, 179
McKim, Mead & White, 59, 65, 71, 77–81, 229n12, 233n67
McQuaid, James, 244n60
Mediterranean Revival style design, 24, 33–36, 38–42, 116, 143; Newcomb's explanation of, 38
Menéndez, Gabriela, 244n60
Menocal, Mario García, 233nn71–72
Meras y Rico Company, 71
Messina, Rab, 119–20
Miahle, Frédéric, 184
Miami: Fontainebleau hotel in, 164, 167, 174, 189–90, 196; high-rise resort hotel building in, 193–94
Minaya, Joiri, 3, *93*; connection between tourism and artwork, 3–4
Mintz, Sidney, 15
Mitchell, Charles E., 232n59
modernity/coloniality project, 6, 8, 10, 15, 17, 69,
89, 113, 126, 136, 196, 211, 213–14, 216
Monmonier, Mark, 47
Monument to Victims of USS *Maine*, 62, *63*, 230n21
Moorish architecture, 35, 109
Moruzzi, Peter, 244n61
Moscoso, Teodoro, 137, 138, 141, 145, 217. *See also* Operación Manos a la Obra
Montaña Hotel, Jarabacoa, 127–28
*mulata*, 185, 243–44n52
Muñoz Marín, Luis, 14, 137, 141, 237n8; defining Puerto Rican identity 146–48. *See also* Operación Manos a la Obra

National Bank of Cuba. *See* Banco Nacional de Cuba
National City Company of New York, 59, 77, 79
National Cuba Hotel Corporation, 59, 65, 70, 77–82
National Finance Company of Cuba. *See* Financiera Nacional de Cuba
National Historic and Artistic Heritage Service. *See* Serviço do Patrimônio Histórico e Artístico Nacional (SPHAN)
Nechodoma, Antonín, 109
Newcomb, Rexford, 38
New York & Porto Rico Steamship Company, 6, 26, 29
*New York Times*: article on future of Havana, 74; report of attack Hotel Nacional, 84–85; review of Caribe Hilton, 151
Neyra, Roderico "Rodney," 167
Niell, Paul, 6, 50
Normandie Hotel, 54, 141, 159–60, *199*, 228n69
Nueva Suiza Hotel, Costanza, 127

Olmsted Act (1909), 27
Operación Manos a la Obra, 6–7, 20, 136, 165, 237n8, 237n12; focus on tourism development, 138, 140; Moscoso's contribution, 137–38; negotiating criticism, 144–46; promotional posters for tourism, 138–39. *See also* Caribe Hilton
Organization of American States, 130
Orientalism, 12
Osuna, Ramon, 244n60

265

Otero, Raúl, *89*
Ovanda, Fray Nicolás de, 118

Palace Hotel in Havana, 75
Palacio Hilton in Chihuahua, 238n26
Pan Am, 140
Pan American Guest House in San Juan, 150
Parque Ramfis in Santo Domingo, 114–16, *115*
Parvin-Dohrman Company, 192
Parvin, Alvin, 192, 244n61
Pastoriza, Andrés, 119
Paz Hotel in Santo Domingo, 129
Pérez, Louis A. Jr., 78, 82, 174, 232n51, 234n83, 241n12
Pérez Montás, Eugenio, 108
*Picturesque Cuba, Porto Rico, Hawaii, and the Philippines* book, 23–24, 50
piña colada, 158, 240n67
Piranesi, Giovanni Battista, 190
Plan Proyecto de La Habana, 229n12
Plant, Henry, 29
plantation system, 6, 7, 24, 11, 158
Platt Amendment (1901), 83, 84, 89, 233n70
Plaza Operating Company of New York, 59, 77, 79
*Pleasure Island*, 232n55
Presidente Hotel, Havana, 75–76
Point Four Program, 140
Polevitzky, Igor, 179, 243n38; Havana Riviera project, 180–82; hotel designing projects, 179
Polevitzky, Johnson and Associates, 179
Ponce Massacre (1937), 227n63
"Porto Rico: The Island of Enchantment" booklet, 26, 44–46, 223n7; Coamo Springs Hotel from, *99*; guest-room suite, *96*
*Porto Rico: The Riviera of the West*, 44–46, 48–49
Porto Rico Steamship Company, 30–31
PRIDCO. *See* Puerto Rico Government Bank and the Puerto Rican Industrial Development Company
Pro Ley y Justicia, 84, 234n76
Puente Dos Hermanos, 31, 33
Puerto Rico, 4, 6, 19, 21, 26, 27, 29, 212, 217, 224n1, 238n35; *bohío* in, 34, 225n32; debt crisis in, 209; dual status, 28; Operación Manos a la Obra project *see* Operación Manos a la Obra projec; Porto Rico Steamship Company, 30–31; promotional brochure for, 26–28, *101–2*; Puerto Rico Coal Company, 30; US mentality in, 238n24
Puerto Rico Government Bank and the Puerto Rican Industrial Development Company (PRIDCO), 137, 237n8, 245n3
*Puerto Rico: Its Conditions and Possibilities* survey (Dinwiddie), 50
"Puerto Rico: 'The Switzerland of the Tropics'" booklet, 28, 44, 51, 224n6; header graphic from, *97*; phrase shift to "Switzerland of America," 28; road map with header graphic of cars, 49, *98*; Roosevelt's promotion, 26–27; science in, 46–48
Purdy & Henderson, 77, 78, 81–82, 232n55, 233n67

Quijano, Aníbal, 6, 10

racism: within Dominican society, 111; in Hispanic Caribbean hotels, 218
Ramírez de Arrellano, F., 32
Rancier, Omar, 104, 108
Randolph, Hunter, 151
Rayneri Piedra, Eugenio, *89*
Río Piedras Massacre (1935), 227n63
Risom, Jens, 155, 214, 240n60
*Ritmo Cubano* (Gelabert), 183–84, *184*, 186, 244n53
Rivera Cusicanqui, Silvia, 7–8
Robbins, J. Stanton, 148–49
Rockefeller, Laurence, 217, 218
Rockefeller, Nelson, 217
RockResorts, 217–18
Rodríguez, Eduardo Luis, 231n36
Rodríguez, Juan Bautista, 31
Rodríguez, Luz Marie, 136
Roig de Leuchsenring, Emilio, 88, 235n93
Roorda, Eric, 107, 108
Roosevelt Corollary, 107
Roosevelt, Franklin Delano, 235n6; funding for Hotel Jaragua, 119–20; Good Neighbor Policy, 238n26
Roosevelt, Theodore, 26–27, 107
Royal Hawaiian hotel, 36, 38
Rosita de Hornedos Hotel, 164

## INDEX

Said, Edward, 12
San Domingo Improvement Company, 107
San Juan, Puerto Rico, 15, 34; San Juan Hotels Corporation, 52–53; San Juan islet, 31
San Juan Viejo, 32, 159, 216; Barrachina restaurant in, 240n68; restoration project in, 148–50
Santo Domingo, Dominican Republic, 15, 20, 118; Ciclón de San Zenón impact, 106; monuments in, 118; Parque Ramfis in, 114–16, *115*; racism within, 111; urbanization in late nineteenth century, 108–9; Villa Francisca neighborhood in, *106*
Schwartz, Rosalie, 82, 232n55, 242n30
Secretaría de Obras Públicas, 69, 81
Seelman, Frederick, 143
Segre, Roberto, 238n36
Seiler, Cotton, 49
Serra, M. Rodríguez, 32
Serviço do Patrimônio Histórico e Artístico Nacional (SPHAN), 148
Sevilla-Biltmore in Havana, 35, 36, 75, 225n35, 226n36, 232n62
Shelbourne hotel in Miami Beach, 179
Sheller, Mimi, 30
Shulman, Allan T., 179, 181, 243n46
Skwiot, Christine, 36, 38, 173, 226n39
*A Small Place* (Kincaid), 6
Smith, Dana C., 177
South Porto Rico Sugar Company, 30
Spanish-American War, 27, 28, 224n3, 228–29n9, 232n52
Spanish Revival style, 35–36, 141, 143
SPHAN. *See* Serviço do Patrimônio Histórico e Artístico Nacional
Stepan, Nancy Leys, 13
St. Johns Hotel, 178
Stone, Edward Durell, 116, 164
Strachan, Ian, 7
Streamline Moderne, 127
*The Structure of Cuban History* (Pérez), 234n83
Suárez, Alex Martínez, 119–20
Suite of the Republic, 69–70
Swartburg, Robert, 143
Swigget, Ralph, 32

Tacón, Miguel, 67
Taft, William Howard, 107
Tampa Bay Hotel, 54–55
Taylor, Will, 88
Theodore Bailey & Company, 71
Thompson, Krista, 13, 14, 223n17, 237n17
Tiffin, Chris, 47
Toro, Ferrer y Torregrosa (architectural firm), 20, 53, *132*, 135, 143, *160*, 161, 218, 238n33, 241n78
Toro, Osvaldo, 143, 238n35
Torregrosa, Luis, 143, 238n33
tourism: connection with colonialism, 3–4; as development, 8–10; historic concept and, 14–15. *See also individual entries*
Trinidad Hilton, Port of Spain, 162, 163, 164, 241n78
tropicalization, 223n17
*Tropical Renaissance* (Manthorne), 239n57
tropical/tropicality, 11, 12-14, 20, 21, 42, 48, 62, 135–36, 144, 147, 148, 151–58, 179, 182, 215 220, 243n37; bound elements, 12–13; conflation of people and landscape, 14
tropical modernism (architecture), 20, 133, 135, 147, 156, 218, 236n3
Tropicana Cabaret, 167
Tropicana Special, 167–68
Trujillo Molina, Rafael Leónidas, 18, 20, 103, 119; Ciclón as nation-building opportunity, 106–11; focus on developing hotels, 127–32; González Sánchez's role in Trujillo regime, 115–17; Haitian Massacre (1937), 18, 113–14, 116–17; projects of agricultural works, 128–29; projects for rural areas, 111–13; racial organization of society under, 125–26
Tugwell, Rexford Guy, 237n8, 245n3
Turits, Richard, 112

Ugalde, José Canaves, 219
United States Ozone Company, 82

Vanderbilt, Frederick, 19, 29, 30, 74
Vanderbilt Hotels Company, 28, 31–33
Varadero, 242n15
Vargas, Getúlio, 148, 239n36
Varona, Ana Gloria, 167
Vedado Hotel in Havana, 178; urban regulations of, 231n44
Venegas Fornias, Carlos, 67

*View of Campo Vaccino* (Piranesi), 190
Volstead Act in United States (1919), 74

Walker & Gillette, 79
Ward, Evan, 218, 240n77
Warren & Wetmore, 19; Bermuda Golf Club design, 36; Grand Central Terminal, in New York, 33; Grand Condado Vanderbilt *see* Grand Condado Vanderbilt; hotel design in Mexico City, 36, 37; Royal Hawaiian, 36, 38
Warren, Whitney, 34, 225n30
Welles, Sumner, 83–84
Wetmore, Charles D., 34, 225n30
Wharton, Annabel Jane, 162, 240n77
Wilson, Woodrow, 107
Winship, Blanton, 52, 53, 228n68
Works Progress Administrations in Puerto Rico, 138
Wright, Frank Lloyd, 109